THE

COMPUTER

IN THE

SOCIAL STUDIES

CURRICULUM

THE
COMPUTER
IN THE
SOCIAL
STUDIES
CURRICULUM

Edward Vockell

Walter Brown

Mitchell McGRAW-HILL

New York St. Louis San Francisco Auckland Bogotá Caracas Hamburg
Lisbon London Madrid Mexico Milan Montreal New Delhi Paris
San Juan São Paulo Singapore Sydney Tokyo Toronto Watsonville

Mitchell **McGRAW-HILL**
Watsonville, CA 95076

The Computer in the Social Studies Curriculum

1 2 3 4 5 6 7 8 9 0 DOH DOH 9 0 9 8 7 6 5 4 3 2

ISBN 0-07-557464-0

Sponsoring editor is Dean Barton.
Editorial assistant is Jennifer Poodry Fish.
Production assistant is Leslie Austin.
Production manager is Christi Payne Fryday, Bookman Productions.
Interior design by Richard S. Mason and Judy Levinson.
Cover design by Juan Vargas, Vargas/Williams Design.
Composition by Patricia Douglass.
Printing and binding by R. R. Donnelley & Sons.

Library of Congress Card Catalog No. 91-066161

CONTENTS

CHAPTER 6

SELECTING AND USING COMPUTERS AND SOFTWARE

CHAPTER 7

WHAT THE FUTURE OFFERS

PREFACE

This book presents an introduction to the use of the microcomputer to promote social studies instruction. It assumes no initial knowledge of computers. It does assume some knowledge of theories of social studies education, but it also summarizes those theories as necessary to give readers the perspective to understand this book properly. This book will be useful to middle school and high school social studies teachers, to elementary teachers who teach social studies, to curriculum supervisors, and to others who are interested in integrating the computer into the social studies curriculum in order to make social studies instruction more effective.

One of the most "negative" comments we received from reviewers of this book stated: "This all sounds wonderful. If only social studies could really be taught like this!" We interpreted this reviewer as suggesting that maybe we should "get real"—that we should be aware that most social studies teachers are going to continue having students memorize definitions so that they can pass tests. In response to such criticism, we have tried to strike a balance between idealism and pragmatism. Our belief is that computerized instruction can be useful to teachers under a wide variety of instructional circumstances. We think this book will be useful to any social studies teacher who has access to computers and is willing to use them for instruction. However, computers themselves do not guarantee good social studies education. Effective software must be integrated with effective teaching to produce effective learning.

THE SERIES

The Computer in the Social Studies Curriculum is a companion volume to *The Computer in the Classroom* by Edward Vockell and Eileen Schwartz. That book can be considered Module 1 in a series on integrating the computer into the curriculum. It is designed for educators in general. It contains a discussion of educational theory applied to the computer across all areas of the curriculum. It also discusses guidelines for software and hardware selection and some programs (such as test generators and gradebooks) that are of interest to teachers in numerous curriculum areas.

The present volume is designed for teachers who teach social studies and for curriculum directors and others interested in applying the computer to their social studies curriculum. While it can be regarded as Module 2 in the series, it is also designed to stand alone or to be used as a supplement to other textbooks. For example, many readers will probably use this book as a supplement in a social studies methods, elementary curriculum, or secondary curriculum course. The present book focuses on specific topics including geography, history, and economics, as well as principles that are applicable in many areas of social studies at all grade levels.

In many cases, information that is presented in greater detail in *The Computer in the Classroom* is summarized at appropriate places in the present book, and a citation is given to the chapter in the other book where readers can find more information. In addition, some basic information (such as general guidelines for evaluating drills and a discussion of major brands of computers) is not repeated in the present book. Readers can decide for themselves whether they wish to pursue more detailed information in *The Computer in the Classroom* or in some similar general book on instructional applications of microcomputers.

Other titles that serve as Module 2 in this series include the following:

- *The Computer in the Foreign Language Curriculum*
- *The Computer in the Mathematics Curriculum*
- *The Computer in the Reading Curriculum*
- *The Computer in the Science Curriculum*
- *The Computer in the English Curriculum*
- *The Computer in the Language Arts Curriculum*
- *The Computer and Higher-Order Thinking Skills*

Although each of these books is designed as a companion volume to *The Computer in the Classroom*, it is not essential that you read the entire series in order to benefit from one of them. Each book presents a complete and useful set of information to introduce educators to instructional applications of microcomputers.

THE STRUCTURE OF THIS BOOK

Social studies teachers are often very narrowly defined specialists. A high school American history teacher may not be interested at all in elementary school social studies or in middle school geography. For this reason, we have tried to write this book in such a way as to enable readers to find the information that is uniquely relevant to their personal interests. Nevertheless, we encourage readers to examine the entire text, in order to get a good impression of all the possibilities of the computer in social studies education. One of the marks of a good program or of an effective strategy is that it can often be used at more than one level of education.

Chapter 1 summarizes many of the major issues in contemporary social studies education and indicates general ways in which the computer can contribute to social studies education. Chapter 2 examines the instructional principles that relate the computer to effective instruction in social studies education. Chapter 3 focuses on social studies education at the elementary school level, and Chapter 4 at the middle school and secondary levels. Chapter 5 focuses on useful hardware components and computer software that are applicable in a wide range of curriculum areas, including spreadsheets, databases, word processors, and graphic packages, and describes ways in which these can be incorporated into social studies instruction. Chapter 6 describes important principles for selecting social studies courseware and for using computerized materials effectively within the classroom. Chapter 7 ventures into the future and predicts ways in which expected developments in computer technology are likely to have an impact on the social studies curriculum. Chapter 8 provides summaries of 25 exemplary social studies programs. The introduction to each chapter provides further details regarding what that chapter covers.

In addition, Appendix A includes a glossary of terms, focusing on technical terms from either social studies education or instructional computing which need to be clearly defined in order to effectively discuss the application of the computer to the social studies curriculum. Appendix B includes very short reviews of a much larger number of programs than could be included in the more detailed reviews of Chapter 8. Appendix C provides an annotated bibliography, briefly describing the contents of several books and articles that shed light on current developments in computer applications to social studies education. Appendix D lists vendors who sell software related to the social studies curriculum.

We would like to express our appreciation to the many people who helped us in this project. We are especially grateful to Dr. Rasjidah Franklin,

California State University, Hayward; Jack Lowry, University of California, Davis; and Rosemary Messick, San Jose State University; who gave us useful feedback on an earlier version of this book. We would also like to express our appreciation to Christi Fryday of Bookman Productions for her help in coordinating the final stages of this project. Finally, we would like to thank the many students at Purdue University Calumet who offered us suggestions during the development of the manuscript.

Edward L. Vockell
Walter L. Brown

CHAPTER *1*

THE COMPUTER IN THE SOCIAL STUDIES CLASSROOM

MICHAEL BROWN AND MARY GREEN were working together in their world history class. Their project was a joint paper dealing with the development of democracies in southern and central Africa. They were seated at the classroom's computer terminal, which was connected to a CD-ROM machine. They needed to see maps of Africa at one-year intervals from 1950 through 1989. A push of a button presented the first map of Africa, and a few keystrokes enabled them to zero in on enlargements of exactly the areas in which they were interested. Michael used a mouse to move the cursor onto Zaire. As he pushed a button, a window appeared on the screen, displaying a table indicating the political structure and other almanac-style information about that country. Another keystroke brought him back to the main map of Africa, and he slid down to Zambia. Again he zoomed in to the political structure information. He then worked backward to examine the political and economic data on Zambia for the past ten years. Mary nudged him and suggested that she saw a pattern. She thought that the likelihood of change in the form of government appeared to be related in a complex way to the amount of rainfall and to the degree of deforestation in the area. Degree of deforestation, in turn, seemed to be related to the percentage of the economy that was controlled by foreign investors. With a few keystrokes, Michael presented on the screen a table showing the name of each country, its average annual rainfall, its rate of deforestation, and the percentage of foreign investment in its economy. To clarify some of the relationships, he had the computer generate bar graphs of some of the data. Mary was dissatisfied with this arrangement of the data, so Michael had the computer generate pie graphs instead. Mary liked this presentation better. She and Michael discussed their ideas, and they realized that they were onto something. Mary transferred the table and the pie graphs onto their private disks so that they could incorporate the information into the paper they were writing on the word processor. They returned to the main map of Africa and continued to scan for other data.

Across the room, Jeff was seated at his desk. Earlier he had accessed several major newspapers via modem on the computer, and now he was reading the description of political turmoil in the Mideast as it had been described the night before in a newspaper in Sydney, Australia. He had already read the parallel reports from New Delhi, London, and Tel Aviv. Treatments ranged from a sympathetic presentation under headlines on the front page to a noncommital summary on page 5. It used to amaze him to see the incredible differences in nuances and emphasis, but Jeff had come to realize that the way information is treated in any newspaper depends on the interests of the readers and the editorial bias of the publisher of the paper. He was disappointed that his "morning mail" had included nothing from either Osaka, Japan, or Reading, Ohio, since he had sent to his correspondents in both of these cities a 350-word essay on the recent elections in the United States and he was eager to see their reactions.

The other students were revising the essays that Miss Peters had returned to them at the beginning of the class. Although they had not been required to do so, most of the students had written their essays with a word processing program on the computers in the writing lab down the hall or had used a home computer. At Miss Peters' suggestion, each student had made two additional copies to share with classmates. The students were using the comments from their peers in combination with feedback from Miss Peters to revise the papers before turning them in for the final grade. Corrections would be easy to make, because the original versions were stored on disk. That morning, Miss Peters had also given the students an update of their progress in the class. Each student had received a personalized letter listing their grades to date and offering suggestions for obtaining the best possible grade in the course. She had accomplished this degree of personalization by using a mail merge feature of her word processor in combination with her database management program.

The next day the students were scheduled to play a game on the computer that simulated a conflict resolution problem. Miss Peters hoped this would help them understand some of the reasons why nations and ethnic groups sometimes fight. This would help them give more meaning to her lectures on various actual historical conflicts. If they had time, Miss Peters hoped to have her class play the same conflict resolution game with a class taught by one of her colleagues in a school system 2000 miles away.

Miss Peters and her class do not exist. The technology is currently available to accomplish everything described in the preceding paragraphs without prohibitive expenditures, but few teachers are actually making such dynamic use of the computer in their social studies curriculum. A major goal of this book is to help teachers make comparably worthwhile applications of the computer to social studies instruction.

THE COMPUTER REVOLUTION

The "computer revolution" has touched nearly every phase of American life. Medical technology, automobiles, office operations, and even household appliances—all have succumbed to the influence of the microprocessor. So it was not without great expectations that *Time* magazine made the computer the "Machine of the Year" in January 1983. With feature articles such as "A New World Dawns" and "The Computer Moves In," the computer was heralded as a panacea, which would not only solve sticky problems in the areas of medicine, office communications, and education, but also free up time around the home by providing greater efficiency in routine tasks such as letter writing and tax computation. And it would not stop there. It would not only create more free time, but it would also fill up that free time by doubling as a purveyor of arcade games to be used to entertain families across America—and right in their own homes.

Continuing its "Machine-of-the-Year" theme, *Time* described with growing anticipation the effect of the computer on the American workplace: the stockbroker who would now work out of his own home rather than making an exhausting commute each day; the car salesman who would use the computer to compute gross profits and commissions with a program written by his 15-year-old son; and the Minnesota business owner who would use a small computer to manage a gourmet cookware store, while her children would use the same machine to compose and print their high school term papers. Even the American farm would change its mode of operation, as computers would be used by farmers to keep track of livestock, feed costs, hybrid seed types, and commodity prices—painstaking tasks which would often have been time-prohibitive using more traditional methods.

At the beginning of 1983, *Time* had essentially declared the American office to be archaic, as methods of preparing payroll, typing letters, and sending memos were being replaced by computers and custom software at what we now describe as "work stations." The article went on to cite Alvin Toffler's *The Third Wave*, which portrays the computer revolution of the 21st century as curing many of the ills created by the Industrial Revolution of the 19th century. Toffler refers to the "electronic cottage" where family members are able to work together and enjoy leisure activities, with the computer providing a backdrop as a sort of "electronic hearth."

Time cited electronic databases as a particularly exciting phase of the revolution, as computers in remote areas could be linked with larger computers containing vast amounts of helpful information. It spoke of the Iowa law student who used his personal computer and a modem to access information from Westlaw on auto insurance precedents. In addition, in medicine the SUMEX-AIM network could be used by local doctors to recognize 4000 symptoms of some 500 diseases, thus enhancing the diagnostic skills of local doctors throughout the country.

Furthermore, in treating the human body, computers were achieving dramatic effects by creating new procedures to provide those suffering from heart disease with controlled pacemakers, by providing diabetes patients with control-release insulin devices, by outfitting the deaf with hearing aids that could translate sounds into vibrations to allow them to "hear," and by creating computer-operated artificial limbs to enable the paralyzed to walk.

COMPUTERS IN THE SCHOOLS

It was against this background of revolutionary changes and medical "miracles" that the computer came face to face with the American educational system, already fraught with problems. Close on the heels of the *Time* article came the release of *A Nation at Risk*, published also in 1983 by the National Commission on Excellence. It offered a scathing indictment of a national school system which had witnessed a series of steadily declining SAT and ACT scores since 1963. Particularly alarming were the continuing low levels of language arts skills, as reading levels often remained two to four grades below age level and writing skills often seemed almost nonexistent.

Given the knowledge of the computer's capability in noneducational fields, it seemed only natural at that time that achieving "miracle solutions" in education would only be a matter of applying time, energy, and money. Indeed, the article continued, "Many Americans concerned about the erosion of the schools put faith in the computer as a possible savior of their children's education, at school and at home." The Yankelovich poll claimed that 57 percent of those questioned thought that the computer would enable children to "read and do arithmetic better."

How far have we come, then, since this period of great anticipation in the early 1980s? It would seem to many critics today that even now in the early 1990s we have achieved only disappointment and disillusionment with a technology that demands increasing amounts of money and training, and most certainly has not produced the much anticipated revolutionary results in educational achievement.

In 1983 U.S. schools had 100,000 computers worth an estimated $200 million. By 1988 there were 1.7 million computers worth some $2 billion.

But what has happened to the widely heralded upheaval in American education? Many educators are now questioning the wisdom of some of our efforts and expenditures. A recent report in the *Wall Street Journal* quotes University of Wisconsin (Milwaukee) Professor Henry Kepner, Jr.: "The computer-learning revolution predicted back in the early 1980s just hasn't happened." Marc Tucker, president of the National Center of Education and the Economy, concurs, "A lot of kids in this country can now distinguish between a computer and a telephone. . . . I think we expect a great deal more."

A 1988 Educational Testing Service study entitled "The Nation's Report Card" supports these criticisms. Nearly 90 percent of the 24,000 students surveyed had used computers, and 95 percent could identify parts of a computer such as a keyboard or a floppy disk. But when it came to serious application of computer skills, the results were not nearly as satisfying. Answers to test questions involving skills applications "barely topped random guessing." And, when frequency of use was questioned, both seventh and eleventh grades reported only about one student in five used a computer once a week for word processing, making graphs, or database applications. Over half of those surveyed claimed they never used computers for these applications.

What is the explanation for this amazing lethargy in incorporating this potentially beneficial technology into our nation's schools? Part of the answer has to be the method of deployment of computer equipment in the school systems. Some 96 percent of the schools in the United States have computers, but the vast majority have 10 to 20 machines housed in a single laboratory, to be shared by classes throughout the school. According to the National Science Foundation, math and science classes averaged less than 15 minutes per day of computer use, and other subjects used them even less frequently. John Schram, senior vice president of publisher Houghton Mifflin Company, cites the ratio of machines per student remains at about one machine for every 35 to 38 students. With limited equipment availability, scheduling of classes often becomes a serious problem.

Another problem involves the availability of good software. Whereas business applications software serves a vast market with large budgets allocated for increasing office efficiency, school systems are often strapped for funds. Under these conditions it is easier to justify an expenditure for a set of $20 textbooks than for a computer costing $2000 per work station or for software which may run several hundred dollars per program. And so publishers of quality software often ignore the educational market in favor of the more lucrative business market. Of the $2.9 billion spent on software in 1987, only $153 million was spent on educational products.

In addition, the types of programs available often do not fit the curriculum design of the individual schools. In cases where the programs do fit the design, teachers are forced to devote much time to preparing the class for making use of the programs. Also, many programs use drill-and-practice approaches that teachers feel could just as easily be covered by handing out more traditional worksheets.

Finally, there has been a marked reluctance by teachers to employ computers in classroom work. They often do not feel confident using a new technology after a few "in-service" workshops or even a college course on computer applications. The result is that many teachers do not attempt to integrate computer usage into their classrooms.

Based on this development, computers as instruments of the educational process seem doomed to suffer the same fate of early educational television, language labs, and teaching machines. The problem with the current state of computer usage is inherent in our approach. The main reason for the failure of technology in these earlier instances was the attempt in each case to "graft" a new technology onto an existing curriculum. Human beings, and especially teachers, are reluctant to incorporate change into their lives, or their classrooms. School systems are not interested in spending $100,000 on either a new language lab or a new computer lab unless they can expect observable improvements in course content or approach. To the frustration of many school boards and administrators, evidence of such improvements has not been provided.

The early 1980s approached the computer as an instrument to be studied; hence the development of the computer literacy curriculum. During this phase, students were introduced to the potential of computers by demonstrations of their strengths and weaknesses as well as some common applications. With regard to actual impact on the traditional curriculum, it soon became apparent that this approach was an effort in futility. It has been likened to a course in studying the potential of the pencil. The real value lies in the use of both computer and pencil to assist the creative learning process.

What then is the future of the computer in education? If it is not destined to fall by the wayside, why not? An essential advantage that the computer has over language lab, educational television, and teaching machine technologies is that these previous systems were essentially dedicated to one particular use. They were expected to fulfill one purpose.

Language labs permitted the practice of a foreign language, using a tape recorder and supervising teacher to create an enhanced environment. Educational television brought the expertise of diverse educators to remote environments via televised programming and either cable set-ups or dedicated educational networks. Teaching machines used a programmed approach to lead students through a maze of concepts much like today's tutorial computer programs do. These machines were even complete with branching, so that a student might receive remediation if appropriate concepts were not fully understood. In reality, the technologies were not at fault; they were simply unused or poorly implemented. Teachers and students had to step outside their normal modes of teaching and learning to use these technologies.

The computer, on the other hand, has greater potential than any of these previous educational enhancements because it is not a technology specifically dedicated to one task, but capable of performing a variety of educational and research duties. Therefore, it should be regarded not as a static approach which either works or doesn't work, but rather as an evolutionary tool, capable of greatly enhancing the efforts of the classroom teacher or of vastly increasing the research and writing capabilities of the student. But more importantly, it is a technology that is constantly striving to improve itself, so that those educators who are using today's technology and are pleased with the results can expect even greater accomplishments with tomorrow's technology.

COMPUTERS AND THE SOCIAL STUDIES CURRICULUM

Before we focus on the role of the computer in the social studies curriculum, it will be useful to summarize the major goals of social studies education. In 1989, the National Council for the Social Studies Task Force on Scope and Sequence defined social studies education as "a basic component of the K–12 curriculum that (1) derives its goals from the nature of citizenship in a democratic society that is closely linked to other nations and peoples of the world; (2) draws its content primarily from history, the social sciences, and in some respects, from the humanities and science; (3) is taught in ways that reflect on awareness of the personal, social, and cultural experiences and developmental levels of learners; and (4) facilitates the transfer of what is learned in school to the out-of-school lives of students" (p. 377). Hartoonian and Laughlin (1989) have pointed out that social studies programs address four goals:

- The development of enlightened democratic citizenship for effective participation in local, state, national, and international affairs.
- The application and understanding of our cultural heritage, including diversity and its role in contemporary society.
- The acquisition of academic knowledge and abilities related to the study of the motives, actions, and consequences of human beings as they live individually as well as in groups and societies in a variety of place and time settings; and the joy of learning about self, others, and human society.
- Learning "how to learn"—how to use prior knowledge to understand complex ideas and how to create new ideas.

These goals are stated in a different way in Table 1.1.

Another way to summarize the scope of the social studies curriculum is to describe the level of sophistication and intensity with which the themes listed in Table 1.2 are covered throughout the K–12 curriculum.

The general goals of social studies can be grouped into three sets: knowledge, values and beliefs, and skills. Knowledge of specific subjects in social studies provides the basis for understanding human affairs and the human condition. In addition, knowledge assists in developing values, beliefs, and skills. The following subjects are covered in the K–12 social studies curriculum (National Council for the Social Studies, 1989, p. 377):

Table 1.1 The major goals of a social studies curriculum in a democratic society. (Based on Hartoonian and Laughlin, 1989.)

- Use reasoning processes in economic, political, social, and personal policy making.
- Appreciate and value the diversity and communality of the human family throughout history.
- Comprehend the vocabulary, logic, and methodology of the several academic disciplines that make up social studies.
- Communicate ideas through speaking, listening, writing, and other use of symbols.
- Use the social and natural sciences, history, geography, literature, social mathematics (statistics, probability, social indicators, data-based management systems), and the fine arts to describe and explain social phenomena.
- Understand the importance of values in people's lives and how values influence our behavior both as individuals and as a society.

Table 1.2 The major themes of the social studies curriculum. The level of sophistication and the intensity with which these themes are covered will vary at different K–12 grade levels (Hartoonian and Laughlin, 1989).

- Cultural Heritage
- Global Perspective
- Politics/Economic
- Tradition and Change
- Social History
- Spatial Relationships
- Social Contracts
- Technology
- Peace/Interdependence
- Citizenship

History: of the United States and the world, understanding change and learning to deal with it.

Geography: physical, political, cultural, economic, worldwide relationships.

Government: theories, systems, structures, processes.

Law: civil, criminal, constitutional, international.

Economics: theories, systems, structures, processes.

Anthropology and Sociology: cultures, social institutions, the individual, the group, the community, the society.

Psychology: the individual in intergroup and interpersonal relationships.

Humanities: the literature, art, music, dance, and drama of cultures.

Science: the effects of natural and physical science on human relationships.

As well as imparting knowledge, the development of democratic values and beliefs represents a second area of emphasis in the social studies curriculum. Values help to set standards for individual and group behavior and beliefs represent a commitment to those values. In American schools, such values include justice, equality, responsibility, rule of law, freedom, diversity, privacy, human dignity, fairness, integrity, honesty, consideration of others, loyalty, authority, and international human rights (National Council for the Social Studies, 1989, p. 378).

Finally, a third category of social studies goals is skills development. A skill is defined as "the ability to do something proficiently in repeated performances. Skills are processes that enable students to link knowledge with beliefs that lead to action." Skills important to the social studies curriculum include the following (National Council for the Social Studies, 1989, p. 378):

Skills Related to Acquiring Information
      Reading skills
      Study skills
      Reference and information-search skills
      Technical skills in the use of electronic devices
Skills Related to Organizing and Using Information
      Thinking skills
      Decision-making skills
      Metacognitive skills
Skills Related to Interpersonal Relationships and Social Participation
      Personal skills
      Group interaction skills
      Social and political participation skills

Because so many of today's curricula are based wholly or in part on specific textbooks, there is a remarkable similarity in both content and goals of social studies courses throughout the country. This is true despite control by local school boards and despite a variety of rationales for different social studies courses.

As subsequent chapters show, the computer can play an important role in achieving almost any of these social studies goals, in the context of individual users, small groups, or whole-class experiences using projection screens. For example, in the early elementary grades, there seems to be an emphasis on the community, the neighborhood, the family, urban and rural studies, and cultural geography. This would seem to be an ideal environment for the use of digitized maps, pictures, and diagrams used in conjunction with an LCD (liquid crystal display) projection system (discussed in Chapter 5). This is not to suggest that teachers should abandon the traditional use of pull-down maps of the United States or hand-drawn charts of the neighborhood for teaching geography lessons. We merely mean that it is *possible* for the computer to play an important role in the presentation of maps, pictures, and diagrams. As Chapter 2 suggests, the actual decision regarding whether to use a computer or a more traditional delivery system will depend on what combination of instructional principles will most effectively enhance academic learning time with regard to the topic of the unit of instruction.

To help develop skills and values, the computer, a modem, and an available phone line can offer students an opportunity to communicate with neighboring or distant communities and make comparisons to their own community. This is actually a revival of an old idea—the "pen pal"—but now the addition of teacher direction and the immediacy of the on-line exchange add a great deal of interest and excitement to the exercise. With a little behind-the-scenes work, the classroom teacher can establish format and ground rules with "sister" communities, so that the information exchanged in this way will have more meaning and relate more directly to the curriculum. The possibilities are endless. This system can be used for subcultural comparisons, for urban and rural studies, for environmental studies, cultural geography, and even climatic studies.

Students in social studies classes often learn to make sense out of large amounts of information by examining maps, searching almanacs, and

Table 1.3 On-line educational databases and services.

SERVICE	DESCRIPTION	CONTACT
National Geographic Kids Network	For grades 4–6 social studies	(202) 775-6580
FrEdMail (Free Educational Mail)	Conference groups students/teachers	Compuserve ID: 76167,3514
Interactive Communication Simulations	Role-playing games	U. of Michigan (313) 763-6716
Einstein	Database searching simulation	(212) 560-6613
McGraw-Hill Information Exchange (MIX)	International electronic mail, K–12	(503) 345-8527 (507) 645-9347
Dialog Classroom Instruction Program	Group instruction on-line searches middle school–12	(800) 334-2564
Pals Across the World	International writing project grades 3–12	(503) 697-4080 Applelink ID: K0591
Long Distance Learning Network	AT&T-sponsored learning circles	(619) 943-1314 Compuserve ID: 76004,1007

doing research in encyclopedias. These tasks can be simplified by permitting students to use the growing number of networks, projects, and services that permit the user to gather information from a remote database or communicate with schools in other communities or even other countries. Three major on-line utility services are COMPUSERVE, THE SOURCE, and PRODIGY. References to similar services are listed in Table 1.3. The nature and use of these services will be explored further in Chapter 5.

The overall purpose of social studies goals is to educate citizens so they are able to participate in social, civic, and political processes and, in some meaningful way, further the values and beliefs that characterize citizens in a democratic society. Many of these skills are developed and encouraged by programs such as OUR TOWN MEETING by Tom Snyder Productions (Figure 1.1), which simulates the decision-making process of a town or village board complete with budget shortfalls, project priorities, and the usual array of local problems. This is a tremendous use for the computer, since students develop their own reasoning and communication skills; the computer merely establishes the environment. (For a more complete evaluation see Chapter 8.)

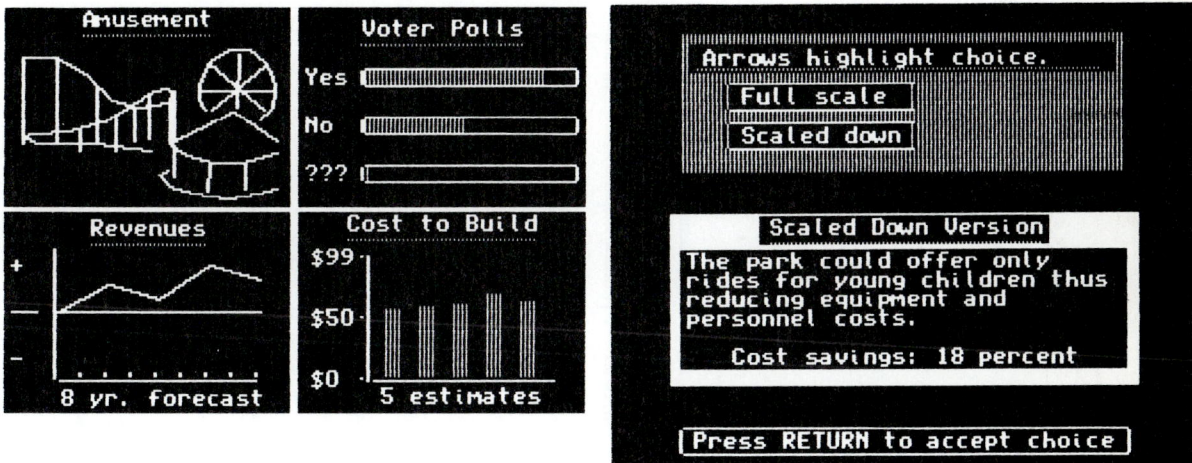

(a)   (b)

Figure 1.1 Two screens from OUR TOWN MEETING by Tom Snyder Productions, which simulates the decision-making process of a town or village board complete with budget shortfalls, project priorities, and the usual array of local problems.

There are several programs that help students develop specialized knowledge in a particular area of social studies (see Figure 1.2). In addition, most textbook publishers now offer test-generating programs to facilitate the construction of testing materials, and many will eventually offer similar programs for computerized workbooks to accompany texts. But these utilities merely remove some of the drudgery for the classroom teacher; they do not take full advantage of the computer's capabilities to access and process information.

Some interesting and creative programs appear to be "naturals" for enticing students to learn more about social studies. For example, the CARMEN SANDIEGO series (Figure 1.3) is not only educational—it's just plain fun. However, as Chapter 2 suggests, in many cases the social studies teacher should not look for "canned" programs but rather seek ways to incorporate the computer as a natural tool to enable students to accomplish more effectively the social studies goals that have been outlined in this chapter. Even when such programs exist, these must be carefully integrated with the curriculum in order to be effective. Simply running a good program with no apparent relationship to the unit of instruction is no more useful than viewing an unrelated filmstrip. Teachers must put together

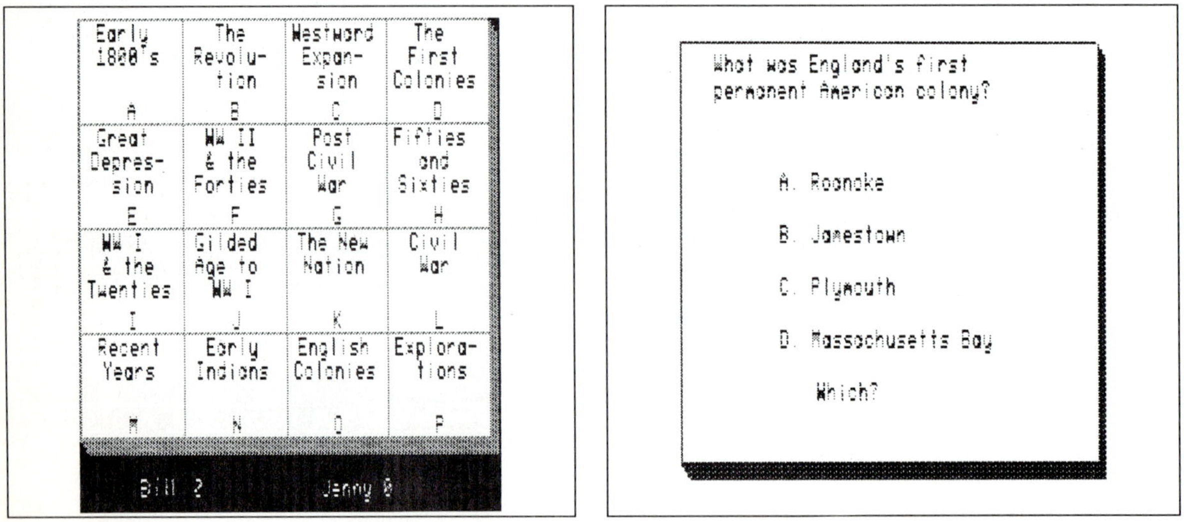

(a)

(b)

Figure 1.2 Two screens from FACTS AND FALLACIES (Hartley), a program that helps students develop specialized knowledge in particular areas of social studies.

(a)   (b)

Figure 1.3 Screens from WHERE IN TIME IS CARMEN SANDIEGO?

lessons which take full advantage of the new technology and make use of it to expand the horizon of the student beyond the conventional classroom or library.

This necessity of additional work and planning is precisely what has kept many social studies teachers from integrating the computer into their classrooms: it appears that they need to go through a great deal of trouble to learn how to use computers, that they must throw out old lesson plans, and that they must replace their old methods with an unfamiliar new technology. However, this perception is simplistic and misleading. One important principle should reassure social studies teachers and make them eager to accept the new technology:

> Ninety-five percent of knowing how to teach social studies with computers is knowing how to teach social studies.

In other words, if you are already a good teacher, it is extremely easy to incorporate the computer into your classroom—provided you have access to computers and software and possess a basic knowledge of computers. If you are not already a good teacher, it is unlikely that the computer alone will turn you into one. To use the computer for instruction, it is vastly more important to understand principles of instruction than to understand computer technology. It is the purpose of this book to enable teachers at all grade levels to incorporate the computer as an effective tool for enhancing social studies instruction.

Table 1.4 presents the "Essential Skills for Social Studies" listed by the National Council for the Social Studies (1989) and indicates ways in which the computer can help students attain these skills. Again, we are not saying that it is *necessary* to use the computer in order to master these skills. Nor are we saying that the computer is better than any other tool for mastering these skills. The listing of skills and computer programs in Table 1.4 merely shows that there are many, many ways in which the computer *can* contribute to the social studies curriculum. Also note that many programs could have been listed in more than one place in the table, and listing them in one place rather than another was done arbitrarily. This table is presented here to give you an idea of the impact the computer can have on social studies education. Without reading the rest of this book, you may be unfamiliar with many of the types of programs listed in this table; therefore, it may be useful to return to this list after you have become familiar with the strategies discussed in the chapters that follow.

In some cases, teachers will use programs to help individual students review skills already mastered by most other students. (For example, although reading skills are listed as an essential skill, many social studies teachers are not reading specialists and they would appreciate the help of a good program for students who are having trouble reading critically in social studies.) In other cases, the computer will be the center of a lessson for a whole class, for small groups, or for individual students. (For example, students could run OREGON TRAIL and use this simulation as a basis for thought and discussion.) In other cases, the computer will be used as a peripheral tool while students learn primarily through some other medium. (Students could use word processors to write reports or store information in databases for effective retrieval.) In still other cases, students who have already mastered material will use the computer to pursue "enrichment" activities for which most students will not have time and which would be major distractions for teachers to try to present without the aid of the computer. Table 1.4 merely lists samples of activities and programs; there are many other possibilities. The rest of this book will help you decide when and how the computer can contribute to instruction in the social studies classroom.

Table 1.4 Examples of ways in which the computer can help teach essential skills for social studies. The skills are based on National Council for the Social Studies (1989).

Essential Skills for Social Studies

I.   Skills related to acquiring information

   A. Reading Skills

      1. Comprehension

        Reading drills and tutorials, described in detail in Whitaker, Schwartz,and Vockell (1989) and in Schwartz and Vockell (1989).

        COMPREHENSION POWER (Milliken), COMPREHENSION CONNECTION (Milliken), DIASCRIPTIVE READING (Educational Activities), THE PUZZLER (Sunburst), READING WORKSHOP (Mindscape)

      2. Vocabulary

        Vocabulary drills and games, described in detail in Whitaker, Schwartz, and Vockell (1989) and in Schwartz and Vockell (1989), many of which come with modules specifically related to social studies or with editing systems that permit the insertion of social studies vocabulary.

        READING AROUND WORDS (I/CT), ROOTS/AFFIXES (Hartley), THE VOCABULARY GAME (J & S Software), WORD ATTACK! (Davidson), CONTENT AREA READING (Gamco), <IN COMMON> Series (Sunburst)

      3. Rate of reading

        Speed-reading drills, described in detail in Whitaker, Schwartz, and Vockell (1989) and in Schwartz and Vockell (1989).

        SPEED READER II (Davidson), SPEED READING (Bureau of Business Practice), SPEEDREAD+ (Inet)

   B. Study Skills

      1. Find information

        Drills and tutorials on how to use books, dictionaries, libraries, and so on; simulated use of information tools; programs that encourage the use of reference sources to answer questions; practice using computerized versions of the tools themselves.

        ANSWERING QUESTIONS LIBRARY STYLE (Learnco), SURVEY TAKER (Scholastic), WHERE IN THE WORLD IS CARMEN SANDIEGO? (Broderbund), SOLVE IT! (Sunburst), COMPTON'S MULTIMEDIA ENCYCLOPEDIA (Encyclopedia Britannica), HOW CAN I LOOK IT UP IF I DON'T KNOW WHAT I'M LOOKING FOR? (Sunburst), APPLEWORKS (Claris), Compuserve

      2. Arrange information in usable formats

        Computerized tools for storing or presenting information, including word processing programs, database management programs, graphic programs, spelling checkers, style checkers, and tutorials helping users learn to use these tools.

        APPLEWORKS (Claris), MAGIC SLATE (Sunburst), RESEARCH MANAGER (Combase), PRO-CITE (Personal Bibliographic Software), INTERPRETING GRAPHS (Sunburst), SENSIBLE SPELLER (Sensible Software), TIMEOUT SPELLCHECK (Beagle Brothers), GRAMMATIK (Want Electronic Corporation), PRINT SHOP (Broderbund), PC:SOLVE (Pacific Crest Software), TIMEOUT GRAPH (Beagle Brothers)

Table 1.4 (continued)

C. Reference and Information-Search Skills

1. The library

Drills and tutorials on how to use libraries; simulated use of libraries; programs that encourage the use of library reference sources to answer questions; practice using computerized library reference tools.

ANSWERING QUESTIONS LIBRARY STYLE (Learnco), COMPTON'S MULTIMEDIA ENCYCLOPEDIA (Encyclopedia Britannica), HOW CAN I LOOK IT UP IF I DON'T KNOW WHAT I'M LOOKING FOR? (Sunburst), COMPUSERVE (Compuserve)

2. Special references

Drills and tutorials on how to use books, dictionaries, libraries, and so on; simulated use of information tools; programs that encourage the use of reference sources to answer questions; practice using computerized versions of the tools themselves.

ANSWERING QUESTIONS LIBRARY STYLE (Learnco), COMPTON'S MULTIMEDIA ENCYCLOPEDIA (Encyclopedia Britannica), WHERE IN THE WORLD IS CARMEN SANDIEGO? (Broderbund), HOW CAN I LOOK IT UP IF I DON'T KNOW WHAT I'M LOOKING FOR? (Sunburst), COMPUSERVE (Compuserve), FACTS ON FILE NEWS DIGEST CD-ROM (Facts on File)

3. Maps, globes, graphics

Drills and tutorials on how to use maps, globes, graphs, and so on; simulated use of these tools; programs that encourage the use of these tools to answer questions; practice using computerized versions of the tools themselves.

LEARNING ABOUT GEOGRAPHY, MAPS, AND GLOBES (Educational Activities), USA GEOGRAPH (MECC), PC GLOBE (PC Globe), CROSS-COUNTRY USA (Didatech), WHERE IN THE WORLD IS CARMEN SANDIEGO? (Broderbund), COMPTON'S MULTIMEDIA ENCYCLOPEDIA (Encyclopedia Britannica), GTV (National Geographic), MACATLAS Series (Micro Maps)

4. Community resources

Programs that facilitate interviewing; programs that facilitate recordkeeping or presentation of information from such sources as interviews, observations, and community newspapers.

SURVEY TAKER (Scholastic), APPLEWORKS (Claris)

D. Technical Skills Unique to Electronic Devices

1. Computer

Programs that teach computer literacy skills, including tutorial programs teaching how to use word processors and database management programs.

APPLE PRESENTS APPLE (Claris)

2. Telephone and television information networks

Programs that teach how to use modem to access networks; the network services themselves or simulations of them.

PRODIGY (Prodigy Services)

II. Skills Related to Organizing and Using Information

A. Thinking Skills

1. Classify information

Drills, tutorials, and simulations that focus on identifying relevant material, grouping based on criteria, sequencing, and tabulating data in charts, graphs, and so on; database programs that require entry of data.

Table 1.4 (continued)

K–12 MEMORY (Sunburst), CONCEPT DEVELOPMENT (Sunburst), GNEE OR NOT GNEE (Sunburst), DATAQUEST series (MECC), U.S. GOVERNMENT DATABASE (Scholastic), <IN COMMON> Series (Sunburst), STATE-SMART 3.0 (Hy PerFormance)

2. Interpret information

Drills, tutorials, and simulations that focus on interpreting information by noting relationships, predicting outcomes, and so on; database programs with guidelines or instructions that require interpretation of data; tools that assist in the interpretation of data.

GRAPHING PRIMER (MECC), U.S. HISTORY DATABASE (Scholastic), APPLEWORKS (Claris), TIMEOUT GRAPH (Beagle Brothers), DATA INSIGHTS (Sunburst), CULTURE 1.0 (Cultural Resources)

3. Analyze information

Drills, tutorials, and simulations that focus on analyzing information by such procedures as organizing, subdividing, and examining the elements of a topic; database programs with guidelines or instructions that require analysis of data; tools that assist in the analysis of data.

PC:SOLVE (Pacific Crest), PROBLEM SOLVING STRATEGIES (MECC), DATA INSIGHTS (Sunburst)

4. Summarize information

Drills, tutorials, and simulations that focus on summarizing information; database programs with guidelines or instructions that require summary of data; tools that assist in summarizing data. Teaching this skill via computer often involves giving a specific (additional) focus to a program that could also be used for a "lower-level" skill.

20TH CENTURY AMERICA (Educational Activities), IMMIGRANT (Sunburst), POINT OF VIEW (Scholastic)

5. Synthesize information

Drills, tutorials, and simulations that focus on synthesizing information by proposing new ideas, reinterpreting events, presenting new charts, communicating orally, and so on; database programs with guidelines or instructions that require synthesis of data; tools that assist in the presentation of synthesized data. Teaching this skill via computer often involves giving a specific (additional) focus to a program that could also be used for a "lower-level" skill.

20TH CENTURY AMERICA (Educational Activities), IMMIGRANT (Sunburst), EARTHQUEST (Earthquest)

6. Evaluate information

Drills, tutorials, and simulations that focus on such tasks as evaluating information and testing validity; database programs with guidelines or instructions that require evaluation of data; tools that assist in the evaluation of data. Teaching this skill via computer often involves giving a specific (additional) focus to a program that could also be used for a "lower-level" skill.

PC:SOLVE (Pacific Crest Software)

B. Decision-Making Skills

Drills, tutorials, and simulations that teach or require decision making. Tools that enable learners to make intelligent decisions. Teaching this skill via computer often involves giving a specific (additional) focus to a program that could also be used for a "lower-level" skill.

Table 1.4 (continued)

DECISIONS, DECISIONS series (Tom Snyder)

C. Metacognitive Skills

Drills, tutorials, and simulations that teach or permit focus on metacognitive skills including time management and effective study skills. Teaching these skills via computer often involves giving a specific (additional) focus to a program that could also be used for teaching other thinking skills.

COLONIAL MERCHANT (Educational Activities), 20TH CENTURY AMERICA (Educational Activities), WAGON TRAIN 1848 (MECC), SIM CITY (Broderbund/ Maxis)

III.   Skills Related to Interpersonal Relationships and Social Participation

A. Personal Skills

Drills, tutorials, and simulations that teach or encourage communication skills, such as expressing ideas, beliefs, feelings, and so on; programs that help clarify values or otherwise help develop affective characteristics. Teaching these skills via computer often involves giving a specific (additional) focus to a program that could also be used for teaching other skills.

DECISIONS, DECISIONS Series (Tom Snyder Productions), GROUPWRITER (MECC)

B. Group Interaction Skills

Drills, tutorials, and simulations that teach or permit learners to interact in groups, such as making or following rules for group functioning and delegating duties. Teaching these skills via computer often involves giving a specific (additional) focus to a program that could also be used for teaching other skills, for example, providing guidelines for cooperative learning at the computer.

DECISIONS, DECISIONS (Tom Snyder), GROUPWRITER (MECC)

C. Social and Political Participation Skills

Drills, tutorials, and simulations that teach or permit learners to participate in social or political activities, such as keeping informed on social issues, working to cooperate with or persuade others, and accepting the responsibilities of citizenship. Teaching these skills via computer often involves giving a specific (additional) focus to a program that could also be used for teaching other skills.

THE OTHER SIDE (Tom Snyder), APPLEWORKS (Claris), COMPUSERVE (Compuserve), PRODIGY (Prodigy Services)

CONCLUSION AND OVERVIEW

Computers can play an important role in our social studies classes at both the elementary and secondary levels. In most cases the major obstacles to making effective use of computer technology are budget constraints of the local school system, staff training, and the imagination of the individual teacher.

This chapter has summarized the principal goals of the social studies curriculum and has shown a few ways in which the computer can help students and teachers meet these goals. The chapters that follow discuss strategies for effectively integrating the computer into the social studies curriculum and describe examples of successful computer implementations.

REFERENCES

Hartoonian, H. M., and M. A. Laughlin. "Designing a Social Studies Scope and Sequence for the 21st Century." *Social Studies* 53 (1989): 388–398.

National Council for the Social Studies. "In Search of a Scope and Sequence for Social Studies." *Social Studies* 53 (1989): 376–387.

Schwartz, E., and E. L. Vockell. *The Computer in the English Curriculum*. Watsonville, CA: Mitchell **McGRAW-HILL**, 1989.

Time, January 3, 1983.

Vockell, E. L., and E. Schwartz. *The Computer in the Classroom* (2nd Ed.). Watsonville, CA: Mitchell **McGRAW-HILL**, 1992.

Whitaker, B., and E. Schwartz. *The Computer in the Reading Curriculum*. Watsonville, CA: Mitchell **McGRAW-HILL**, 1989.

CHAPTER 2

HOW THE COMPUTER CAN ENHANCE SOCIAL STUDIES SKILLS

THE FOLLOWING CHAPTERS provide examples of courseware that can help teach social studies skills more effectively. The present chapter provides a practical introduction to the underlying theory of *how* the computer can help produce this desirable impact. It examines a few of the principles important to social studies instruction and shows how the computer can be integrated with these principles. Subsequent chapters demonstrate how these principles can be applied at different grade levels to various subject areas within the social studies curriculum.

ACADEMIC LEARNING TIME

Academic learning time (ALT) is defined as the amount of time a student spends attending to relevant and worthwhile academic tasks while performing those tasks with a high rate of success (Caldwell, Huitt, and Graeber, 1982; Berliner, 1984). In any designated subject area, ALT is likely to be more strongly linked to academic success than any other variable over which the teacher can exercise control. The concept of academic learning time and its relation to instructional computing is covered in detail in Chapter 1 of *The Computer in the Classroom* (Vockell and Schwartz, 1992). At this time, ALT will be discussed as it relates to social studies education.

Even if there were no research to verify it, most teachers would assume students learn more about any given topic or skill when they spend more time on the task. Research has proven this relationship exists for many academic activities, including social studies instruction. Simply assigning more study time to social studies, however, will not automatically increase the student's learning regarding that topic. The relationship is a bit more complicated. For example, not all the time officially scheduled for social studies is likely to be allocated to that activity. If an hour is assigned to working in a laboratory, but the teacher devotes 5 minutes at the beginning of the session to returning papers, 10 minutes to setting up the lab equipment, and 15 minutes at the end to cleaning up and making announcements, then only 30 minutes have been allocated to working on experiments during that period.

Scheduled time for instruction merely sets an upper limit on *allocated time*. Likewise, *allocated time* for a subject merely sets the upper limit to *engaged time*, which refers to the amount of time students actively attend to the subject matter under consideration. Finally, even when they are actively engaged in studying social studies, students learn effectively only when they are performing mental activities at a high rate of success. This smaller amount of time during which students are actively performing at a high rate of success is the factor most strongly related to the amount of learning that takes place. In the social studies classroom, students learn efficiently to the extent that they turn their class and study time into effective academic learning time.

Neither "class time" nor "study time" automatically qualifies as ALT, but both may become ALT if the learner actively attends to relevant tasks with a high rate of success. A student who devotes 100 hours to academic learning time in a course will learn more than an equally capable student who devotes only 50 hours. However, a person allocating only 50 hours to study and spending 90 percent of that time in active academic learning will learn more than an equally capable student who allocates 100 hours but spends only 30 percent of those hours in active academic learning. ALT will be a critical factor no matter which of the general theories of social studies instruction is embraced by the teacher or school.

ALT can be increased not only by lengthening the school year or school day, but also by enabling the teacher to manage a classroom more efficiently and enabling students to study more efficiently and with a higher rate of success. Although computers cannot lengthen the amount of time spent at school, they *can* help teachers and students perform their tasks with greater efficency and success. In addition, students may simply be motivated to spend more time on a task when using computers for instruction. But it is not imperative that social studies students have access to computers to make effective use of academic learning time. Good social studies teachers are good precisely because they help students make efficient use of that time. However, it is obvious that the computer *can* make an important contribution to ALT in social studies. Simply stated, in situations where computers have enhanced learning, they have done so by increasing effective academic learning time. When computers have failed to improve learning, it is very often because they have not increased ALT. In looking for areas in which computers can contribute positively to social studies instruction, therefore, it is important to seek ways in which they can increase the academic learning time available for effective use by students.

Computers with good instructional software can enhance ALT for social studies in three ways: (1) by permitting learners to study specific social studies information, (2) by enabling students to apply social studies skills to real or simulated problems, and (3) by helping students develop basic tools of learning that they can apply in a wide variety of settings. The following chapters describe specific ways in which the computer can help increase ALT in various areas of the social studies curriculum.

Important Note: If you have somehow understood our discussion of academic learning time as indicating that it is better to have students actively involved 100 percent of their time in the pursuit of trivia than to have them actively involved only 75 percent of the time in the pursuit of more important goals, then we have failed to communicate a very important concept to you. This failure in communication probably occurred because you held a previous "alternative conception" of academic learning time and let that override the concept as we have described it. We emphatically recommend devoting academic learning time to significant educational objectives. If you did not take this as our intent, we urge you to reexamine the preceding paragraphs in this section before continuing with this chapter.

This book, therefore, does not recommend that the microcomputer become one more subject area for students to study, but rather that it become a means to facilitate and enhance social studies teaching and learning. In the social studies curriculum, the computer can provide a method of integrating social studies with various thinking skills to provide a more meaningful experience for the student. In addition, the computer can play a vital role because it has the capacity to both motivate learners and focus their attention more effectively on the task at hand.

IMPORTANT PRINCIPLES OF EDUCATIONAL PSYCHOLOGY

Chapter 3 of *The Computer in the Classroom* provides a detailed discussion of several principles of educational psychology that the computer can help incorporate into the classroom to make instruction more effective. Nearly all of these principles (summarized in Table 2.1) are applicable to social studies instruction. The present section focuses on nine specific principles that are especially relevant to the social studies curriculum: mastery learning, direct instruction, overlearning and automaticity, grouping and peer interactions, feedback, individualization, questions asked by teachers, reading comprehension, and interactive activities. Many of the other principles are also very important for social studies instruction, as they are for all curriculum areas. For a more in-depth look at these other principles, readers should refer to *The Computer in the Classroom*.

Even without computers, these principles are important elements of social studies instruction. A major premise of this book is that the computer should serve as a useful tool to help apply these and other effective instructional strategies in the social studies curriculum.

Table 2.1 Summary of major instructional principles and guidelines for using the computer. (Based on Vockell and Schwartz, 1992.)

Principle: Mastery Learning
Summary: Given enough time, nearly all learners can master objectives.
Guidelines: 1. Use programs that provide extra help and practice toward reaching objectives.
              2. Use programs to stimulate and enrich students who reach objectives early.
              3. Use record-keeping programs to keep track of student performance.

Principle: Direct Instruction
Summary: If teachers describe objectives and demonstrate exact steps, students can master specific skills more efficiently.
Guidelines: 1. Use programs that specify exact steps and teach them clearly and specifically.
              2. Show the relationship of computer programs to steps in the direct teaching process.

Principle: Overlearning
Summary: To become automatic, skills must be practiced and reinforced beyond the point of initial mastery.
Guidelines: 1. Use computer programs to provide self-paced, individualized practice.
              2. Use computer programs that provide gamelike practice for skills that require much repeated practice.
              3. Use computer programs that provide varied approaches to practicing the same activity.

Principle: Memorization Skills
Summary: Recall of factual information is a useful skill that enhances learning at all levels.
Guidelines: 1. Use computer programs to provide repeated practice and facilitate memorization.
              2. Use programs designed to develop memory skills.

Principle: Peer Tutoring
Summary: Both tutor and pupil can benefit from properly structured peer tutoring.
Guidelines: 1. Have students work in groups at computers.
              2. Use programs that are structured to help tutors provide instruction, prompts, and feedback.
              3. Teach students to give feedback, prompts, and instruction at computers.

Principle: Cooperative Learning
Summary: Helping one another is often more productive than competing for scarce rewards.
Guidelines: 1. Have students work in groups at computers.
              2. Use programs that promote cooperation.
              3. Provide guidelines for cooperative roles at computers.

Principle: Monitor Student Progress
Summary: Close monitoring of student progress enables students, teachers, and parents to identify strengths and weaknesses of learners.
Guidelines: 1. Use programs that have management systems to monitor student progress.
              2. Use record-keeping programs.
              3. Use computer to communicate feedback.

Table 2.1 (continued)

Principle: Student Misconceptions
Summary: Identifying misconceptions helps develop an understanding of topics.
Guidelines: 1. Use programs to diagnose misconceptions.
             2. Use programs to teach correct understanding of misunderstood concepts.

Principle: Prerequisite Knowledge and Skills
Summary: Knowledge is usually hierarchical, and low-level skills must be learned
             before higher-level skills can be mastered.
Guidelines: 1. Use programs to assess prerequisite knowledge and skills.
             2. Use programs to teach missing prerequisite skills.

Principle: Immediate Feedback
Summary: Feedback usually works best if it comes quickly after a response.
Guidelines: 1. Use programs that provide immediate feedback.
             2. Use programs that provide clear corrective feedback.

Principle: Parental Involvement
Summary: Parents should be informed about their children's progress and assist in
             helping them learn.
Guidelines: 1. Use computers to communicate with parents about educational
                activities and progress.
             2. Exploit home computers.

Principle: Learning Styles
Summary: Learners vary in preference for modes and styles of learning.
Guidelines: 1. Use programs that appeal to students' preferred learning styles.
             2. Use programs that supplement your weak teaching styles.
             3. Use programs that employ a variety of learning styles.

Principle: Classroom Management
Summary: Effective classroom management provides more time for instruction.
Guidelines: 1. Use the computer as a tool to improve classroom management.
             2. Use programs that have a management component.

Principle: Teacher Questions
Summary: If teachers ask higher-order questions and wait for students to answer,
             higher-level learning is likely to occur.
Guidelines: 1. Select programs that ask higher-level questions.
             2. Use programs that individualize pace of instruction, since wait time is
                likely to be better than with traditional instruction.

Principle: Study Skills
Summary: Effective study skills can be taught, and these almost always enhance
             learning.
Guidelines: 1. Teach students to use the computer as a tool to manage and assist
                learning.
             2. Use programs that teach thinking skills.
             3. Teach generalization of thinking and study skills across subject areas.

Principle: Homework
Summary: When homework is well planned by teachers, completed by students, and
             related to class, learning improves.
Guidelines: 1. Assign homework for home computers.
             2. Have students do preparatory work off the computer as homework.

Table 2.1 (continued)

Principle: Writing Instruction
Summary: Writing should be taught as a recursive process of brainstorming, composing,
                revising, and editing in all areas of the curriculum.
Guidelines: 1. Use word processors for composition.
                2. Use programs that prompt writing skills.
                3. Teach students to use grammar and spelling checkers effectively.

Principle: Early Writing
Summary: Encourage even very young children to write "stories."
Guidelines: 1. Use simple word processing programs.
                2. Use programs that combine graphics with writing.
                3. Use graphics programs to stimulate creativity.

Principle: Level of Abstraction
Summary: Concrete experience helps students understand and master abstract
                principles.
Guidelines: 1. Match programs to children's level of cognitive development.
                2. Use programs that provide concrete demonstrations with clear graphics.

Principle: Reading Comprehension
Summary: Students often learn better if reading lessons are preceded by preparatory
                materials and followed by questions and activities.
Guidelines: 1. Use programs that have pre and post activities to accompany them.
                2. Use computer programs before or after traditional reading materials.

Principle: Social Studies Experiments
Summary: Students learn social studies best if they can do concrete experiments to see
                social studies in action.
Guidelines: 1. Use computer simulations.
                2. Use tutorial and drill programs with concrete graphics.
                3. Use database and word processing programs to manage and report
                   noncomputerized social studies experiments.

Principle: Transfer of Learning
Summary: Students will generalize what is learned in one situation to other settings if
                specific steps are taken to assure transfer of learning.
Guidelines: 1. Focus attention on what was successful.
                2. Ask reflective questions at end of unit.
                3. Use the "Remember when . . . ? Now let's. . . . " rule.

Mastery Learning

Mastery learning holds that given enough time and help, about 95 percent of the learners in any group can come to a complete mastery of the designated instructional objectives. Traditional instruction holds time constant and allows achievement to vary within a group. For example, a history unit may last nine weeks, and at the end of that time students who have mastered the subject thoroughly receive grades of A, while those who have mastered very little get grades of F. Mastery learning reverses this relation-ship by holding achievement constant and letting vary the time students spend in pursuit of the objectives. In the same history unit, a few students might meet the standards in 3 weeks, most might take 9 weeks, and a few students might take up to 15 or 20 weeks.

Mastery learning is not synonymous with pass/fail grading, nor does it imply that "standards should be lowered." When mastery learning is successful, high standards are articulated, and students receive ample time and help to meet them. Additional information about mastery learning can be found in Guskey and Gates (1986), Slavin (1987), and Levine (1987).

Mastery learning has received formal emphasis only in the past 20 years; informally, students and teachers have known about this principle for a long time. For example, students having trouble in any subject usually believe they can master it if they are given enough time.

Two problems often arise with mastery learning: (1) Grouping and scheduling may become difficult. It is easier to force people to work at a constant pace and to complete tasks at a predictable rate than to permit wide variations in activities within a class. (2) While slower learners spend extra time on minimum standards, the faster learners may be forced to wait, when they could be progressing to higher levels of achievement. These problems are not insurmountable. They are overcome by providing in-dividualized attention, setting high but attainable standards, and making additional materials available for those students who master objectives more quickly.

Computers can aid mastery learning in three ways:

1. Many students need additional time and individualized practice with feedback to meet objectives. Computer programs can often provide opportunities to study at times and at a pace suited to the individual's needs.
2. Additional programs can be made available for students who master objectives quickly. These programs can provide more intense study of the same objectives, move on to higher objectives, or integrate the objectives covered in the unit with other objectives.
3. Gradebook and other recordkeeping programs can help teachers keep track of student performance.

As mastery learning overlaps considerably with other principles dis-cussed in this chapter, these three contributions of the computer are cited in later sections. (For example, applications of mastery learning will appear in the sections on Direct Instruction and Overlearning.) Mastery learning has for many years worked quite well without the aid of computers. However, the wise use of computers can often make this approach work more effectively.

In subjects for which there is an abundance of software, computers can make an easy and obvious contribution to mastery learning. For example, if students are expected to learn the names, locations, and capitals of all the states, there are several programs designed to help them reach this objective. Programs such as STATES (Queue), STATES AND CAPITALS (Gamco), STATES AND TRAITS (Britannica), and U.S. ATLAS ACTION (Edu-Tron) provide useful and interesting drills. Students who need additional practice could run one of these programs repeatedly until attaining mastery. To add variety and avoid monotony, they could be permitted to use more than one of these programs. Students who achieved mastery more quickly than others could move on to games that include additional information about the states, such as SPACE COMMANDER (Gamco) and AMERICA COAST TO COAST (Mindscape), or more detailed information about a single state, such as KNOW YOUR STATE (Right On). They could also run programs that involve problem-solving skills, such as ROAD RALLY U.S.A. (Edu-Tron) and CROSSCOUNTRY U.S.A. (Didatech), or they could work with database programs that focus on specific states, such as U.S.A. IN PROFILE (Active Learning Systems) and U.S.A. GEOGRAPH (MECC).

The availability of computer programs makes it possible to promote mastery learning on higher-order objectives as well. For example, while some students would reach the objective of "understanding what it was like to travel west as a pioneer" by running OREGON TRAIL just once or twice, others might need several trials to come to this understanding. What do the faster students do while these others continue to enjoy themselves by mastering OREGON TRAIL? Having them leave the computers and do worksheets is almost a form of punishment. Having them continue a simulation they have already mastered may become boring; and they may ruin the simulation for others by simply telling them the answers and reducing their creative thought. One solution is to offer these early finishers a second simulation on the same objective. SANTA FE TRAIL (Educational Activities), LEWIS AND CLARK EXPEDITION (MicroEd), SETTLING AMERICA (Edu-Tron), and WAGONS WEST (Focus Media) all simulate similar pioneer journeys. Students who enjoy adventure games could be permitted to start GOLD RUSH! (Sierra Online), which is described in Chapter 4. Another follow-up activity would be to let the early finishers develop their own simulation, using Hartley's SIMULATION CON-STRUCTION KIT. The computer can help keep students at all levels of proficiency on task, while the teacher interacts with them as necessary to monitor and assure mastery. In this way, all students can master legitimate, higher-order objectives without any inefficient waste of academic learning time.

The large number of programs listed in Appendix B indicates the abundance of good software currently available for most subjects in social studies. However, in many cases the programs do not match up properly with textbooks, and therefore a teacher may be unable to find good software to support mastery of a specific unit of instruction. To overcome this problem, teachers can use programs such as CLAS (Touch Technologies), INTERACTIVE AUTHORING SYSTEM (McGraw-Hill), or HYPERCARD (Claris) to fashion their own curriculum-correlated practice materials. These programs permit the creation of custom-made lessons that allow the student to achieve mastery learning, without straining the resources (or the patience) of the teacher. A common format of such programs includes:

1. On-screen instructions for using the program.
2. A tutorial section for introducing instructional materials.
3. Short-answer, multiple choice, and true/false questions.
4. Branching elements that offer additional instruction for areas where weakness is indicated.

Authoring programs offer other advantages such as student-controlled pace, effective use of graphics for reinforcement, and automatic recordkeeping (Vockell and Schwartz, 1992). In addition, some existing programs (such as Hartley's MEDALISTS series on history and geography) provide a useful game format into which teachers or students can insert questions relevant to their own needs. Finally, to promote mastery of higher-order skills, teachers should consider Hartley's SIMULATION CONSTRUCTION KIT.

Direct Instruction

The term *direct instruction* refers to academically focused, teacher-directed classrooms using logically sequenced instructional materials or teacher guidance to keep students on task effectively. Further characteristics include goals that are clear to students, sufficient and continuous time allocated for instruction, monitoring of student performance, questions at an appropriate cognitive level so that students can produce numerous correct responses, and immediate and academically oriented feedback. The teacher controls instructional goals, chooses materials appropriate for the students' abilities, and paces instruction. Interaction is structured, but not authoritarian. Learning takes place in a convivial atmosphere. For basic skills in such areas as reading, language arts, social studies, and mathematics, direct instruction has consistently proven to be more effective than informal or nondirective strategies (Rosenshine, 1986).

Direct instruction is most useful in those areas of social studies that focus on specific information or skills, such as learning geographical information or concepts in history. We are not aware of a large number of good programs that provide self-contained units of direct instruction on social studies concepts. However, there are many programs that teachers can easily integrate with the direct instruction normally conducted in an effective classroom. For example, a teacher might first use direct instruction methods to teach an American geography unit, and then use one of the programs cited in the Mastery Learning section or Hartley's STATES to verify whether the students have mastered the unit's objectives. Likewise, a geography teacher could use Sunburst's NORTH AMERICAN DATABASES as a basis for a direct instruction unit to develop specific skills related to collecting, organizing, locating, and reporting facts about North America.

Direct instruction can also play an important though limited role even in areas of the social studies curriculum where the objectives are more vague. For example, it would be difficult to teach "an appreciation of the impact of mercantilism on American history" through direct instruction. However, this general goal requires as prerequisites several more specific subskills, such as defining mercantilism and knowing how to read and interpret graphs. The teacher could use INTERPRETING GRAPHS (Sunburst) as part of a direct instruction subunit that would enable students to develop skills for a more discovery-oriented overall approach to the topic of appreciation of mercantilism.

Overlearning and Automaticity

With many skills and concepts in social studies, it is important to continue studying them and applying them well beyond the point of initial mastery. When teachers work with large groups of students, they are often forced to violate this principle. In most classes, some students master objectives quickly, a large number learn at a medium rate, and others learn very slowly. Because of the way class time must be structured, the teacher is practically forced to move on to the next objective as soon as the middle group of students demonstrates an initial understanding of the topic. Therefore, the students who get the most overlearning are the brightest students, who mastered the objectives quickly and then may have continued to practice beyond the point of initial mastery. Paradoxically, the students who *need* overlearning the most are the slowest students—who probably get none at all. This is especially unfortunate with regard to basic concepts, which must be mastered to a point where they become automatic, so that they can be incorporated into subsequent higher-level objectives.

Computers can help solve this problem. Just as computers can help learners achieve mastery learning (see the first principle), they can help students practice skills well beyond the point of initial mastery until they become overlearned or automatic. The interest, variety, and gamelike atmosphere provided by the computer offer a considerable advantage when students practice an activity beyond initial mastery. The simple fact is that there are numerous skills that must be practiced in spite of the fact students "already know them." By selecting computer software that provides repeated practice in different contexts and through different formats, students can achieve this necessary repetition without the stultifying monotony that might otherwise occur.

For example, most elementary social studies curricula in the United States include a unit where students are required to make a study of the location and identifying facts of the individual states. Traditionally, this type of unit requires poring over maps and historical descriptions. The program STATES AND TRAITS by DesignWare (Figure 2.1) offers an exciting alternative. Instead of enduring the drudgery of memorization, the program challenges the students by awarding points for correct locations of states or correctly identifying a state by its traits or historical facts. When learning is placed in the context of a game or contest, the challenge of competition becomes the incentive. As we stated in our previous discussion of mastery learning, if there is a sufficent amount of good software on a topic, the computer can easily help students cover the same objectives from various perspectives and with different motivational strategies until these objectives are thoroughly mastered and overlearned to the point where they become automatic.

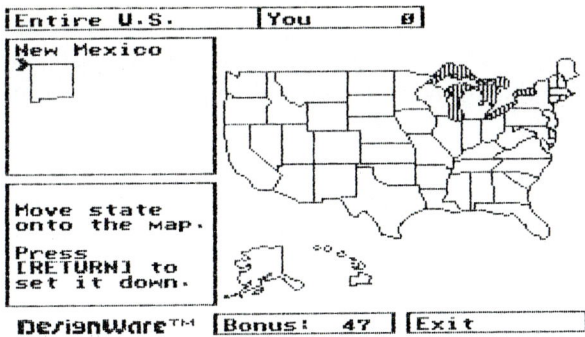

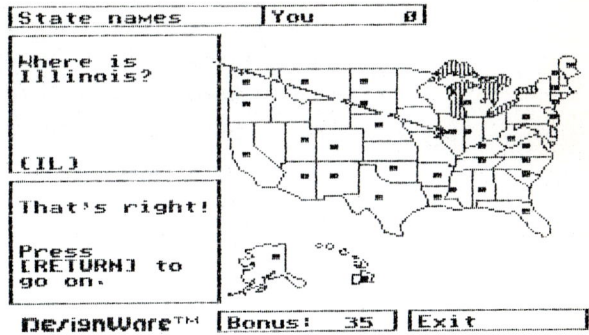

(a)

(b)

Figure 2.1 Screens from STATES AND TRAITS by DesignWare, which challenges students by awarding points for correct locations of states or correctly identifying a state by its traits or historical facts.

(c)

Grouping, Cooperative Learning, and Peer Tutoring

When students work alone at computers, the following disadvantages are likely to occur: (1) the social isolation involved can create mood states (such as loneliness, boredom, and frustration) that interfere with sustained effort to complete learning tasks; (2) students are denied the opportunity to summarize orally and explain what they are learning; and (3) computers cannot provide social models to be imitated and used for social comparisons (Johnson and Johnson, 1987). Working as a whole class with the teacher can solve these problems, but the cooperative learning and peer tutoring literature suggests that small groups can also overcome these difficulties.

At the computer, students can work in groups in many different ways. For example, they can work individualistically and take turns using the computer, they can compete to see who is best, or they can cooperate. Current research suggests that the cooperative approach is usually the best. The key components of effective cooperative learning are positive interdependence, individual accountability, and shared responsibility for one another. This means that the success of the group requires that each person have a role, be accountable for that role, and be interested in helping the group as a whole attain important goals. Closely related to the concept of cooperative learning is that of peer tutoring. Research on this topic indicates that when students tutor their peers, both the tutor and the tutee benefit from the process.

Investigation programs like THE RIPPLE THAT CHANGED AMERICAN HISTORY (Tom Snyder Productions) offer the opportunity for peer tutoring. In this program a distortion or warp in time is moving through the historic events normally studied in American history. It is the job of the student, or in this case the team, to locate and stop this destructive ripple. Two-person teams create an opportunity for a meaningful exchange or dialog, which may lead to the successful completion of this game.

The research on cooperative learning and peer tutoring is discussed in greater detail in Cohen, Kulik, and Kulik (1982), Slavin (1983, 1986), Slavin et al. (1985), Wang and Walberg (1985), and Vockell and Schwartz (1992).

What this all amounts to is that when students are working on programs that teach higher-order thinking skills, small groups at the computer are almost always preferable to individual students at the computer. And large-group (whole-class) presentations are often preferred over solitary work at the computer. But once important skills have been thoroughly learned by some members of the class and at least partially mastered by everyone, then small groups may provide a better use of academic learning time than a continued large-group session.

Small-group activities at the computer will support the learning of social studies skills only if the group sessions are structured to promote their occurrence. Usually, this means incorporating the direct instruction approach described in this chapter, assigning group activities only after the unit has been appropriately introduced to a large group, ascertaining that group members have actual roles they understand and objectives they can meet, and teaching students to interact properly with the program and with one another.

For example, after completing a unit of study on the colonial period of U.S. history, small-group work might include writing, editing, and publishing a newspaper. This sort of activity offers practice in gathering research information, in writing and editing, and in critical thinking skills. Division of labor can be left to the individual group members. One advantage to this is the need for only one member of each group to be proficient at keyboarding. Other members can perform other duties. Desktop publishing programs such as PUBLISH IT! (Timeworks) and CHILDREN'S WRITING AND PUBLISHING CENTER (Learning Company) provide an attractive final copy. This is a good project to run just before parents' night or open house.

There is a very important distinction between the *learning phase* and the *practice phase* of instruction. During the learning phase, students who have not yet mastered knowledge or skills need feedback to focus attention correctly, to detect and clarify misconceptions, and to come to a relatively clear understanding of concepts or principles under consideration. During the practice phase, external feedback from a skilled teacher is less important, since the student is practicing skills previously learned, and feedback will arise automatically from the situation or from the student's own insights. Because they can become more actively involved in more communication with peers, it is probably true that students can greatly benefit from practicing social studies skills in small groups.

Our belief is that many teachers make the mistake of sending students off to practice skills they have not yet learned. Students can (and should) practice together, and sometimes they can help each other understand and master complex skills—although this is comparatively rare. Peer tutoring of *factual* information is extremely effective. Peer *modeling* of process skills is also extremely effective. But peer *teaching* of process skills is not likely to be effective; the teacher should maintain responsibility for monitoring progress in social studies skills and prompting their development through effective interaction and discourse.

We are not suggesting that if you find a group of children deeply engaged in vivacious discourse about social issues you should tell them to stop thinking until you have time to teach them how to do it. Many students can and do learn by arriving at insights and making discoveries on their own. What we are suggesting is that teachers should assign students to small-group or individual work on social studies software—especially when it deals with fairly complex objectives—only when they have a good reason to believe the students are likely to be in the practice phase and therefore likely to benefit from the software. Turning a group of students loose on a program such as ECONOMICS (Merrill), containing subtitles like "Law of Demand," "Law of Supply," "Fractional Reserves," and "Stock Market Simulation," would be futile and frustrating without proper background instruction.

Several companies (such as Tom Snyder Productions, the makers of the DECISIONS, DECISIONS series) have begun to introduce software that is designed to stimulate normal classroom discussion and activities. Good social studies teachers have sometimes resisted using computers because they already had developed effective strategies to promote communication skills and felt the introduction of computer software would require them to abandon successful techniques in favor of an unknown novelty. These doubts can be overcome if teachers emphasize using the computer as an effective tool within existing sound instructional frameworks.

Feedback

In order for learners to receive maximum benefit from feedback, it should be supplied as soon as possible after the performance of an activity. Actually, mature learners can often wait for a few days or even weeks to find out whether their response was a good one. There is even research to indicate that sometimes learners do their own assessments of correctness when teacher feedback is lacking, and these self-assessments are useful. But in general, the best time to tell learners whether they were right or wrong is when they are most interested in this information—usually right after they have given their answer. For various reasons, classroom feedback is often delayed for several minutes, hours, days, or even weeks. Positive feedback (knowledge that you are right) is obviously important, but negative feedback (knowledge that you are wrong) is sometimes even more crucial, since a blissfully ignorant student may spend several minutes, hours, days, or weeks mispronouncing a word or applying a misconception before discovering the nature of this error.

The computer has the capacity to give almost instantaneous feedback. Rapid positive or corrective feedback and branching based upon student responses are important components of drill and tutorial software. Another feature that computerized feedback can add is objectivity. If a student gives a disastrously inappropriate answer, the computer neither attacks the personality of the learner nor helps out with inappropriate hints: a wrong answer or bad decision simply leads to its logically programmed consequences. Because they are warm, compassionate human beings, teachers often sympathize with students who are making errors (for example, by following blind leads) and inadvertently supply hints that prevent them from learning through their mistakes. The impersonal objectivity of the computer sometimes offers the advantage of taking the teacher out of the evaluative process and letting him/her join the learning team on the side of the students. In MECC's OREGON TRAIL students are challenged to successfully negotiate a journey from St. Louis to the West Coast by joining a wagon train (see Figure 2.2). This provides an interesting class exercise using an LCD projection panel. If the students are merely left to their own inclinations, they usually die on the trail. The teacher should resist the urge to help out too much, and should even risk "death on the trail" as a result of poor student decisions. By commiserating with them but allowing them to learn from their mistakes, she can increase their chance of success on subsequent trips and promote student/computer interaction to develop important understandings. In this way, the teacher can supply the personal touch missing in the computer program, without jeopardizing the instructional setting.

Individualization

A major advantage offered by the computer is individualization. In the typical classroom, students vary widely in their instructional needs with regard to thinking skills. As this chapter has indicated, students effectively learn social studies skills if they spend useful instructional time on tasks suited to their own needs. The teacher is faced with major difficulties because in a class of 30 students, some will have mastered all the prerequisite skills to begin working toward mastery of a more advanced skill, while others will have mastered none of them. In between are students with a tentative mastery of some and a solid mastery of others. If all the students have mastered the prerequisite skills, it is a fairly straightforward task to help them master the new strategies. However, teachers are often overwhelmed by the need to give attention to individual weaknesses while simultaneously trying to "enrich" the curriculum for the students who have mastered the prerequisite skills and course objectives at a speed and level dictated by their own needs.

Moreover, since basic social studies concepts need to become automatic to provide a basis for more advanced skills, it is important to provide repeated practice for important skills. Repeated practice can be boring,

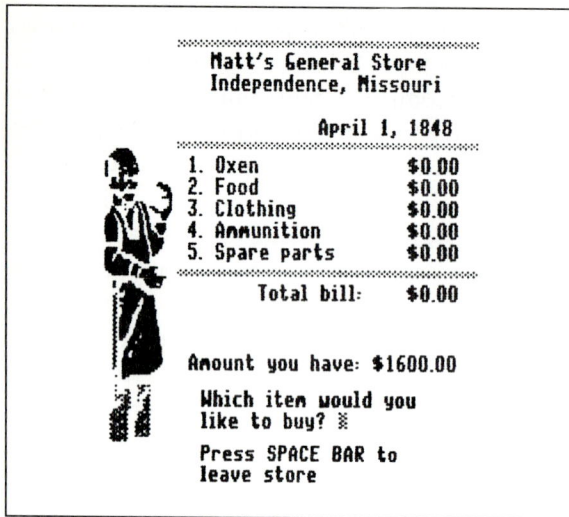

(a)

(b)

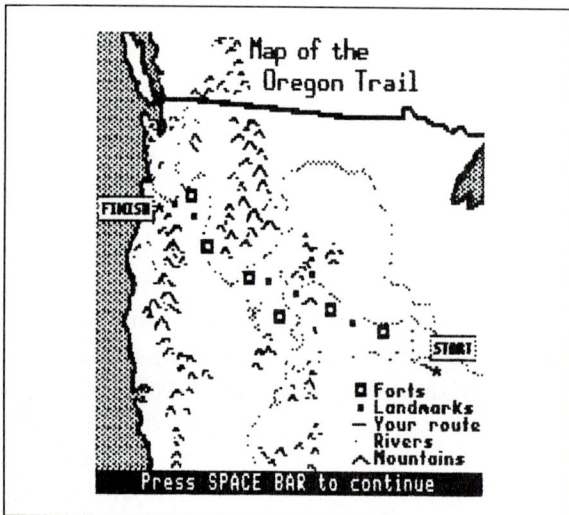

(c)

(d)

Figure 2.2 Screens from MECC's OREGON TRAIL, in which students are challenged to successfully negotiate a journey from St. Louis to the West Coast as members of a wagon train.

painful, and frustrating. This is why many students "turn off" to academic subjects. A computer can help reduce the repetition for those who do not need additional practice. For students who do need the extra practice, creative teachers can use the computer to help overcome this difficulty by making the practice interesting (even gamelike), by supplying informative feedback, and by making the repeated practice relevant to the present or future needs of the students. A microcomputer can assist by making the practice more interesting or by changing the repetitive drill into a challenging game.

The principle of individualization does not contradict the principle of cooperative learning. When students are focusing on objectives of unique interest to themselves alone, working alone at the computer is the most effective strategy. However, such solitary objectives are indeed rare in the social studies curriculum. It is the contention of this book that very often the best strategy is to have the students work in small groups or even to have the entire class work at a single computer. The computer can become the focal point for class activity, thinking, and discussion.

The key point is that individualization is *not* synonymous with individualistic learning. Research supports the concept of individualization, which suggests that students learn best when instruction is suited to their individual needs. Individualization does not by any means require that students work alone. The key requirement of individualized instruction is that each student be working at his/her maximum level of performance on tasks related to his/her needs.

Students experiencing individualized instruction can definitely benefit from interacting with peers: for example, they may profit from modeling, motivating social interactions, or feedback from their peers. They can also benefit from interacting with a knowledgeable teacher, who can keep them on task, model useful strategies, and provide feedback and insights as needed. On the other hand, research does *not* support the concept of individualistic instruction, which suggests that students should pursue their own instructional objectives without concern for the needs or interests of their classmates. As this chapter has indicated, a cooperative approach is likely to be more effective for most educational topics in most classrooms.

Questions Asked by Teachers

Student achievement rises when teachers ask questions that require students to apply, analyze, synthesize, and evaluate information in addition to simply recalling facts. Students also do better when given time to think before answering these questions. Two of the factors that seriously inhibit learning are that teachers tend to ask only questions that require rote memorization and that they expect students to answer within about one second after a question is asked. Studies show that when teachers ask higher-order questions and give appropriate feedback for answers, students learn higher-order skills more effectively. In addition, if teachers pause a few seconds longer and provide appropriate prompts, students can often answer higher-order questions and benefit accordingly. Excellent summaries of research on teacher questioning and wait time can be found in Barell (1985) and Tobin (1987).

Computers are not automatically superior to teachers at asking higher-order questions that involve nonrote skills. In fact, a very large number of computer drills require nothing more than rote responses. Note, however, that even if all computer programs required merely rote answers, they would be freeing teachers to engage students in more higher-order thinking. Of course, it is also possible to program the computer to ask higher-order questions, as Figure 2.3 indicates. If teachers are seriously interested in promoting nonrote skills, then they should examine programs carefully and select software that requires higher-order performance.

Computers do have an inherent advantage over teachers with regard to how long they are willing to wait for the student to respond. When a teacher asks a question, a lengthy silence may signal a coming disruption in the teaching process. Many teachers feel compelled to indicate that the student is "wrong" or to call on another student almost immediately. Actually, the most sensible way to approach a difficult question is to pause, analyze the problem, bring to mind relevant information, develop a tentative answer, check the validity of this tentative answer, and then give the answer out loud. It's difficult to do this within the short time provided by most teachers, so students (at best) "think on their feet." If they understand the question, they either give a memorized (or previously thought out) response or start talking and develop their answer while they are giving it. This may be a useful strategy for winning prizes on a game show, but it hardly enhances effective thinking. (In fact, the students who benefit are probably the other thoughtful students, who go through all the appropriate steps while the teacher is calling on the first student.) The computer solves this problem simply by waiting as long as necessary for the student to respond. There is no ominous silence after the computer presents a question, and no pressure to answer before the teacher calls on another student. When asked a higher-order question, the student can pause, go through the appropriate steps, and then respond.

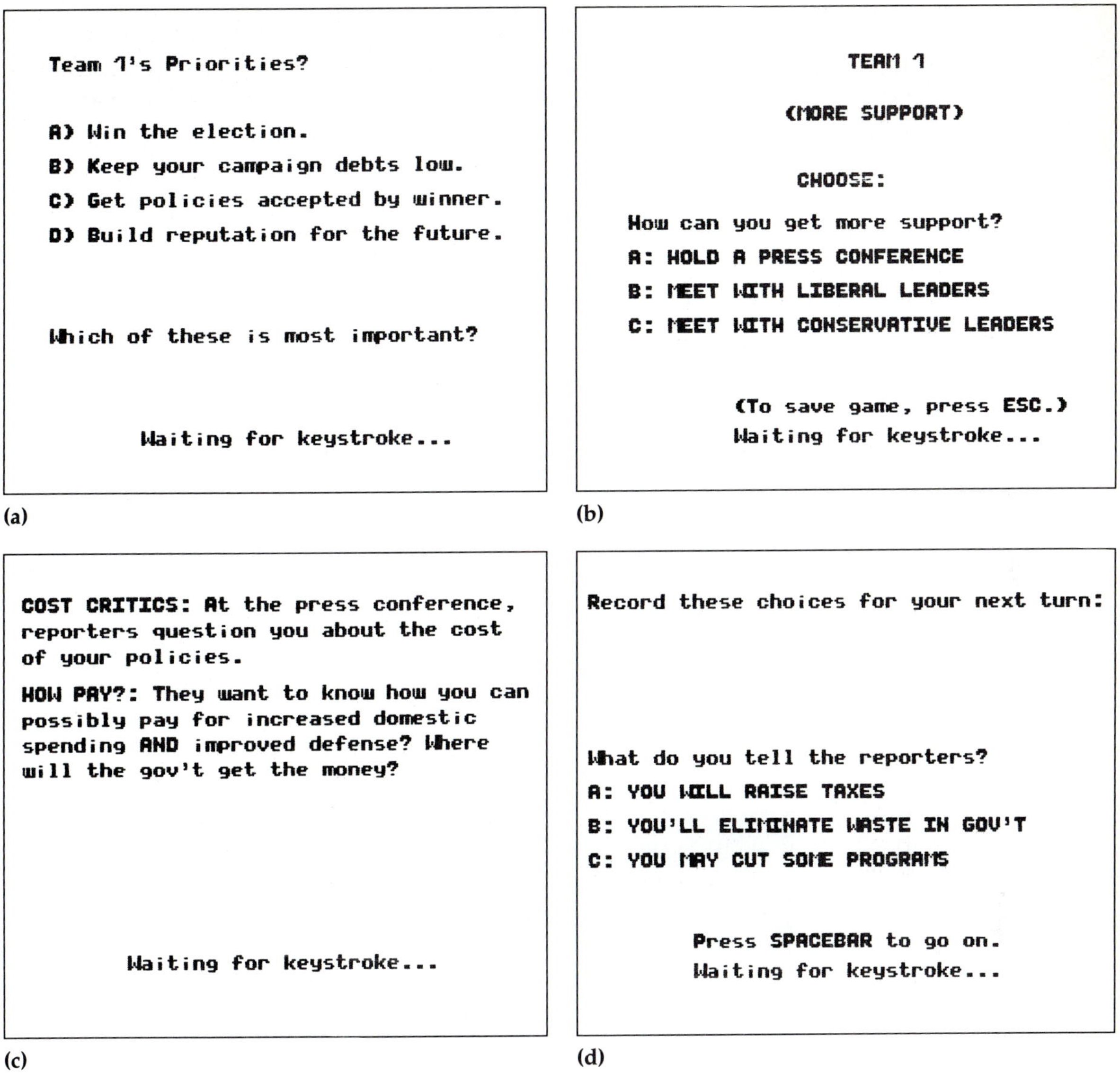

(a)

```
Team 1's Priorities?

A) Win the election.
B) Keep your campaign debts low.
C) Get policies accepted by winner.
D) Build reputation for the future.


Which of these is most important?


          Waiting for keystroke...
```

(b)

```
              TEAM 1

           (MORE SUPPORT)


             CHOOSE:

How can you get more support?
A: HOLD A PRESS CONFERENCE
B: MEET WITH LIBERAL LEADERS
C: MEET WITH CONSERVATIVE LEADERS


        (To save game, press ESC.)
        Waiting for keystroke...
```

(c)

```
COST CRITICS: At the press conference,
reporters question you about the cost
of your policies.

HOW PAY?: They want to know how you can
possibly pay for increased domestic
spending AND improved defense? Where
will the gov't get the money?




          Waiting for keystroke...
```

(d)

```
Record these choices for your next turn:




What do you tell the reporters?
A: YOU WILL RAISE TAXES
B: YOU'LL ELIMINATE WASTE IN GOV'T
C: YOU MAY CUT SOME PROGRAMS


        Press SPACEBAR to go on.
        Waiting for keystroke...
```

Figure 2.3 A screen from DECISIONS, DECISIONS: ON THE CAMPAIGN TRAIL (Tom Snyder), showing a higher-order question. The computer has presented several questions and will branch in response to this one.

Reading Comprehension

Students get more out of a reading assignment when the teacher precedes the lesson with background information and follows it with discussion. For this reason, good social studies teachers begin lessons by introducing key vocabulary words and concepts with which the students may be unfamiliar. They stimulate the interest of the students. Afterwards, they ask questions that probe the major elements of the reading passage. These follow-up questions serve two purposes: they help verify understanding, and they make it more likely that the students will remember the information they read and be able to use it on future occasions.

An increasing number of computer programs provide introductory and follow-up activities for social studies passages. For example, the program shown in Figure 2.4 provides questions to ascertain whether students have understood that story (which they read in the normal hardcopy format). Likewise, OREGON TRAIL (shown in Figure 2.2) provides a gamelike opportunity for students to make major decisions that will determine the success of their trip along the Oregon Trail to the Pacific Coast. Correct planning enables students to use this program either as a preliminary activity to stimulate their curiosity about the dangers the pioneers faced, or as a follow-up activity for those who have studied the westward movement in some other context.

Programs like OREGON TRAIL that include rich and informative reading passages are also useful because they counter a trend which may

Figure 2.4 A screen from CHARLOTTE'S WEB (Sunburst), which provides questions to ascertain whether students have understood the story (which they read in the normal hardcopy format).

When Wilbur grew bigger, Fern's father said that Wilbur must leave. So, Wilbur was

_____.

1 sold to Fern's Uncle Homer

2 given to Fern's Aunt Mandy

3 taken to Doctor Dorian's

occur when students use computerized or other programmed materials. If students never read complete passages of continuous text, they may get the false impression that reading and studying consist of reading a short passage and answering questions about it. Although there is good reason to use programs that provide these testlike passages and short drills, it is also essential to use programs that encourage students to use their reading and study skills beyond the world of the computer—for learning and enjoyment.

Interactive Activities

Students learn many subjects best when they become actively involved in the study activities. Young children need concrete experience with their studies; they cannot understand abstract principles unless they can base them on concrete experience. Even older students and adults, who are capable of more high-level reasoning, can understand abstract principles of social studies more clearly if they can relate them to concrete experiences.

At first thought, it might seem that the best way to experience social studies in action is to do actual, nonsimulated activities. However, some concrete activities are too dangerous, expensive, complicated, or for some other reason impractical to conduct in the classroom. In many cases, it is possible to simulate such activities with the computer. Even if it is possible to carry out a nonsimulated activity, the computer offers the advantage of efficiency: it may be able to conduct the same activity 20 times as rapidly. By using the computer to simulate interaction with other people, for example, the student may be able to repeat the process several times within a single class period and not be distracted by extraneous factors, such as artificial time constraints or inattentiveness of other group members.

OREGON TRAIL is an excellent example of a good social studies simulation. Students easily become actively involved in this program, and they often prefer it to more specifically recreational computer games. Note, however, that it is probably not a good idea to exclude easily accessible real-life activities by replacing them with simulated experiences. For example, it would not be desirable to run ecology simulations *instead of* studying actual events in the newspapers or becoming actively involved in a project to improve the environment. It is most effective to employ a combination of actual and simulated activities. In many cases, computerized strategies such as databases, graphing programs, and word processors can be incorporated into these real-life activities. The mechanical, time-consuming process of recording, tabulating, and graphing data can be done by computer and related software, so that the student can spend time planning the activities and understanding the processes under observation.

SUMMARY

This chapter has examined a few of the principles that are important in social studies instruction and has shown how the computer can be integrated with these principles. In addition to the principles discussed in this chapter, many of the other principles briefly summarized in Table 2.1 can also be applied to social studies instruction. For example, the principles related to learning styles, classroom management, and prerequisite knowledge are obviously applicable to the social studies curriculum. More detailed discussions of these other principles can be found in *The Computer in the Classroom*.

The key point of this chapter is that computers will help students improve their social studies skills if (and only if) they lead to more effective use of academic learning time. This chapter has also shown how procedures for promoting mastery learning, direct instruction, automaticity, peer tutoring, cooperative learning, feedback, individualization, and effective teacher questioning can be integrated with the computer to facilitate social studies instruction. Subsequent chapters apply these strategies to more specific instances of bringing the computer into the social studies classroom.

REFERENCES

Barell, J. "You Ask the Wrong Questions." *Educational Leadership* 42 (May 1985): 18–23.

Berliner, D. "The Half-Full Glass: A Review of Research on Teaching." In P. Hosford (Ed.), *Using What We Know About Teaching*. Alexandria, VA: Association for Supervision and Curriculum Development, 1984.

Caldwell, J. H., W. G. Huitt, and A. O. Graeber. "Time Spent in Learning: Implications from Research." *Elementary School Journal* 82 (1982): 471–480.

Cohen, P. A., J. A. Kulik, and C. C. Kulik. "Educational Outcomes of Tutoring: A Meta-Analysis of Findings." *American Educational Research Journal* 19 (1982): 237–248.

Guskey, T. R., and S. L. Gates. "Synthesis of Research on the Effects of Mastery Learning in Elementary and Secondary Schools." *Educational Leadership* 43 (May 1986): 73–80.

Johnson, D. W., and R. T. Johnson. *Learning Together and Alone: Cooperative, Competitive, and Individualistic Learning.* Englewood Cliffs, NJ: Prentice-Hall, 1987.

Levine, D. U. *Improving Student Learning Through Mastery Learning Programs.* San Francisco: Jossey-Bass, 1987.

Rosenshine, B. V. "Synthesis of Research on Explicit Teaching." *Educational Leadership* 43 (7) (1986): 60–69.

Slavin, R. E. *Cooperative Learning.* New York: Longman, 1983.

Slavin, R. E. *Educational Psychology: Theory into Practice.* Englewood Cliffs, NJ: Prentice-Hall, 1986.

Slavin, R. E. "Mastery Learning Reconsidered." *Review of Educational Research* 57 (1987): 175–213.

Slavin, R. E., S. Sharan, S. Kagan, R. Hertz-Lazarowitz, C. Webb, and R. Schmuck (Eds.). *Learning to Cooperate, Cooperating to Learn.* New York: Plenum, 1985.

Tobin, K. "The Role of Wait Time in Higher Cognitive Level Learning." *Review of Educational Research* 57 (March 1987): 69–95.

Vockell, E. L., and E. Schwartz. *The Computer in the Classroom* (2nd Ed.). Watsonville, CA: Mitchell **McGRAW-HILL**, 1992.

Vockell, E. L., and R. van Deusen. *Using the Computer to Teach Higher-Order Thinking Skills.* Watsonville, CA: Mitchell **McGRAW-HILL**, 1988.

Wang, M., and H. Walberg (Eds.). *Adapting Instruction to Individual Difference.* Berkeley, CA: McCutcham, 1985.

CHAPTER 3

THE MICRO-COMPUTER IN THE ELEMENTARY SCHOOL YEARS (K–6)

THE PREVIOUS CHAPTER SHOWED that the microcomputer is compatible with the goals of elementary and secondary educational systems and serves as a useful medium for integrating mastery learning, peer tutoring, cooperative learning, and other individualized and group techniques into the curriculum. The present chapter focuses on practical applications of the computer in the elementary social studies curriculum. It discusses ways in which computer technology can benefit students by helping them master the concepts, skills, and principles typically covered in this curriculum.

At the elementary level, the social studies curriculum is usually closely integrated with other subject areas—especially with the language arts curriculum. One of the most effective ways to teach social studies is to offer a language-rich environment that stimulates activities involving geography, history, economics, information retrieval, social skills, and other topics related to the social studies curriculum. In such an environment, students are encouraged to interact not only with the teacher and materials provided, but also with one another; thus, they develop skills in communication as well as social studies. The physical setting, the characteristics of the students, and the teacher's style of communicating combine to establish the learning atmosphere. The computer and appropriate software influence the physical setting while providing numerous opportunities for student-to-teacher and student-to-student communication in a language-rich environment.

The physical setting of such an environment provides a warm, cheerful place in which the student feels at ease. The classroom is filled with books, newspapers, magazines, and other reading as well as listening material. This setting respects the student's need for individual space, while also encouraging group interaction. By providing a suitable furniture arrangement and "something to talk about," it promotes student thought and talk. Often a teacher inadvertently discourages student interaction by arranging desks in rows facing the front of the room. While this arrangement is convenient for some purposes, it may encourage a passive, receptive, individualistic style of learning. Research tells us (Mayer and Brause, 1986) that students benefit most from talking with each other in guided activities. It is possible to set up desks and other furniture—including computers—in a way that promotes orderly activity and minimizes distractions without introducing obstacles to the communication.

Many teachers find that they can facilitate communication by arranging desks in groups or having students sit at tables. This set-up encourages student interaction and cooperative learning. Proper classroom organization can lead to the use of the computer and other materials in peer teaching as well as facilitate the cooperative learning model discussed in Chapter 6. The placement of computers within a learning environment can often determine the computer's capacity to promote social studies and communication skills in the classroom.

Besides the arrangement of desks, the physical setting can enhance a language-rich environment by providing "things to talk about." For example, bulletin boards can invite discussion. Displays that focus on current events, hobbies, or other favorite topics can initiate conversation. A bulletin board that requires interaction is a perfect spot for study partners to discuss a subject and learn together with or without assistance from the computer. The computer placed adjacent to the bulletin board can be a part of that learning experience. Figure 3.1 shows a screen from HYPER ATLAS. This output could be an effective part of a bulletin board display for fifth graders about Middle East oil resources. By discussing responses to various questions in this program, a student and study partner partake in verbal practice while sharing their own background experiences and insights. This example shows how the computer and bulletin board can mutually supplement each other: the bulletin board draws attention to and motivates students to use the computer, while the computer augments information introduced on the bulletin board.

Many elementary classrooms also feature learning centers—nooks, corners, or tables in the classroom where related materials are collected for individual or group exploration. A center may include an assortment of reading materials, manipulatives, artist's tools, or whatever is appropriate

Figure 3.1 A screen from HYPER ATLAS. By discussing responses to various questions while using this program, a student and study partner gain verbal experience while sharing their own background experiences and insights.

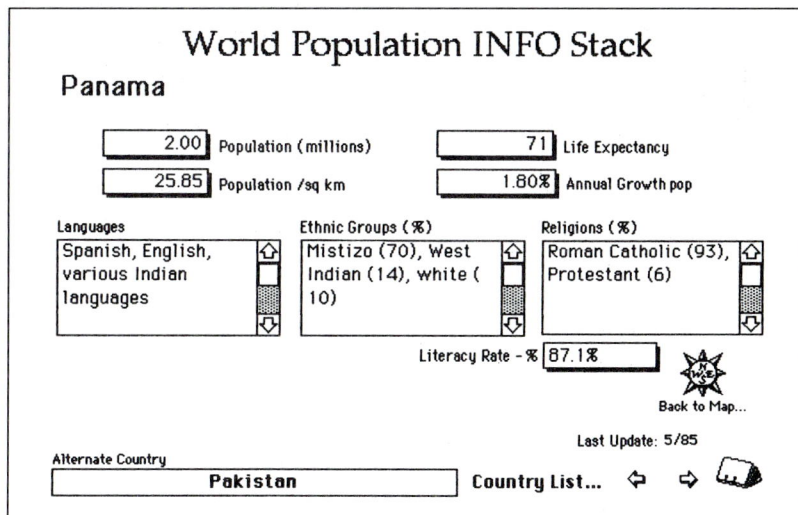

World Population INFO Stack

Panama

2.00 Population (millions)   71 Life Expectancy
25.85 Population /sq km   1.80% Annual Growth pop

Languages
Spanish, English, various Indian languages

Ethnic Groups (%)
Mistizo (70), West Indian (14), white (10)

Religions (%)
Roman Catholic (93), Protestant (6)

Literacy Rate - % 87.1%

Back to Map...

Last Update: 5/85

Alternate Country
Pakistan   Country List...

for the topic under consideration. The inclusion of a computer in the center provides numerous possibilities. The learning center can become a study and writing center that provides a word processing program such as KIDWRITER (Spinnaker) or MAGIC SLATE (Sunburst) to create journals or short stories and a graphics program like PRINT SHOP (Broderbund) to generate posters and banners on class topics. It can become a vocabulary development center that includes a database package to create a classroom glossary or personal dictionary of new words. It can become a desktop publishing center that gives students the chance to create their own newspaper. A major advantage of the computer is its flexibility. The computerized learning center is not restricted to any *one* of these applications mentioned. The insertion of a different disk and the press of a button can instantly change a social studies center into a mathematics center or into a desktop publishing center.

An example of a physical setting that promotes a language-rich environment is pictured in Figure 3.2. Note the simple but revolutionary "technological innovation" that vastly enhances the impact of the computer in this classroom: a second chair at the computer station. It is amazing how

---

Interactions at the Computer

Teachers are sometimes concerned that the use of computer will reduce interaction among students. Many educators fear that students who were glued to the computer screen will miss out on the conversational give-and-take in a classroom of peers. They don't want their pupils to become isolated learners. Actually the computer often has accomplished the opposite impact! In Mr. Young's classroom for example, Becky is a student who usually sits quietly and observes the daily routines of the classroom. She seldom volunteers answers, nor does she interact with other students. But her behavior changes dramatically when she and another student sit together at the computer. Becky not only discusses the software on screen, but frequently shares personal stories that relate to the topic of the program which they are running. Why the change of behavior? Perhaps the computer provides a non-judgmental backdrop for conversation. Or maybe Becky simply feels more confident working in tandem. Whatever the reason, Becky's time at the computer is filled with language experiences that are difficult to replicate at any other time of her school day. Far from isolating her, the computer connects Becky to her peers. Teachers should be aware that the computer often has this socializing impact.

Figure 3.2 An example of a physical setting that promotes a language-rich environment.

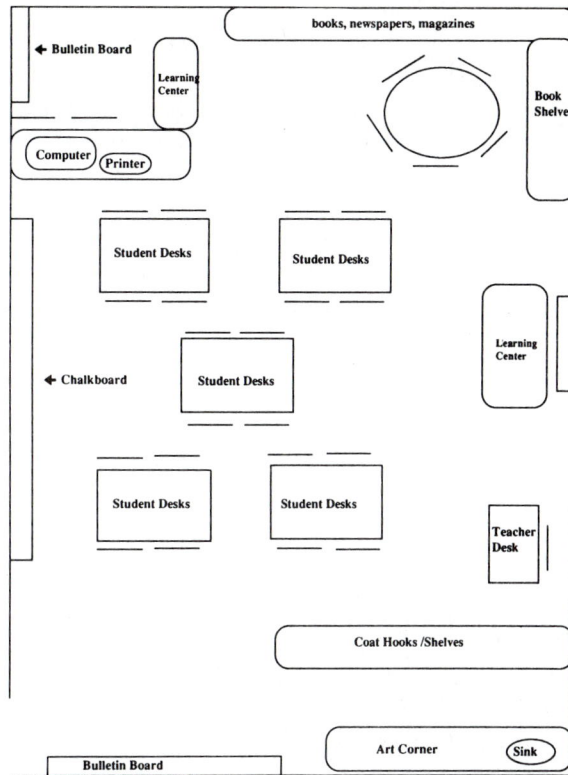

often schools will spend $2500 on computer hardware and additional money on software but not an extra $10 to enable a second student to share the computer. Making it easily possible for students to work together at the computer can greatly increase the opportunities for cooperative learning and peer tutoring discussed in Chapter 2 and later in this chapter. Of course, a mere "floor plan" cannot support a language-rich environment unless it is complemented by effective teacher guidance in communication experiences.

The remainder of this chapter describes some programs related to specific subject areas within the social studies curriculum. Most of these are designed for upper elementary students, and many are also appropriate for middle school and high school students. As you read these examples, keep in mind that the primary use of the computer in the elementary social studies curriculum will often be to support the language-rich environment which we have discussed in this introductory section.

GEOGRAPHY

In the early elementary grades, "geography" consists of studying the local community or communities in general. THE WHOLE NEIGHBORHOOD (Pelican) provides graphics that can serve as story starters to enable young learners to write about their neighborhoods. Weekly Reader Family Software offers STICKYBEAR TOWN BUILDER (see Figure 3.3). With this program (geared toward students in grades 1 through 3) learners construct an entire community on the screen using a joystick or arrow keys to move buildings into place. By doing this, children acquire a sense of the important features of the community—hospitals, schools, fire stations, stores, and so on. Once the town is completed, it may be used for a game or saved for future use. Most games consist of following directions for moving an automobile from one location to another. Games consist of multiple stops, and students are scored by how efficiently they complete their task before they run out of fuel. The "Find the Key" game develops a sense of direction in reading and using maps by having students locate 12 hidden keys from compass direction references. There are many desirable learning objectives that are achieved by this program including map reading, compass use, vocabulary development, and the sense of community. This is a program

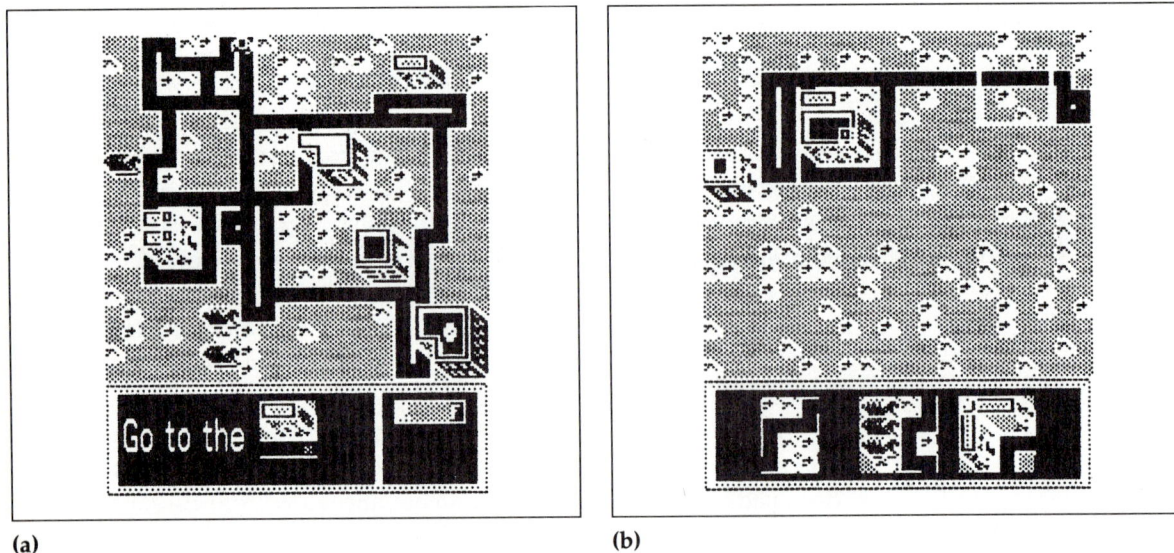

(a)   (b)

Figure 3.3 Screens from STICKYBEAR TOWN BUILDER (Weekly Reader Family Software). With this program learners construct an entire community on the screen using a joystick or arrow keys to move buildings into place.

that may be used as a small-group activity, with three or four students clustered around a single computer, or as a whole-class activity using an overhead projector and an LCD projection screen. Programs like TOWN BUILDER coordinate well with many social studies goals of the early grades.

The computer has already proved to be of great assistance in geography because of its graphics and game-playing capabilities. One of the most popular sets of programs among elementary and secondary school students is the Broderbund series, WHERE IN THE WORLD IS CARMEN SANDIEGO?, WHERE IN THE U.S.A. IS CARMEN SANDIEGO?, and WHERE IN EUROPE IS CARMEN SANDIEGO? (Figure 3.4). With these programs (suitable for grades 5 and up) the user is challenged to recover a stolen art object or other artifact by using scant clues gathered at various stops to track down the criminal. If the clues are not interpreted carefully, valuable time is wasted and the mission may not be completed in the required time frame. These programs can be used as an individual, small-group, or whole-class activity. The artificial incentive of successfully tracking down a criminal encourages students to use reference books such as the atlas, the almanac, and Fodor's *U.S.A.* In small-group environments, sometimes heated verbal communication will take place, as students use their knowledge of geography and reference skills to draw each case to a successful conclusion. These programs and similar programs such as Polarware's ADVENTURERS IN SOUTH AMERICA and ADVENTURES IN NORTH AMERICA can be very rewarding for students who have a basic knowledge of geography and who are able to use standard reference books. In addition, they make excellent use of the sound and graphics capabilities of the computer. Programs like these provide a gamelike format for practicing geography and problem-solving skills.

SEE THE U.S.A. (Compu-Tech) invites students to take a trip on a high-resolution map across the United States. Learners can either plan a simple trip from one state to another or can play a quiz version, where they answer questions about each state as they travel. CROSSCOUNTRY USA (Didatech) also provides a very realistic opportunity for children to drive a simulated truck across the country (Figure 3.5). The learner must pick up a load designated by the computer and deliver it to a specified destination. The program's graphics are very motivating (like an arcade game), and the routes and strategies actually represent those employed by real truckers. Students must overcome realistic obstacles such as fatigue and bad weather while they drive their trucks. By making the deliveries, the child learns

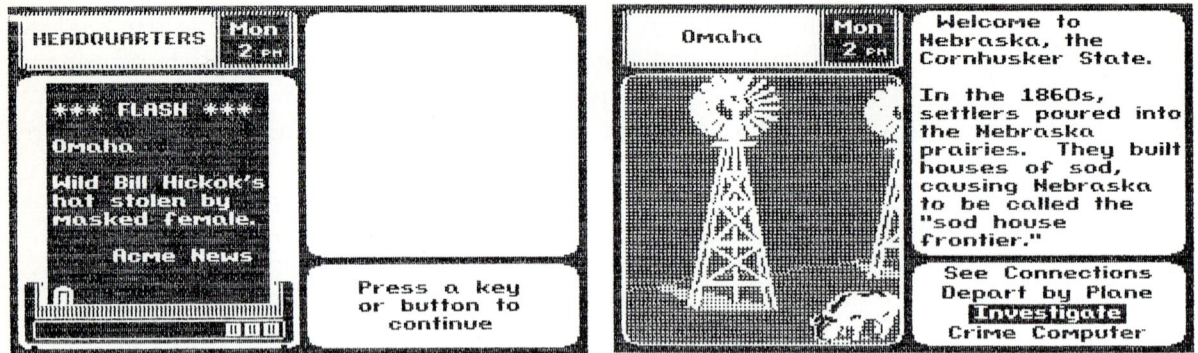

(a)   (b)

(c)   (d)

Figure 3.4 Screens from the Broderbund series WHERE IN THE U.S.A. IS CARMEN SANDIEGO?

about the basic geography of the United States, as well as about goods produced in various regions. The series also stimulates higher-order thinking skills by requiring effective planning and decision making along the route.

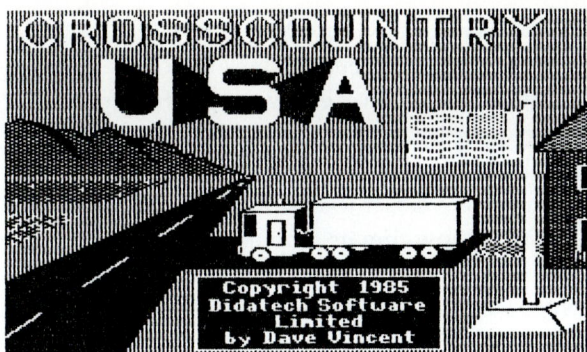

(a)

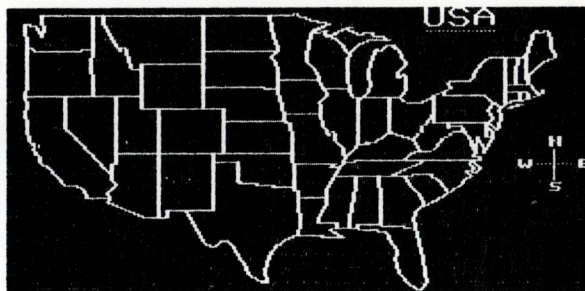

(b)

STEVE >'

Figure 3.5 Screens from CROSSCOUNTRY USA (Didatech), which provides a very realistic opportunity for children to drive a simulated truck across the country. The learner must pick up a load designated by the computer and deliver it to a specified destination.

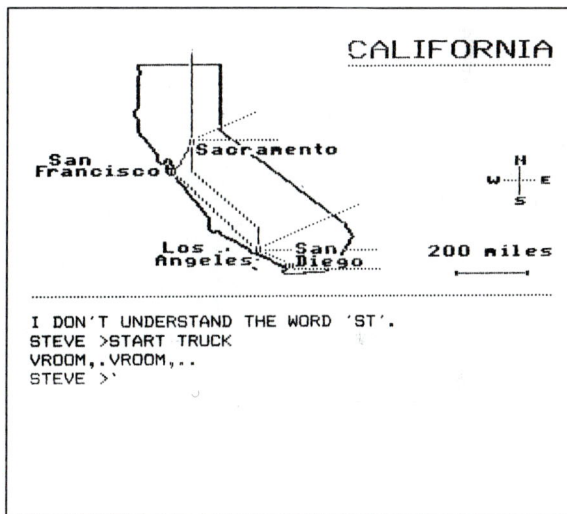

(c)

GLOBAL EXPRESS ATLAS: THE UNITED STATES and GLOBAL EXPRESS ATLAS: THE WORLD (Orange Cherry) provide excellent maps on the Apple II GS, but these programs offer fewer opportunities for instructive interaction than do similar programs. Recommended programs for map generation and map study include QUICK MAP (Micro Maps) and ATLAS * MAPMAKER (Strategic Mapping).

Springboard's ATLAS EXPLORER and MECC's WORLD GEO-GRAPH are computerized databases that enable the students in grades 5 and up to use a mouse or keyboard to zoom in easily on specific information about important aspects of geography. For example, WORLD GEOGRAPH (Figure 3.6) provides a database of significant information on 177 nations. The student is able to zoom in for a closer look at a continent, country, or region, or select a themes map to show climate, population density, or some other characteristic. A push of a button can immediately convert information to a bar graph for easy comparison. Students can easily print out tables, maps, or raw data for inclusion in reports they are writing about a designated country or region.

HISTORY

U.S. history and world history present special problems for most software publishers. Because both topics cover vast amounts of material, many early programs were drill and practice programs such as the MECC SOCIAL STUDIES series or the Hartley MEDALIST series. These programs (typical-

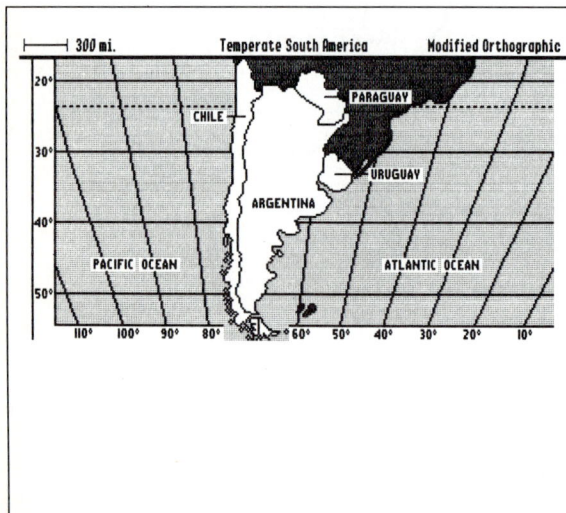

(a)

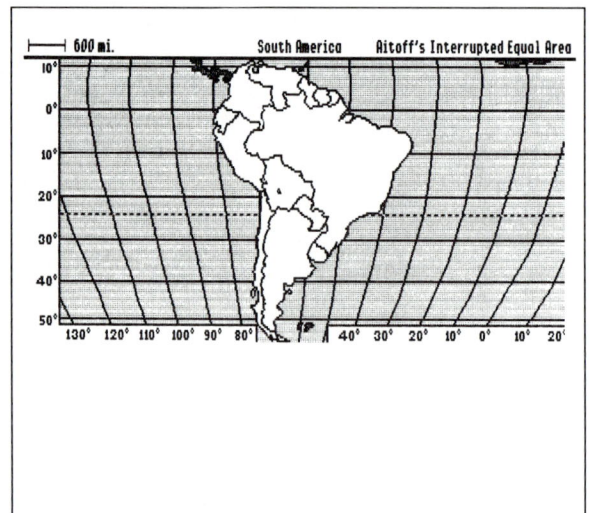

(b)

Figure 3.6 Printed output from WORLD GEOGRAPH, which provides a database of significant information on 177 nations. The student is able to zoom in for a closer look at a continent, country, or region, or the student may select a themes map to show climate, population density, or some other characteristic.

ly designed for grades 4 or higher) permit students to review a set of material in order to help them remember important facts. Unfortunately, these programs are not always correlated with the objectives of individual curricula, and for this reason can interfere with rather than clarify the learning process. Recently updated programs such as the Hartley series do permit teacher modification of the original data, so that these programs can be brought into line with course objectives. In addition, the Hartley MEDALIST series, which includes U.S. HISTORY, FACTS AND FALLACIES, WOMEN IN HISTORY, and others reviews factual information using a game format (Figure 3.7), which is somewhat more exciting than simply a question-and-answer format.

Broderbund's WHERE IN TIME IS CARMEN SANDIEGO? is similar to the CARMEN programs described in the "Geography" section of this chapter, except that the players must use a time machine to track villains. The program promises to be as motivating and enjoyable as its predecessors. MECC's TIME NAVIGATOR offers a similar opportunity to study history through a simulated time machine. However, our opinion is that with their present content these programs are not likely to correspond with the K–6 social studies curriculum.

The computer also offers the opportunity to simulate historical activities, permitting students to participate in the events and problems of history, thereby coming to a more thorough understanding of the topics being studied. Historical simulations are covered in Chapter 4. Although

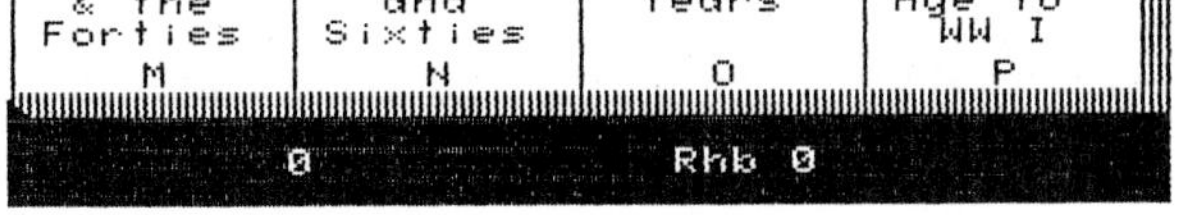

Figure 3.7 A screen from U.S. HISTORY FACTS AND FALLACIES from the Hartley MEDALIST series, which reviews factual information using a game format. Students choose questions from the above categories in a game similar to "Jeopardy."

discussed in the context of secondary education, many of these same programs (and certainly the same principles) are applicable at the elementary level of social studies. Most of the simulations available at the present time are more directed toward middle school and higher grade levels, but some of the programs may be useful with fifth or sixth graders. We expect that more simulations directed toward younger learners will be produced within the next few years.

Although computers can provide great assistance in situations where repetitive practice is required, they need not be the focus of classroom activities. There are occasions where computers provide the backdrop or the atmosphere for classroom interactions. Such is the case with programs such as THE RIPPLE THAT CHANGED AMERICAN HISTORY and OUR TOWN MEETING (Tom Snyder Productions), which are geared for fifth graders and up. In both cases, the computer is used to stimulate discussion in small- or medium-sized groups of students. In the RIPPLE program (Figure 3.8) students use their knowledge of American history to track down a "ripple" or flaw in the normal sequence of events in our history. Once this is done, the ripple can be "unripped." To accurately accomplish this, the individual or group must work in close collaboration to be sure of the accuracy of their information, as the user is given only one chance to accomplish the task.

OUR TOWN MEETING, on the other hand, encourages group work by simulating the decision process of a town or village board, complete with project decisions, budget balancing challenges, and the usual array of subcommittee work. With both programs, the computer acts as a catalyst for group cooperation and discussion. Especially with OUR TOWN MEET-ING (Figure 3.9), much of the actual work is done away from the computer. Programs such as these offer intriguing possibilities by encouraging active interaction and participation by students. Additionally, they elicit problem-solving behavior, which finally allows educators to attack the long sought-after but seldom accomplished higher-level objectives of analysis and synthesis. (Note that these same programs, with a different emphasis and context, could be used for secondary-level students.)

Reference Books and Student Reports

Important process skills also include library research and the subsequent preparation of written reports. Correctly using card catalogs, vertical files, and the Dewey decimal system are important skills which should be encouraged. Selecting an appropriate reference or resource book is an old research problem that can be approached in a modern way using computer-

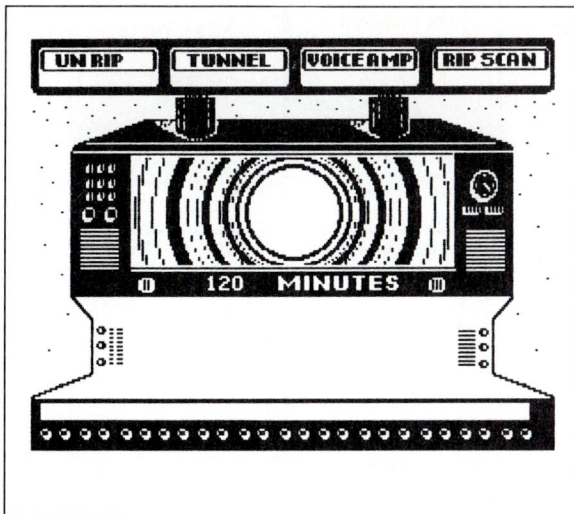

(a)

(b)

Figure 3.8 Screens from THE RIPPLE THAT CHANGED AMERICAN HISTORY (Tom Snyder Productions), in which students use their knowledge of American history to track down a "ripple" or flaw in the normal sequence of events in our history. Students use the time machine (a) to obtain clues from history, (b) and (c).

(c)

assisted instruction (see Figure 3.10). Several software publishers offer programs to give students the opportunity to practice finding the correct reference: HOW CAN I FIND IT IF I DON'T KNOW WHAT I'M LOOKING FOR? (Sunburst), STUDY SKILLS (Houghton Mifflin), LET'S LEARN ABOUT THE LIBRARY (Troll Associates), SKILLS MAKER (Follett), and RIPLEY'S BELIEVE IT OR NOT! LIBRARY RESEARCH SKILLS (SVE).

(a)

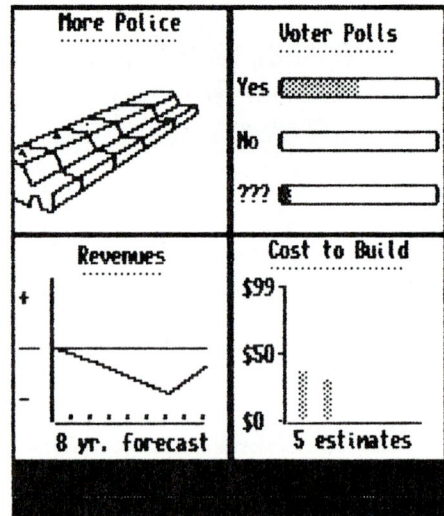

(b)

Figure 3.9 Two screens from OUR TOWN MEETING (Tom Snyder Productions), which encourages group work by simulating the decision process of a town or village board, complete with project decisions, budget balancing challenges, and the usual array of subcommittee work. The computer acts as a catalyst for group cooperation and group discussion. Much of the actual work is done away from the computer.

Likewise, Broderbund's CARMEN SANDIEGO programs (cited earlier in this chapter) encourage children to look up information efficiently in order to win the game.

Libraries, including school libraries, have begun to purchase reference materials in a CD-ROM format. Social studies teachers should encourage students to use the computer as an effective tool in retrieving information. For example, COMPTON'S MULTIMEDIA ENCYCLOPEDIA (described in detail in Chapters 7 and 8) provides access to all the information of a traditional encyclopedia (including excellent graphics)—with the additional advantage of immediate access through several effective search strategies. Any child who is capable of using a hardcopy encyclopedia is probably also capable of using this kind of electronic encyclopedia. In addition, teachers should consider the possibility of displaying the electronic image on a large screen to provide instant access to accurate information on topics that come up in student discussions. While the present COMPTON'S is the equivalent of a traditional encyclopedia, it is safe to anticipate that similar CD-ROM reference packages will soon be-

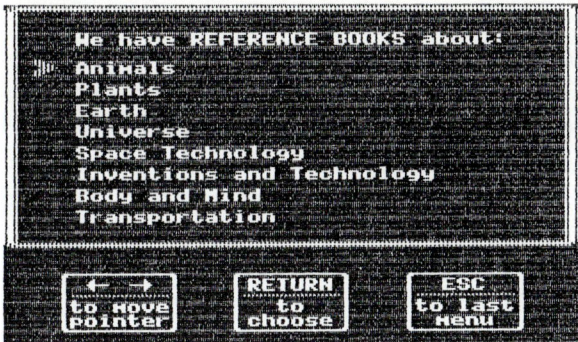

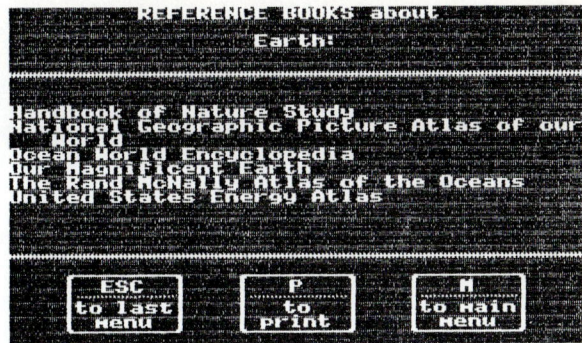

(a)

(b)

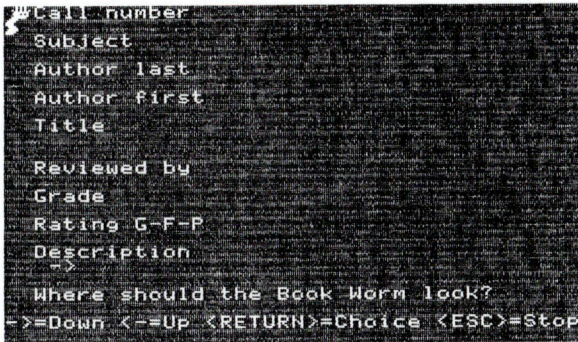

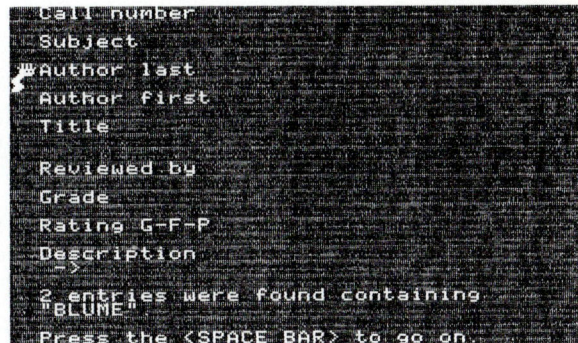

(c)

(d)

Figure 3.10 Screens from Sunburst's HOW CAN I FIND IT IF I DON'T KNOW WHAT I'M LOOKING FOR? (a) and (b) and from MECC's BOOKWORM (c) and (d), programs that help students in choosing and using the most appropriate reference or resource book.

come available for specifically younger audiences. (CD-ROM technology is discussed in Chapter 7.)

The computer can also be used by students to record information relevant to the books they have read. MECC'S BOOKWORM is a commercial database that lends itself specifically to this task, but any database could be used for this purpose. Many teachers find this hard to believe; but it is because they themselves have not used databases—usually because they have not been introduced to this invaluable aspect of technology. We have seen even fourth and fifth grade students use database management programs effectively. While BANK STREET FILER by Broderbund is specifically designed for children as young as the second grade, AP-PLEWORKS by Claris, or even MICROSOFT WORKS are reasonable choices for fourth or fifth graders, as long as the children are not overwhelmed by complex functions that they don't need for simple applications. Each of these programs is easy to use and does not require unusual hardware configurations. In creating a personal database of books read, students are not bound by a publisher's choice of data categories. This freedom gives students the opportunity to choose the information that they deem important in the book. Teachers can learn about students by simply reading their choice of categories.

Once research materials have been secured, they can be easily assembled into a finished report using traditional word processors such as BANK STREET WRITER, MAGIC SLATE, APPLEWORKS, or MICRO-SOFT WORKS. An attractive alternative is using desktop publishing programs, which have been simplified for use by younger students. Examples of this type of program are CHILDREN'S WRITING AND PUBLISHING CENTER (The Learning Company), ONCE UPON A TIME ... II (Compu-Tech), and KIDWRITER (Spinnaker). These programs offer self-contained graphics and pictures, which may be used to illustrate or enhance the story line. They are easy to learn and operate, so that students just learning keyboarding can concentrate on the creative process rather than feel the frustration that can be caused by more difficult programs. Yet they all retain the main advantages of word processing—namely, an easy method of entering and revising text materials and an attractive presentation of the final product. (For further review of these programs, see Chapter 8.)

A program developed for science students opens up exciting possibilities for the fields of history and geography. In THE DESERT (Figure 3.11), a program from William K. Bradford, the computer presents basic scenes and lets students add items, insert captions, and develop story lines. The graphics are extremely attractive and include animation. Stories can be

Figure 3.11 A screen from THE DESERT (William K. Bradford), in which the computer presents basic scenes related to social studies concepts and lets students add items, insert captions, and develop story lines.

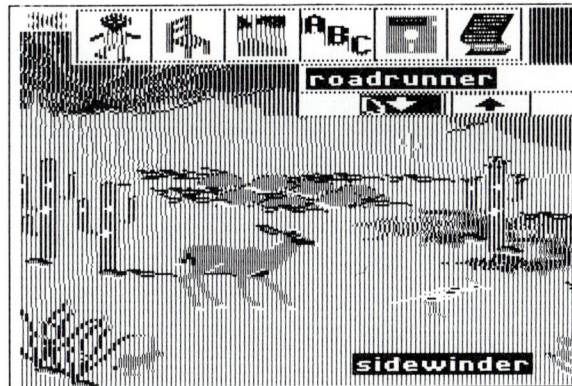

saved to disk and read by other students on the computer screen, or they can be printed out in a book format. Students using this program must understand accurate information about the desert in order to write good stories. It seems safe to expect that software vendors will see the advantage of developing similar programs that will encourage students to think about and write about topics typically covered in geography and history classes.

GOVERNMENT

In order to encourage good citizenship habits and otherwise satisfy certain state mandates concerning knowledge of the federal, state, and local governments, many school districts require some coverage of the U.S. Constitution and state constitutions. In most cases some sort of basic competency test is involved, and passage of this test requires the recall of a large amount of factual information. Some drill and practice programs, such as THE U.S. CONSTITUTION (Scholastic Software), are dedicated to this task. Other programs provide a gamelike format to enliven this process of recalling facts. Hartley's CREATE YOUR OWN BINGO+ provides an excellent alternative. This utility program permits the teacher to generate a set of randomly jumbled bingo cards using whatever terms need to be reviewed. For example, Figure 3.12 shows a bingo game designed to review information about amendments to the U.S. Constitution. Once the set of cards has been printed, the game can proceed as usual, only instead of

(a)

	B	I	N	G	O
	FATHER CHARLES COUGHLIN	HENRY C. WALLACE	PWA	AMERICAN FEDERATION OF LABOR	CORDULL HULL
	WAGNER ACT	LAISSEZ-FAIRE	BOONDOGGLING	TVA	FDIC
	SOCIAL SECURITY ACT	CCC	ROBERT LAFOLLETTE	ALF LANDON	GLASS-STEAGALL ACT
	CWA	FREE	FARM CREDIT ADMINISTRATION	FRANCES PERKINS	NRA
	RAYMOND MOLEY	WPA	PROHIBITION	AAA	BRAIN TRUST

(b)

NEWDEAL MASTER LIST

	B	I	N	G	O
	WPA	PWA	CCC	NRA	AAA
	TVA	FDIC	BRAIN TRUST	PROHIBITION	BOONDOGGLING
	SOCIAL SECURITY ACT	LAISSEZ-FAIRE	ALF LANDON	FARM CREDIT ADMINISTRATION	CWA
	GLASS-STEAGALL ACT	HENRY C. WALLACE	RAYMOND MOLEY	CORDULL HULL	FRANCES PERKINS
	ROBERT LAFOLLETTE	FRANCIS TOWNSEND	FATHER CHARLES COUGHLIN	WAGNER ACT	AMERICAN FEDERATION OF LABOR

Figure 3.12 Output from CREATE YOUR OWN BINGO+ (Hartley), a utility program which permits the teacher to generate a set of randomly jumbled bingo cards, with whatever terms need to be reviewed. This example shows a bingo game designed to review information about amendments to the U.S. Constitution.

reading "B5" the teacher would describe the contents of a constitutional amendment. Students recognizing the correct amendment would tab that square on their individual cards. Otherwise, all normal bingo rules would apply. By creating a game out of a routine memory task, the teacher offers an extrinsic reward for acquiring this body of knowledge. (In addition, students will find that the dexterity gained from poring over their bingo cards has great training potential for later life.)

ECONOMICS

Athough the formal study of economics is reserved for high school, elementary-age students can benefit from understanding selected basic concepts, such as supply and demand, profit and loss, and inventory control. These concepts can be explored with the programs on the MARKET PLACE disk from MECC (Figure 3.13). LEMONADE STAND permits the student to order an inventory of anticipated supplies for each day. Ordering too few supplies will cause a loss of potential profit; ordering too many can also result in a loss, since supplies are perishable. As the program progresses

SAM 2's Refreshing Lemonade DAY 1

Weather Forecast:
partly cloudy and
warm with no chance
of rain

Cash on hand: $ 4.00

How many glasses will you make? ▓

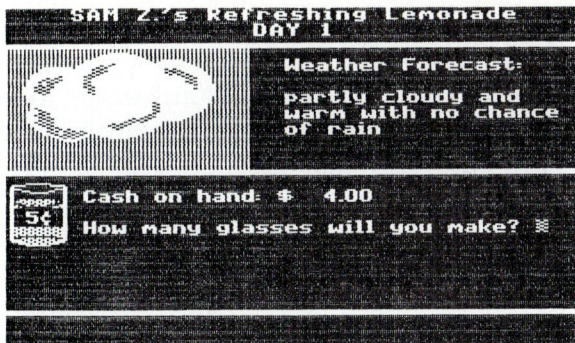

SALES REPORT, DAY 1		
	SAM	SAM	SAM
glasses made	80	80	60
signs made	0	0	4
price	$ 0.25	$ 0.25	$ 0.30
glasses sold	9	9	15
income	$ 2.25	$ 2.25	$ 4.50
expenses	$ 4.00	$ 4.00	$ 4.00
profit	$ -1.75	$ -1.75	$ 0.50
cash on hand	$ 2.25	$ 2.25	$ 4.50

Press SPACE BAR to continue

(a)   (b)

Figure 3.13 Screens from MECC's MARKET PLACE. The LEMONADE STAND program permits the student to apply basic economics principles to ordering an inventory of anticipated supplies for each day in order to make a profit.

from one day to the next, weather conditions change. Students must adjust both inventory and price to fit these changing conditions, as continued poor decision making will lead to a loss of profits or even to bankruptcy. HOT DOG STAND uses the same approach, only more products are involved; hence, decisions become more complex. Both programs can be played by individual students, by teams of students, or by an entire class using an LCD projection system. The obvious benefit here is mastering of difficult concepts such as supply and demand, achieved in an intuitive and informal manner using interactive computer simulation.

SOCIAL SKILLS/ COMMUNITY DEVELOPMENT

One of the most exciting yet least developed areas of elementary social studies is the use of what the industry refers to as "distance learning." According to the U.S. Department of Education's Office of Educational Research and Improvement, distance learning is defined as:

> . . . the application of telecommunications and electronic devices which enable students and learners to receive instruction that originates from some distant location. (Bruder, 1989)

In the 1960s and early 1970s, distance learning consisted of educational television and correspondence courses. The basic intention was to reach students who, because of limitations of distance or physical disability, were deprived of contact with normal channels of instruction. Distance learning in the 1980s has taken on new meaning with the introduction of electronic communications devices—specifically the computer modem and the fac-simile or "fax" machine.

Modems and fax machines can facilitate direct communication to help establish a sense of national and community identity and to help students understand how various communities differ in some ways and are the same in others. Consider the following example.

A sixth-grade class in Lansing, Illinois, is doing a unit of study on local government and its operation. The students wonder if the village board and mayoral system they have are common throughout the country. To create a perspective on local government, their teacher establishes contacts via modem with six other communities, one each in Massachusetts, Vir-ginia, Ohio, Texas, California, and Washington. The size of the communities varies from 2,000 inhabitants to 85,000 inhabitants. The class soon discovers through their Dayton, Ohio, contact that a type of government called the city manager system exists. The children exchange views on the operation of their respective systems, including their perception of local community problems such as toxic waste disposal. This dialog on community govern-ment and problems takes place once a week for the entire school year. In the course of these exchanges, students of both schools gain greater ap-preciation of community activities. Sonoma, California, for example, is intrigued by Lansing's Good Neighbor Day Parade. Student drawings of parade activities are part of a Lansing class art project, so some of these were "faxed" to California. The California class wonders if this sort of tradition might be established in their town. The students of all com-munities are so interested in their newly established friends that com-munications continue throughout the summer, and several students form pen pal relationships.

The Daedulus Project, operated out of the University of Connecticut, uses telecommunications in a creative manner to stimulate the writing abilities of learning-disabled and physically handicapped students. The strategy is amazingly simple. Students are told that "Mysterious Mel" or someone else at the other end of the modem will answer any letters they write. With this assurance, students who have never previously shown any interest in writing begin communicating and improving their writing skills via modem. Not only do writing skills improve, but students also show dramatic improvements in self-esteem and social interaction.

It is clear from these examples that electronic communication devices open up a wide range of distance learning opportunities, limited only by constraints of equipment, funding, and teacher-student imagination. To encourage this kind of learning exchange, states like Indiana, Florida, and Texas have established state-funded bulletin boards, and schools are actively encouraged to exchange ideas. Distance learning, once a nearly dead issue, appears to be regaining the attention of many educators.

In addition to distance learning, several other computerized applications help students acquire personal and social skills normally associated with the elementary social studies curriculum. For example, Sunburst's THE CHOICE IS YOURS! offers children in grades 5 through 9 an opportunity to explore a broad range of career possibilities.

Finally, several programs focus on the problem of substance abuse. For example, THE SMOKING DECISION (designed by Sunburst for grades 6 through 12) uses an interactive approach to present facts that will help students make decisions about smoking.

INTERDISCIPLI-NARY PROGRAMS

As we emphasized at the beginning of this chapter, at the elementary level the study of social studies is usually closely integrated with the rest of the curriculum. This integration can often be accomplished be creating a language-rich environment. For example, the learning center opens up a wealth of language experiences that can be integrated with the social studies curriculum. While using ZANDER from SVE, social studies middle school students can simulate the creation of their own cultures. This program gives them opportunities for using language arts skills to voice opinions on everything from the structure of the government to conservation of resources.

In addition, it is possible to employ computerized instructional packages that deliberately integrate social studies with other subject areas. For example, Chapter 4 describes the VOYAGE OF THE MIMI, which is more appropriate for older students. Although some fifth or sixth graders might use the MIMI materials, at the present time we are aware of no such integrated packages specifically designed for the K–6 audience. However, it is likely that the next few years will witness the publication of similar programs that use several different media (including videotapes, maps, books, and computers) to integrate social studies skills with science, mathematics, language arts, and other areas of the elementary curriculum. We recommend that elementary teachers read Chapters 4 and 7 to get ideas about what they can expect to come.

SUMMARY

This chapter has suggested ways in which the computer can assist in the elementary social studies curriculum. It has described several self-contained, stand-alone programs that help students master concepts and principles in geography, history, and economics. In addition, the chapter has suggested ways to use the computer as a tool to carry out more efficiently many of the tasks that have traditionally been effective in mastering social studies skills. Finally, strategies have been given for expanding the classroom by using the computer's modem to access information in other classrooms, in other buildings, or even in other countries.

REFERENCES

Bruder, I. "Distance Learning: What's Holding Back This Bottomless Delivery System?" *Electronic Learning* 8, (April 1989): 31–35.

King, R., and E. L. Vockell. *The Computer in the Language Arts Curriculum.* Watsonville, CA: Mitchell **McGRAW-HILL**, 1991.

Mayer, J. S., and R. S. Brause. "Learning Through Teaching: Is Your Classroom Like Your Grandmother's?" *Language Arts* 63 (1986): 617–620.

CHAPTER 4

THE MICRO-COMPUTER IN THE SECONDARY GRADES (7–12)

SOCIAL STUDIES AT THE SECONDARY school level generally refers to specific courses such as geography, U.S. history, and world history for middle school and early high school; economics, psychology, sociology, political science, and other electives are usually studied by high school juniors and seniors. Course outlines and instructional sequences for secondary social studies are most often based on the textbook of a specific publisher. As a result, independent software publishers find it very difficult to meet the needs of such a wide diversity of textbook coverages; hence, the major software vendors have not marketed programs on "American history" or "western civilization." However, many textbook publishers now include on disk some sort of review exercises covering the chapters in the book, as well as a test-generator program keyed to the content of individual chapters or units of study.

In addition, both textbook publishers and independent vendors have developed separate units of instruction for topics covered in secondary social studies. For example, ANCIENT ROME (Teach Yourself by Computer) provides a unit on customs of ancient Rome, which could be integrated with any textbook on ancient history or world civilization that discussed Rome. Furthermore, textbook publishers sometimes develop a utility disk containing background data or other related materials pertinent to the topic covered by the textbook. For example, Merrill Publishing Company has put together a disk keyed to topics contained in its book ECONOMICS PRINCIPLES AND PRACTICES. The disk contains useful simulations on the stock market, supply and demand, fractional reserves, and amortization tables. Because these concepts are covered in most economics courses, demonstrations done using this disk could prove useful in any economics course, no matter what textbook is being used.

All social studies courses rely heavily on information. Until recently, a search for information generally meant a trip to the school library or resource center to gather pertinent printed data for individual subjects. The latter part of the 1980s witnessed the beginning of a fundamental change in the way students and teachers can access research information. The microcomputer in conjunction with the CD-ROM (see Chapter 5) and new software products promises not only a "one-stop shopping" approach to research, but will inevitably permit the infusion of important instructional information directly into the classroom. The first CD-ROM encyclopedia offered for general public use was produced by Grolier Inc. The entire encyclopedia was contained on a single CD-ROM disk, offering the user the ability to "search" all volumes simultaneously for any article that mentioned the desired topic. Unfortunately, the Grolier product offered few enhancements beyond the basic printed page. It failed to make complete use of computerized CD-ROM capabilities. Students often became discouraged with this "print on screen" approach, and complained that they often were inundated with information they didn't want, just because an article had contained a relevant keyword. Most students seemed to prefer the traditional hardcopy encyclopedia, which made it easy to browse, to follow a natural path in searching for information, and to examine pictures and tables relevant to the article they were reading. At the time of this writing, the Grolier electronic encyclopedia is undergoing revision.

COMPTON'S MULTIMEDIA ENCYCLOPEDIA goes beyond the rather simplistic approach employed in the original Grolier computerized encyclopedia. It permits the user to access information in several different ways, enabling learners to find all articles in the entire encyclopedia that mention a designated topic or combination of topics, as well as following more traditional approaches, such as moving quickly from one topic to another without having to pull another volume off the shelf or moving from a general topic to a more specific topic as the need and interest naturally dictate. The program provides seven different ways to access the information on the CD-ROM disk and permits the user to move easily from one access method to another.

Applications of this new type of product will be obvious in the context of the individual subjects discussed in this chapter. Chapter 5 describes additional applications that can be used for these subjects. In addition, this chapter offers an examination of some of the possibilities for computer usage in the social studies classroom using available technology and other computer programs.

Many of these applications will work best with a single computer and an LCD projection system. There are three reasons for this. First, many middle schools and high schools offer limited computer lab availability—often one or two labs for the entire school. Trying to schedule computers for two or three geography classes during the school day can prove very difficult. Second, many current programs, such as the Tom Snyder series, are intended to be used as a catalyst in generating group discussions and projects. A single screen visible to all the students is all that is needed for applications of this kind. And finally, demonstration programs such as ECONOMICS PRINCIPLES AND PRACTICES and other database programs work best as sources of information in units of instruction requiring direct teacher input and supervision. The computer serves as an electronic blackboard or demonstration device to provide information which would otherwise be hard to present to an entire group.

The following pages offer a subject-by-subject look at how the personal computer might contribute to improving social studies classroom instruction.

GEOGRAPHY

Secondary school geography can cover a wide variety of information, ranging from simple map study to cultural geography. It often includes a thorough study not only of the people but also of the climate of a particular region. Many of the geography programs discussed in Chapter 3 (such as WHERE IN THE WORLD IS CARMEN SANDIEGO?) can also be motivational tools for learning geography at the secondary level. Some programs, on the other hand, are more specifically appropriate for older learners.

ATLAS EXPLORER by Springboard Software indicates the direction for future computer-assisted instruction in geography. It makes excellent use of the computer's graphic capabilities by first presenting a world map, then allowing the user to zero in on the hemisphere, continent, or country to be studied (see Figure 4.1). Although it can be used by a single student seated at an isolated computer, its main strength may lie in its use on a large screen for a whole class. Thirty-seven maps are available for classroom use, and the program offers basic demographic information about each location, giving statistics about the size and population of the area in question. Although the program can accommodate either keyboard or mouse input, it can be used most easily with a mouse. Its arrangement of information in some ways resembles the hypertext database strategies discussed in Chapter 5, which permit the user to narrow the scope of study to the desired area.

A shortcoming of ATLAS EXPLORER is its lack of depth of coverage. It is able to present only a limited amount of demographic information about any particular geographic area. This weakness will be overcome either when Springboard or other vendors devote an entire disk to a single area (such as one disk for each continent or major country) or when the computer is able to devote greater memory to the atlas (as by employing the CD-ROM or laserdisc strategies described in Chapter 5). In addition, it would be possible to create partial, unfinished databases into which individual users could insert appropriate information relevant to their interests or to the objectives of a unit of instruction. Similar programs include PC GLOBE and PC USA (PC Globe),

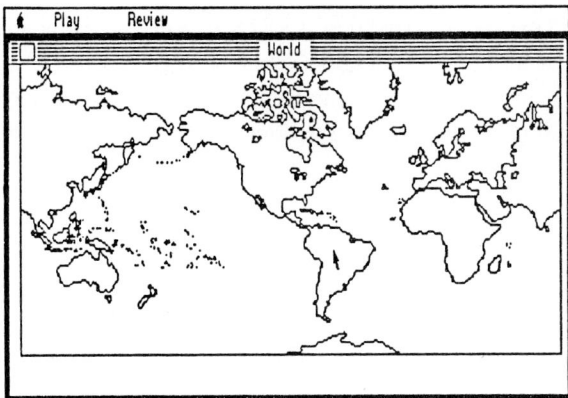

(a)

(b)

(c)

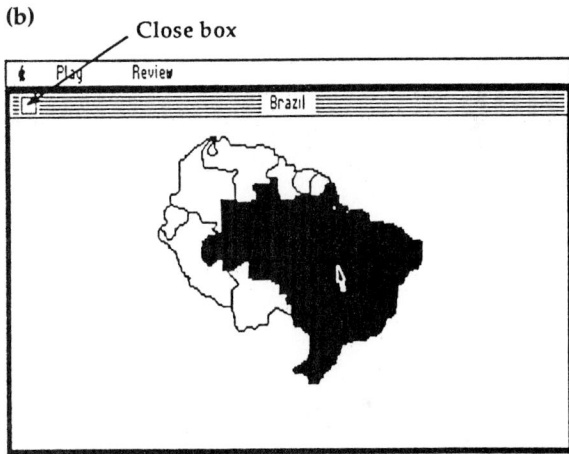

(d)

Figure 4.1 Screens from ATLAS EXPLORER by Springboard Software, which makes excellent use of the computer's graphic capabilities by first presenting a world map, then allowing the user to "zero in" on the hemisphere, continent, or country to be studied.

ELECTRONIC MAP CABINET (Highlighted Data), the MACATLAS series (Micro Maps), and ATLAS*MAPMAKER (Strategic Mapping).

COMPTON'S MULTIMEDIA ENCYCLOPEDIA (described in more detail in Chapter 5) offers similar advantages for the study of geography. The atlas section of this computerized encyclopedia gives the user a view of global projections, with excellent use of graphics. A student or teacher may then narrow down the desired area of study to a particular hemisphere, continent, country, or even city. At any one of these stops, the learner may view accompanying text, pictures, or other related data (see Figure 4.2). In addition, the use of the MULTIMEDIA ENCYCLOPEDIA along with an LCD projection system can create an opportunity for lessons involving

---

Computers in Action

A Midlands High School eleventh grade geography class is studying the connection between climate and culture. Their teacher, Mrs. Snyder, hands out a study guide entitled "Habitat Regions of the World," which appears as follows:

Habitat Region	Climate	Natural Vegetation	Growth Potential
Dry Lands			
Tropical Forest Lands			
Tropical Woodlands and Savannas			
Mediterranean Woodlands			
Mid-latitude MixedForest Lands			
Boreal Forest andWoodlands			

the entire class. Because the study of geography for grades 7–12 frequently involves cultural development, physical environments, and land forms, a further advantage of this comprehensive, computerized encyclopedia is that the user can access the main portion of the encyclopedia almost instantaneously from the atlas and return to the atlas as necessary. For example, a student or class researching Chile could move to an encyclopedia article on the Andes, on Latin American customs, or on Simón Bolívar, from there to another topic as interests dictate, and return whenever necessary to the map and demographic information provided in the atlas.

Polar Lands

Mountain Lands

Mrs. Snyder then boots her IBM-compatible laptop computer, which is connected to a CD-ROM and an LCD projection system [Note: In applications where clarity is essential, a large monitor-receiver should be substituted for the LCD projection system]. Using the atlas feature of COMPTON'S MULTIMEDIA ENCYCLOPEDIA, she proceeds to preselected areas of the globe, where pictures showing various climatic conditions are shown. At each stop, data on temperature, rainfall, altitude, and population density are displayed. She asks the class to fill out the study sheets by placing the name of the location under the appropriate habitat region. The students then use the visual displays as input to complete the remaining portion of the study guide. At the conclusion of the written portion of the assignment, the class is subdivided into small study groups of four or five students each, where they compare their classifications and reach a consensus on the wisdom of their selections.

Because of the type and range of data available in COMPTON'S ENCYCLOPEDIA, Mrs. Snyder can use it very effectively for studies of latitude and longitude, map projections, seasons, and land forms. She also uses a scanner to save on disk and project on the large screen pictures from textbooks, atlases, and other resource books. She uses these scanned images in classroom presentations as well as in written handouts and tests, using desktop publishing.

Figure 4.2 Main menu of COMPTON'S MULTIMEDIA ENCYCLOPEDIA. The atlas section of this computerized encyclopedia permits the user a view of global projections, with excellent use of graphics. A student or teacher may then narrow down the desired area of study to a particular hemisphere, continent, country, or even city. At any one of these stops, the learner may view accompanying text, pictures, or other related data.

In addition, simple database management programs and predesigned database files can often contribute substantially to an understanding of geography. Atlases, almanacs, and other reference books have always provided useful, systematic lists of information related to geography. Now these are available in electronic form, which promotes easy access and efficient comparisons. The MACATLAS series (Micro Maps), STATES OF THE UNION DATABASE (Heizer), CANADIAN FACTS STACKS (Palm Island), and FACTS ON FILE (Facts on File) are examples of programs that provide an exhaustive amount of information in carefully structured files. Sunburst offers a series of files on its NORTH AMERICA DATABASE that are easily accessed by BANK STREET FILER. Scholastic has a set of WORLD GEOGRAPHY, CULTURES, and ECONOMICS databases that are accessed through PFS: FILE.

Many high school geography courses include some study of resource distribution and geology. One of the best of the recent wave of simulation programs is GEOWORLD by Tom Snyder Productions. Students are asked to explore for, test for, and engage in the mining of various valuable resources in virtually any location of the world (see Figure 4.3). Through elaborate graphics, the user gets a true feeling for some of the steps necessary to operate a successful mining venture. The results can then be documented in a report format and later transferred to AP-PLEWORKS (Claris), so that students use their logic and thinking skills

(a)

(b)

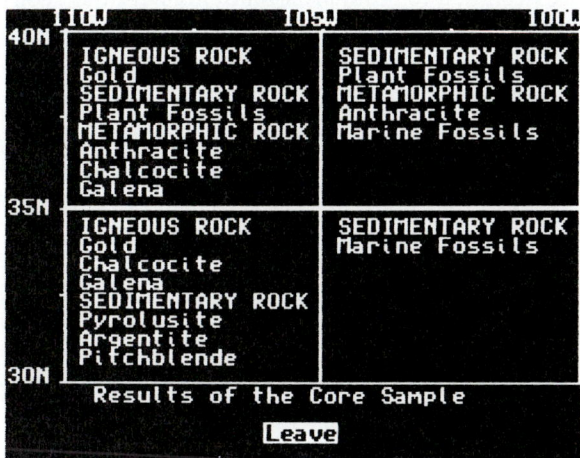

(c)

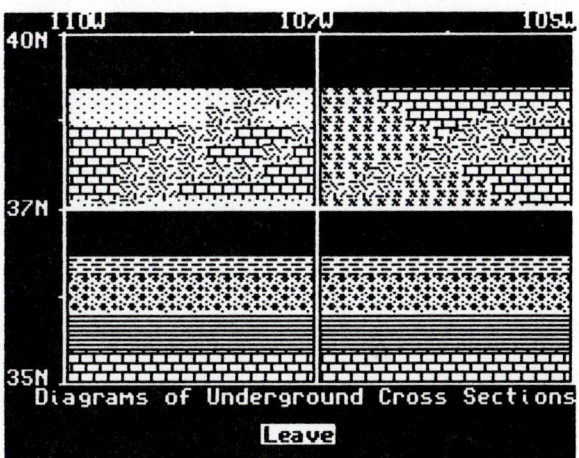

(d)

Figure 4.3 Screens from GEOWORLD by Tom Snyder Productions. Students are asked to explore, test for, and engage in the mining of various valuable resources in virtually any location throughout the world.

in locating and mining resources, while using their writing skills in preparing a report on their findings.

Computers in Action

Mr. Payne is teaching a unit of study of South American countries. He has found that GEOWORLD (Tom Snyder Productions) offers an opportunity to create an exciting "discovery" situation for his students. Because the program is available in lab packs of ten programs, he uses it in a computer lab environment with small "task force" groups of two or three students at each machine. Each task force receives a checklist of valuable mineral resources and is challenged to locate and quantify the resources of the country currently being studied. Once completed, the results of their findings along with a commentary on the economic impact is prepared and turned in as a written assignment. The same assignment is repeated as different countries are covered during the semester. Not only are investigative and writing skills used, but map skills are reinforced as well.

Several programs are designed to familiarize students with the geography, history, culture, language, and customs of other cities and countries. For example, Blue Lion Software's TICKET TO PARIS simulates a trip to that city. The student must answer questions about food, politics, colloquialisms, and other matters in order to complete a successful trip and obtain a ticket back to the United States. Other programs in the same series include TICKET TO LONDON, TICKET TO SPAIN, TICKET TO WASHINGTON D.C., and even TICKET TO HOLLYWOOD.

WORLD HISTORY

There have been very few programs created exclusively for world history. Some of the U.S. history programs overlap into world history, and programs such as DISCOVER THE WORLD by Hartley Courseware can be used for either. A more common application of the computer to world history courses is to employ various tool programs to amplify or facilitate the delivery of noncomputerized teaching strategies. For example, the use of word processors and databases can remove the drudgery from routine assignments and sometimes even generate additional interest in the subject.

Creating a world history database can be a very useful and time-saving exercise. (Database management systems are discussed in detail in Chapter

Computers in Action

Miss Figueroa has her students select an individual from the following list of Renaissance contributors. She asks them to do a brief biographical sketch by filling in a page that asks for the following: data of birth, place of birth, primary life residence, area of contribution, example or examples of the contribution, place of death, and date of death.

Boccaccio	Castiglione	Cervantes	Erasmus
Machiavelli	More	Donatello	Guttenberg
de' Medici	Petrarch	Shakespeare	Brueghel
Durer	van Eyck	Rembrandt	Titian
Michelangelo	da Vinci		

Once the information has been gathered, the students will enter the data on the page. A typical entry might resemble the example below.

NAME: Leonardo da Vinci

DATE OF BIRTH: April 15, 1452

PLACE OF BIRTH: Florence, Italy

LIFE RESIDENCE: Florence/Milan, Italy

AREA OF CONTRIBUTION (art, science, literature, etc.): painting, sculpture, architecture, science (anatomy)

EXAMPLE(S) OF CONTRIBUTIONS: Mona Lisa, Adoration of the Magi, Virgin of the Rocks, The Last Supper; left over 5000 pages of drawings and manuscripts including work on human anatomy, hydraulics, weapons, and airplanes

PLACE OF DEATH: Amblise, France

DATE OF DEATH: May 2, 1519

Miss Figueroa checks the completed forms for accuracy and then has the students enter the information into an APPLEWORKS database. By the end of the year, each student has added fifteen entries to the database, and students have been able to make easy comparisons among famous persons of various eras of history.

5.) Information in a database format offers a number of advantages over more traditional biographies. These are discussed in Chapter 5.

There are also numerous instances in which students can benefit from using a word processor in history class. For such applications of the computer to be effective, it is necessary for students using the word processor to have learned word processing skills in some setting other than history class. It would be frustrating and counterproductive in terms of academic learning time to take time away from history to learn these skills. However, with the expanded availability of computers in homes and the increased use of computers in composition and computer literacy classes, it is not at all unusual to find students who can effectively use the computer as a tool. Social studies teachers should be aware of the abilities of their students to use the computer and should encourage their students to use the computer as a tool whenever possible. Incorporating the computer as a word processing tool in the social studies class serves two purposes: (1) It enhances academic learning time in the social studies class, and (2) It promotes the

---

Computers in Action

Mr. Peters has created a problem-solving situation by selecting characteristics of features of the life of a "mystery person," and challenging students to identify the person in question in a fashion similar to the "crime computer" section of the CARMEN SANDIEGO program.

Example:
1. Born: between 1450 and 1460
2. Left over 5000 pages of notes and drawings.
3. Studied biology, chemistry, and anatomy.
4. Designed buildings, canals, and weapons.
5. Typifies what has been called the "Renaissance man."
answer: Leonardo da Vinci

By revealing these clues one at a time, Mr. Peters encourages his students to run "searches" of their database and narrow the field of possible candidates until the correct one is found. On some occasions, he gives a printout of all clues to the class as a computer lab exercise. In either instance, his students gain valuable experience using databases while reinforcing material from the current unit of study. Some of them have even begun revising the database Mr. Peters gave them, because they have found a way to make searches much more efficient. These students can now get in three steps answers that used to take five steps.

transfer of computer literacy skills into a wider variety of areas of application.

For example, all world history textbooks contain a unit of study on feudalism in Europe during the Middle Ages. It is not unusual for teachers to make as assignment such as:

> Write a one-act play illustrating the relationships among the following persons of the feudal period: knights, serfs, lords, clergy, peasants, and women. The setting can be England during the early 1200s and can involve the fictional character Robin Hood and his accomplices.

In this case, computer technology can allow students to concentrate on the creative portion of the assignment. Word processing and the computer lab can make a substantial difference in academic learning time, as the computer can remove much of the drudgery from creating and revising scripts. In addition, the teacher can more easily make critical suggestions for improvement without drawing the usual moans and groans from those saddled with the task of retyping the script. Entire new parts can even be added without unnecessary burdens to typists. Also, the quality of the end product is often improved, because most of the errors and inaccuracies are removed in the revised scripts.

One of the areas of study that generates a great deal of student interest is the unit on world exploration. Typically, this involves background study of important inventions such as the magnetic compass and astrolabe, and important contributors such as Sir Francis Drake, Bartholomeu Diaz, Vasco da Gama, and others. One of the best supplements to this unit of study is the simulation DISCOVER THE WORLD by Hartley Courseware. Students make decisions regarding the hiring of crew and the purchase of supplies and equipment such as ships, guns, cannon balls, and water. They then embark on a voyage beginning in 1412 and face a variety of changing conditions involving weather, skirmishes with pirates, encounters with natives, and discoveries of land (see Figure 4.4). If learners make successful discoveries and trades, and if they are able to correctly answer questions in the "Explorer's Notebook," they earn points. There is a student recordkeeping feature that keeps track of accumulated points for each student. The major advantage of this program is its ability to approximate the decision-making environment faced by the early explorers. It also encourages students to learn about instruments such as the compass and to find out as much as possible about known territories, so that game decisions will be enlightened.

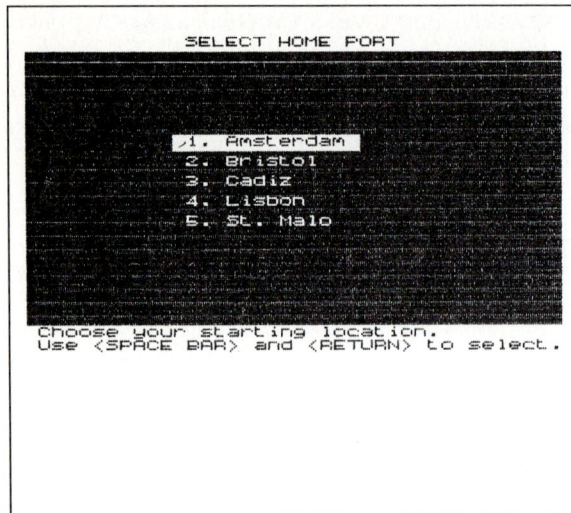

(a)

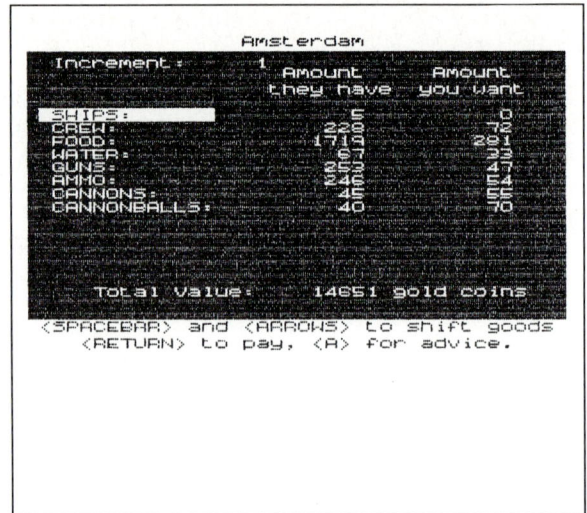

(b)

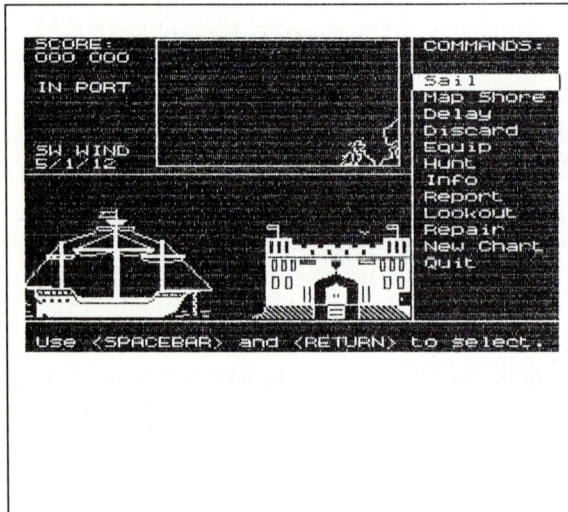

(c)

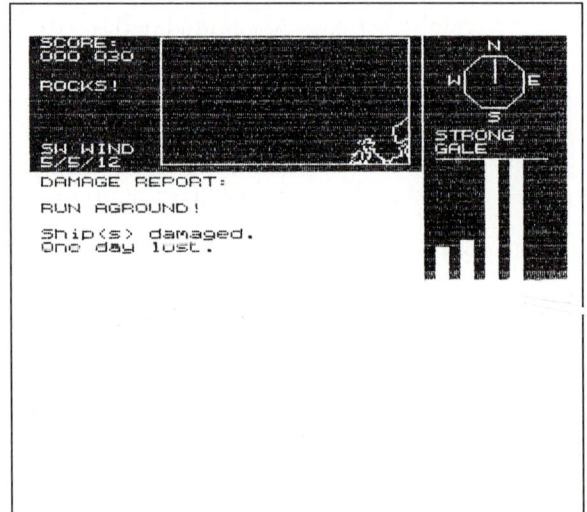

(d)

Figure 4.4 Screens from DISCOVER THE WORLD by Hartley Courseware. Students make decisions regarding the purchase of supplies and equipment such as ships, guns, cannon balls, water, crew, etc., as they embark on a voyage beginning in 1412 and encounter a variety of changing conditions involving weather, encounters with pirates, encounters with natives, and discoveries of land.

In some cases, it is even helpful to bring into the history classroom software from other disciplines that demonstrate events or principles that have influenced history. For example, the Galileo controversy consisted of a series of important scientific discoveries that forced changes in the way people viewed themselves and their universe. Because they normally are not science teachers and do not conduct their classes in a science lab, history teachers can usually do no more than mention the importance of Galileo's discoveries or (at best) show a film that touches upon them. However, Module 1 of Broderbund's SCIENCE TOOLKIT contains a highly accurate on-screen speedometer, which shows speed and elapsed time of moving objects. This can be used to effectively recreate Galileo's experiment involving falling weights of different magnitudes. As ball bearings of varying sizes and weights are rolled down an inclined plane, SCIENCE TOOLKIT Module 1 measures the speed of each sphere as it reaches the bottom of the plane (see Figure 4.5). The results of several trials should uphold the validity of Galileo's claim that the weight of an object has no influence over how fast it falls, disproving Aristotle's theory that it is a body's weight that determines how fast it will fall. This reenactment will appeal to all social studies teachers who long for some of the excitement of classroom physics demonstrations. Whereas in a science classroom this software might best be used by small groups of students creating and conducting their own experiments with SCIENCE TOOLKIT, in the history classroom the software would work best as part of a demonstration in which the teacher and a few volunteers from the class would conduct the experiments with the computerized results appearing on an LCD display for the entire class to see.

The American Revolution often heralds in a unit on world revolutions and offers some opportunity for computer assistance. COLONIAL MERCHANT (Educational Activities) enables students to understand the mercantile complexities leading up to the Revolution. For a period of twenty years, students try to carry on trade, while dealing with such factors as slavery and taxation. Especially in courses that emphasize a topical approach to revolution, HIDDEN AGENDA (Springboard) sets up a simulation to relate the volatile conditions in eighteenth-century United States and France to those of more modern times. In this simulation, a student or small group of students is challenged to maintain power in a fictitious Central American country named Chimerica. In so doing, the ruling junta must deal with three political parties, with appointing or firing government officials, and with the changing economic and social conditions. The program does

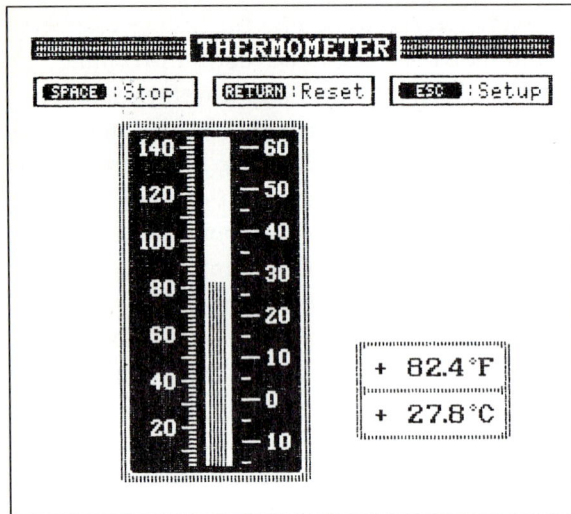

(a)

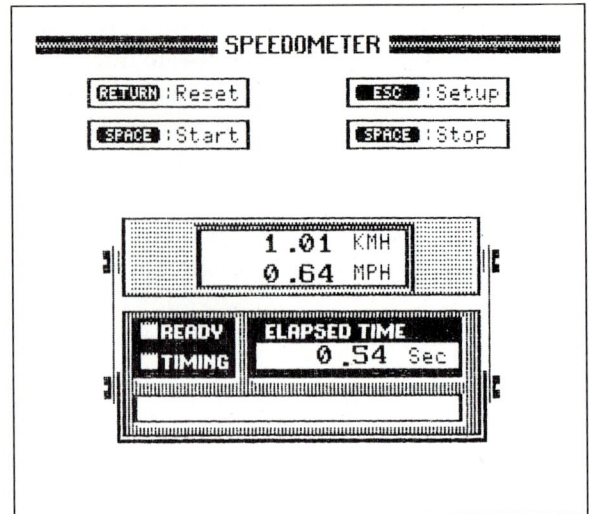

(b)

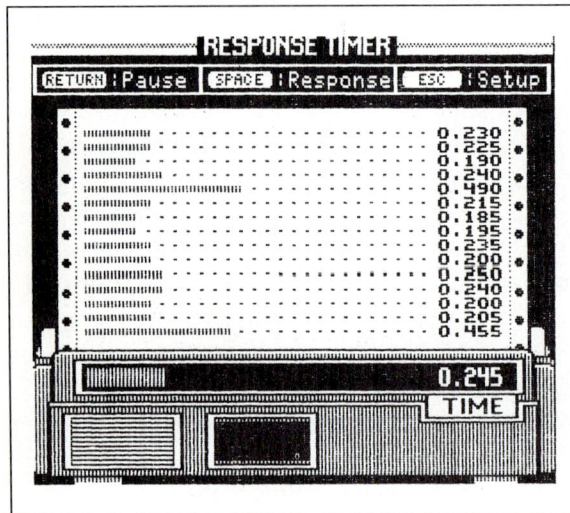

(c)

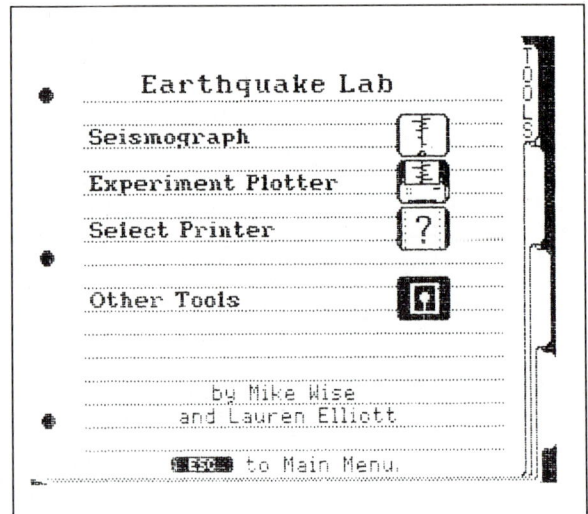

(d)

Figure 4.5 Screens from Broderbund's SCIENCE TOOLKIT, which can be used to effectively recreate Galileo's experiment involving falling weights of different magnitude.

an excellent job of presenting information. Data is available in graph form on decision areas including military spending, social spending, infant mortality, land distributions, food crops, export crops, currency earnings, currency reserves, and loans and aid (see Figure 4.6). As "presidente," the learner must make important decisions while responding to questions at occasional press conferences, gaining experience through contact with the people, and balancing the various political and social interests of the country in a changing environment. The student's objective is to stay in power for three years. HIDDEN AGENDA is a sophisticated simulation which will challenge students on many different levels of understanding.

For world history courses organized in topical rather than chronological fashion, REVOLUTIONS, PAST, PRESENT, AND FUTURE by Focus Media offers insight into the concept of "revolution." Using background events drawn from the American, French, and Russian revolutions, the program offers a tutorial on how to analyze specific events and how to evaluate their impact on the social and political order of each country. Although REVOLUTIONS, PAST, PRESENT, AND FUTURE lacks some of the appeal of more recently developed programs in that it uses screen text rather than graphics to convey information and concepts, it nevertheless encourages logical thinking and critical analysis, and it promotes outside library research as well. By using the computer as a catalyst rather than as the main contributor of study information, it also cultivates improved study habits.

Focus Media has also produced a simulation that may help students understand some of the futility and frustration surrounding the tremendous loss of life during World War I. THE TRAGEDY OF WAR: A SIMULATION teaches students about battle conditions and military logistics, using the Battle of the Somme as the setting. Teachers should make sure that students are familiar with trench warfare and World War I weaponry, or this simulation could degenerate into another arcade game. With proper planning, this program offers some authentic insights into the battlefield conditions and strategy of the First World War. This may work very well as a whole-class simulation, using the overhead projector and an LCD-projection system so that on-screen activities can be viewed by the entire class.

TIMELINER from Tom Snyder Productions is a unique tool for helping students develop a historical perspective. Students feed into the computer information about various historical events. The computer generates timelines of these events, which can be posted at the front of the classroom. The company also sells carefully researched data disks on various topics, including American history, world history, the arts, and science. This program becomes particularly interesting when several timelines are merged.

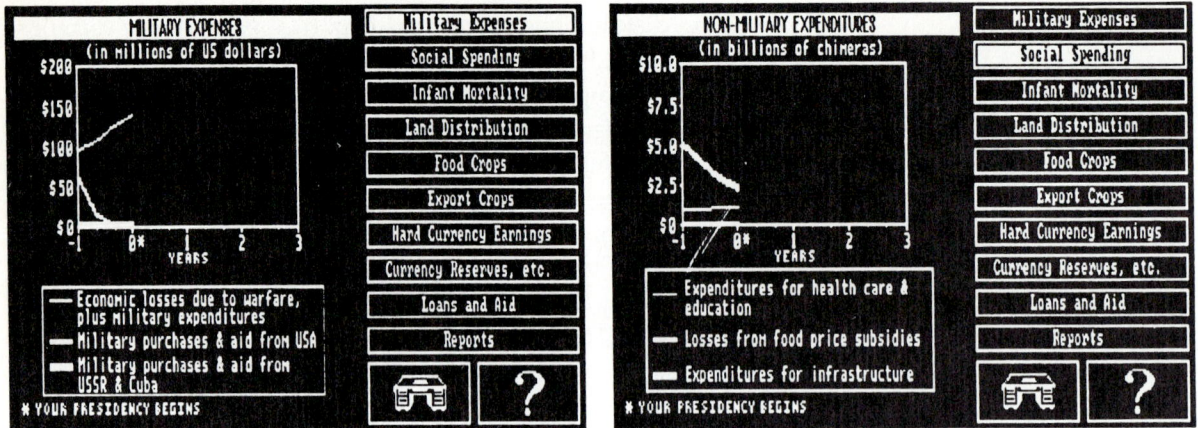

(a)   **(b)**

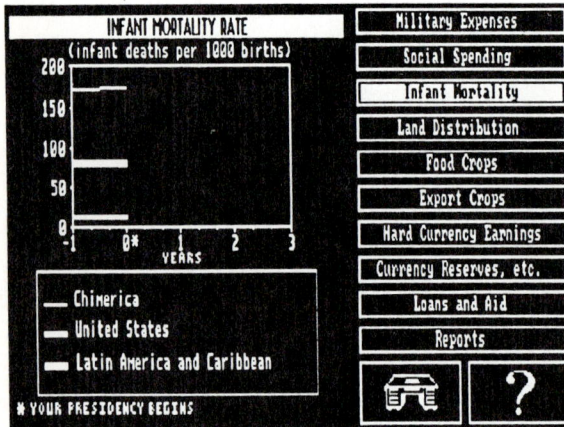   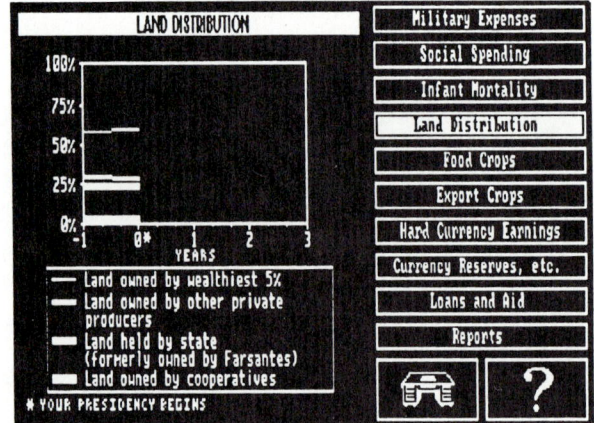

(c)   **(d)**

Figure 4.6 Screens from HIDDEN AGENDA (Springboard). In this simulation a student or small group of students is challenged to maintain power in a fictitious Central American country named Chimerica. In so doing, the ruling junta must deal with three political parties, with appointing or firing government officials, and with the changing economic and social conditions.

For example, a student may compose a timeline for her family history, which would be very specific for her own and her parents' lives but relatively sketchy for her great grandparents and more remote ancestors. By merging this self-created timeline with the pre-designed American history, world history, arts, and science timelines, she would be able to gain interesting insights into linking her family's evolution with events in the world, and be motivated to explore the nature of the relationships between these events.

UNITED STATES HISTORY

U.S. history is taught more frequently and at more levels of schooling than probably any other single social studies course. As a result, more computer software is available for it than any other course. This section will offer a brief look at a few computer-assisted learning strategies for U.S. history courses for grades 7–12. A more complete look at software is available in Chapter 7 and Appendix B.

With the many similarities between world history and U.S. history, many of the computerized techniques that are successful in one will also prove successful in the other. For example, the self-constructed database we did for the Renaissance unit (see page 81) works quite well when doing a U.S. history unit on any of the following areas: exploration, the American Colonies, the Industrial Revolution, the New Deal, or any of the modern decades—the fifties, sixties, seventies, or eighties. Because any of these units offers a large body of related information, the database becomes the ideal organizational and management tool. Students usually cringe at the thought of memorizing the "alphabet soup" programs of the New Deal. Why not organize these as a database? This offers some opportunities for library research. The completed database gives students the ability to quickly retrieve information vital to the understanding of the Roosevelt years. And remember that, if needed, the database can be printed out for classroom use. A sample database format and a specific entry appear in Figure 4.7.

If student-designed databases do not lend themselves well to your particular course structure, there are published databases that offer a number of opportunities for classroom exercises. Even more than for world history, software vendors for U.S. history materials have emphasized

```
NAME OF PROGRAM:

DATE OF CREATION:

CHIEF ADMINISTRATOR:

PROGRAM DESCRIPTION:




FINAL DISPOSITION:
```

```
NAME OF PROGRAM: National Recovery Administration
                 (NRA)
DATE OF CREATION: 1933

CHIEF ADMINISTRATOR: General Hugh S. Johnson

PROGRAM DESCRIPTION: The NRA sought to create a
better business atmosphere by creating some 500
"codes of fair practice" to regulate competition,
limit production, and set minimum prices.

Under its provisions, President Roosevelt established
a minimum wage of $12 to $15 per week and a maximum
work week of 35 to 40 hours.

Section 7A gave unions the right to organize.

Businesses which voluntarily cooperated displayed a
flag or decal depicting a blue eagle.

FINAL DISPOSITION: Declared unconstitutional in May,
1935 in SCHECTER POULTRY CORP. v. UNITED STATES.
```

(a)   (b)

Figure 4.7   A teacher-constructed database for a U.S. history unit.

databases, with more recently published programs offering greater degrees of sophistication.

The COLONIAL TIMES DATABASES (Sunburst) use BANK STREET FILER to access data based on sets of information compiled from records of the colonial period of U.S. history. Sets of information include the following:

- travelog—providing demographic, geographic, historical, and settlement data
- era news—providing information about significant events of the colonial period
- patriots—containing information about persons prominent in the Revolutionary War
- jobs—describing jobs performed and the necessary training and tools
- bazaar—describing period games, crafts, recipes, and remedies
- families—providing information about five colonial families

Databases of this type can be used effectively in a number of ways. The publisher includes sets of sample exercises, which can be useful especially for elementary and middle school students. Learners can also use these databases for retrieving information to enhance class assignments.

Among Sunburst's additional database offerings, UNITED STATES DATABASE offers recent information on climate and economies of the fifty states. Scholastic likewise offers U.S. HISTORY DATABASE, which presents a historical cross section of U.S. history. It uses PFS: FILE to access information. Table 4.1 shows a small sampling of its topics. A do-it-yourself module also permits inserting entries of local importance. Therefore, this approach might work well in courses that include a unit on state history. The "created" database becomes more feasible as students become more at ease using PFS: FILE. Detailed instructions and documentation are included. APPLEWORKS versions of the same database files are also available. A more specialized database is Sunburst's IMMIGRANT, which provides detailed data related to the Irish immigrant experience in Boston.

The TIMELINER program from Tom Snyder Productions is highly applicable to American history. In addition, this same company has com-

---

Computers in Action

Ms. Harris has her students choose one of the families detailed in the "Families" section of the COLONIAL TIMES DATABASE and write a brief sit-com skit (à la "The Cosby Show," "Family Ties," "Growing Pains," etc). They try to create plots which illustrate social and economic life of the period. They are expected to take special pains to accurately reflect activities in the following areas:

1. Games, dances, and other social activities.
2. Economics—What were some typical vocational activities of the period?
3. Major news event—Include a discussion of at least one. Try to portray real, historical attitudes toward this event.
4. Popular persons—Indicate through discussion some reaction to controversial figures of the time, e.g., Patrick Henry, Samuel Adams, etc.

Ms. Harris has her students work in groups of four to six. She finds that this activity offers opportunities to apply information taken from the database. Since this particular database does not contain any pictures, it acts only as a starting point. Students still need to gain access to additional information from the school library or resource center. In this case the computer is acting as a catalyst to encourage research rather than as the only source of information.

Table 4.1 Topics covered in Scholastic's U.S. HISTORY DATABASE.

1. The expanding american frontier.
   a. Texas independence
   b. California gold rush
   c. the final frontier—space
   d. Louisiana Purchase
   e. Mexican War
   f. Monroe Doctrine
   g. War of 1812

2. Inventions and technology.
   a. communications
   b. textiles
   c. military
   d. information processing
   e. transportation
   f. medicine
   g. home/leisure

3. Twentieth-century America.
   a. population
   b. education
   c. birthrates
   d. life expectancy
   e. gross national product
   f. unemployment

4. American presidents.
   a. previous occupations
   b. achievements
   c. political parties
   d. home states

5. Fun with American history.
   a. lifestyles of twentieth-century America
   b. popular history

bined concepts from TIMELINER and its SOCIAL STUDIES TOOL KITS to produce TIME PATTERNS TOOL KIT. This database program provides easy access to information on the history of the United States and encourages students to look for patterns and relationships.

An area of computer applications that holds great promise for future development is that of computer simulation. One of the oldest and best known of these is MECC's OREGON TRAIL (Figure 4.8). The program takes students on a fascinating journey from Independence, Missouri, to the Pacific Coast, with excellent graphic depictions of certain landmarks such as Chimney Rock and Fort Mandan. To prepare for their trip, students must carefully select appropriate supplies. Along the way, they encounter

(a)

The Willamette Valley, Oregon
January 16, 1849
Press SPACE BAR to continue

(b)

Congratulations! You have
made it to Oregon! Let's see
how many points you have
received.

The Willamette Valley, Oregon
January 16, 1849
Press SPACE BAR to continue

Figure 4.8 Screens from the conclusion of MECC's OREGON TRAIL, which takes students on a fascinating journey from Independence, Missouri, to the Pacific Coast. This program was described more fully in Figure 2.2.

an array of hardships including bad water, disease, river crossings, famine, and the like. Without careful planning, few members of the original wagon party will successfully reach the mouth of the Columbia River. It is, of course, possible for students to vicariously experience the problems and tribulations of the westward pioneering movement without the computer. For example, they could read a good book on the topic or watch a good movie, and many teachers do incorporate books and movies into their courses. However, the computer has the advantage of enabling the students to *interact* with the events they as pioneers would typically encounter—to make decisions and to experience the results of good or bad decisions. This personal involvement can often enhance both motivation and under-standing of the topic being studied.

The success and popularity of OREGON TRAIL have spurred the development of other simulations. One of the most promising is REVOLU-TION '76 by Britannica Software. As the name implies, this program takes students through the Revolutionary War from the American viewpoint. Along the way, they must assign qualified leaders, raise and train an army, place ambassadors in strategic European locations, decide economic issues such as taxation, assign generals, and move troops in and out of theaters of action (see Figure 4.9). REVOLUTION '76 is time consuming, as it takes a good deal of preparation to give students enough background to make enlightened decisions. However, games in progress can be saved so that this simulation can be suspended and resumed later. Other interesting simulations related to American history include ELECTION OF 1912 (Eastgate Systems) and LINCOLN'S DECISIONS (Educational Activities). CONVERSATIONS WITH GREAT AMERICANS (Focus Media) encourages students to use primary sources by interviewing historical figures to learn about various time periods.

GOLD RUSH! (Sierra On-Line) is an "adventure game" with obvious educational implications. Adventure games are popular, enjoyable, computerized activities in which the user pursues an adventure—the quest for the Holy Grail, freeing a princess from a dungeon, fighting dragons, or similar adventurous activities. GOLD RUSH! simulates a journey to California around 1850 in search of gold. The learner makes a large number of very realistic choices (such as whether to sail around the tip of South America, to cross the isthmus of Panama, or to travel across country from New York to California), and is also faced with very practical decisions (such as finding food and staying off the deck of the boat during storms at sea). The simulation is much more complex than OREGON TRAIL—eight double-sided disks for the Apple II version—but this complexity results in considerable realism. Students running this program would come away with a realistic understanding of what it was like to take part in the California gold rush. One problem with this kind of program is that not all students enjoy the adventure-game format. Programs of this type require a unique type of input and persistence; adventure game players can almost be regarded as a subculture within our society. However, a very large number of young people *do* enjoy adventure programs, and for those students this type of program provides an excellent way to make history come alive. A further problem with GOLD RUSH! is that it is very time-consuming; students would not be able to complete this program within an hour-long time period. Most users would have to spend several days to succeed. However, the fact that both children and adults *are* indeed willing to spend hours and even days trying to make it to California as efficiently as possible is a strong indication that this is a very worthwhile program for students who take an interest in it. Teachers need to become aware of programs of this kind and offer them as possible activities for students who are interested in and have time for programs of this type.

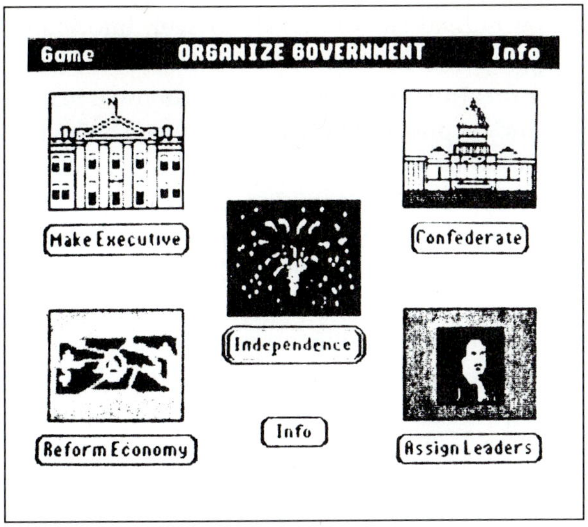

(a)

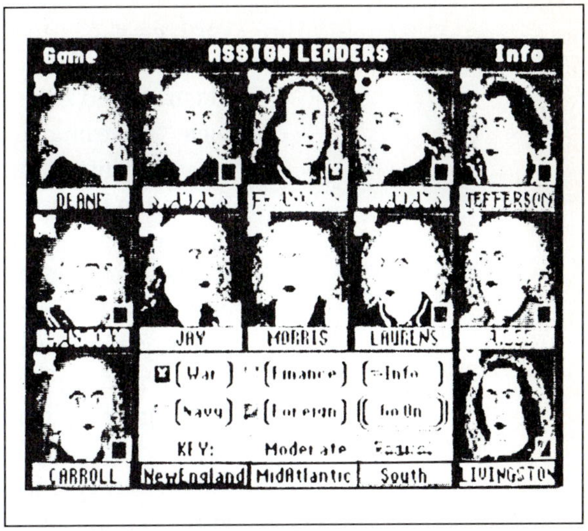

(b)

Figure 4.9 Screens from REVOLUTION '76 by Britannica Software, which takes students through the Revolutionary War from the American viewpoint. Along the way, they must assign qualified leaders, raise and train an army, place ambassadors in strategic European locations, decide economic issues such as taxation, and assign generals and move troops in and out of theaters of action.

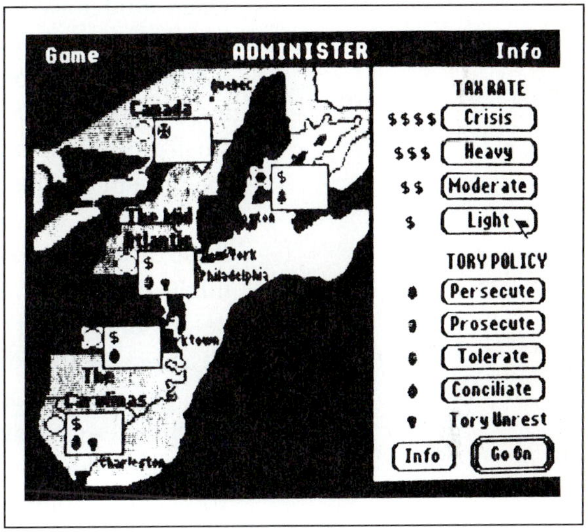

(c)

POINT OF VIEW (Scholastic) is a CD-ROM application providing a detailed database that includes not only factual information about American history but also copies of original documents, eyewitness testimony, pictures, maps, and statistics. It enables users to sift information, place data in context, and test historical hypotheses. The program can be used as a research tool by individuals or classes to seek information traditionally found in encyclopedias or textbooks. Teachers can use it to illustrate and enhance their presentations, and students can use it to complete "electronic term papers" to present to their classmates. The logic of accessing information is creative: for example, students can access information either by topic or from a timeline. Demographic data can be presented in columns, tables, or graphs. It is easy to move among these several formats, and they can even be set to "evolve," enabling students to see changes from year to year.

A program of this type can be used in many ways. As an electronic chalkboard, it can enrich lectures or stimulate discussions. By being thoroughly familiar with the program and topics under discussion in class, the teacher could easily call up on the screen maps, charts, pictures, and data to support lecture topics or to answer questions raised by students. However, the most vital use would be to get a tool like this into the hands of students. The program could stand alone in the library or media center, where students could access it to perform their own research. It could also be used in a cooperative learning environment, with small groups of learners working on research questions. To make the cooperative environment work most effectively, students should have specific roles within the small groups: for example, one student could search for information within the present database, another could look elsewhere for information to be inserted into an expansion of the original database, another could synthesize this information and actually insert it into the database, and another might digitize information from another source to be inserted into the database. The roles can be changed from time to time, so that students learn all aspects of this kind of research.

This program is an example of software that requires some training for effective usage. Students cannot be expected to profit from it by simply turning on the computer, inserting the disk, and doing their own research. To use the program effectively, students would have to possess a basic understanding of the hypertext environment (using icons, pointing, clicking, and so on) and of using and resizing windows. Without these basic skills, students are likely to flounder uselessly or, at best, overlook the opportunities offered by this kind of program. A very useful strategy would be to begin with a whole-class presentation, encouraging students to offer input and suggestions for deriving data on the screen in front of the entire class. The teacher should carry out instructions given by the class, offer insights and ideas of his own, and make it clear to the students how he achieves the interesting output that appears on the screen. Then he should be prepared to help the students work in small groups as they follow their own research interests. Instruction of this type works best when the teacher himself is well prepared (by running the program numerous times himself) and when he supplies useful guidelines to help the students run the program effectively.

Note, however, that as programs like this become more prevalent, we can expect both teachers and students to become more proficient in their use. For example, students who have used similar CD-ROM and hypertext programs in their literature or science class during their sophomore year would require very little introductory instruction to use POINT OF VIEW as an effective research tool in their junior American history class.

Tom Snyder Productions has emphasized the development of computer programs that are designed to supplement, rather than replace, a teacher's ordinary style of teaching. Many of the programs from this company are designed to operate off a single computer (even without a large screen). The teacher carries on a good discussion with the class, and the computer serves as a sort of reference tool and discussion guide. The DECISIONS, DECISIONS series applies this concept to American history. For example, in the COLONIZATION program, students are presented with dilemmas faced by European nations as they explored and colonized the New World in the 15th through 17th centuries. The students talk over possible solutions to a dilemma and then, as a group, make a choice of action. The computer then provides a revised setting with a new dilemma and a new set of choices, and the students continue their discussion. Upon request, the computer provides information on various topics. The computer's main function is to serve as a storehouse of information and a prompter of students. In traditional, noncomputerized teaching, social studies teachers often feel they are making the most progress when they are thoroughly informed on a topic and get their students intimately involved in a discussion on that topic. The DECISIONS, DECISIONS programs enable the teacher to have such stimulating discussions by focusing on discussion skills while letting the computer provide the informational component. The series also includes REVOLUTIONARY WARS, IMMIGRATION, and URBANIZATION, all of which fit into recognizable units of American history. For teachers employing a topical rather than chronological approach, Tom Snyder's CRITICAL ISSUES PACK of the same series offers FOREIGN POLICY, TELEVISION, THE BUDGET PROCESS, and finally one entitled ON THE CAMPAIGN TRAIL. These programs can be employed in a whole-class setting or in a cooperative atmosphere using smaller groups.

A large number of news programs have become available on CD-ROM with hypertext interfaces. These strategies are discussed in Chapter 5. Examples include VIETNAM REMEMBERED (Wayzata), IN THE HOLY LAND and the '88 VOTE (Optical Data), and THE GREAT QUAKE OF '89 (The Voyager Company).

Several programs have applied the concept of "time travel" to the study of American history. Broderbund's WHERE IN TIME IS CARMEN SANDIEGO? follows a format similar to the CARMEN programs described in the Geography section of Chapter 3, except that the players must use a time machine to track villains. The program promises to be as motivating and enjoyable as its predecessors. MECC's TIME NAVIGATOR and TIME NAVIGATOR LEAPS BACK programs offer a similar opportunity to study history through a simulated time machine. Tom Snyder's THE RIPPLE THAT CHANGED AMERICAN HISTORY challenges the user to locate a destructive "ripple" by listening into conversations from the past and doing "ripscans" over a U.S. map to find the location of the problem.

A difficulty with the time machine games is that they do not permit the student or teacher to select the time period to be covered. For example, TIME NAVIGATOR covers events from 1900 through the 1980s, and TIME NAVIGATOR LEAPS BACK covers 1776 through 1900. A student in the second month of an American history course might be reading about and discussing the process of ratifying the Constitution. She won't study the Civil War for another two months. If she runs TIME NAVIGATOR LEAPS BACK, she *may* get clues involving the time between 1776 and 1788 (which she has studied), but she is equally likely to get clues about the Civil War or Reconstruction (which she has not studied). While this very creative program can be used to teach students critical thinking skills and the effective use of reference books even very early in an American history course, it can serve as a useful review only after they have moved past the turn of the century in their textbooks. The problems are even more overwhelming for WHERE IN TIME IS CARMEN SANDIEGO?, which covers the entire scope of recorded history and would therefore serve a useful review purpose for almost no pre-college students.

Time travel programs would be much more useful if students or teachers could select particular time periods to correspond to what students are expected to know and need to review. In fact, the MECC TIME NAVIGATOR programs accomplish this simply by letting students select the terminal (most recent) date and having the computer select clues exclusively from events prior to that date. The main reason this is not done in more programs is because a very large number of clues would be required for early terminal dates. Our guess is that a company with a huge number of "clues" already on CD-ROM (such as the publisher of an electronic encyclopedia) will realize that they can add a time travel game with very little additional effort. The result will be a truly useful time travel educational game.

We anticipate a time travel game integrated into a program like GTV: A GEOGRAPHIC PERSPECTIVE ON AMERICAN HISTORY. The student will travel back into American history, and the screen will present a photograph or chart describing the targeted time. When students go to the same time on different runs of the game, it will even be possible for the visual clues to be varied to prevent trivial, rote memorization of details. The game could consist of identifying the time period as rapidly as possible in a "Name That Tune!" format (I can name that historical period in seven frames . . . "). Or it could incorporate a CARMEN SANDIEGO theme of looking for a villain somewhere in history. At the present time, the time travel games—although they are ingenious and enjoyable—often focus on trivia. Integrating them with high-quality CD-ROM materials will change that.

POLITICAL SCIENCE AND GOVERNMENT

Political science and government courses are a natural environment for databases and simulations. This section provides a sample of good programs and effective strategies. Chapter 8 offers additional choices and reviews.

Scholastic Software's U.S. GOVERNMENT DATABASES provides resource materials in the following areas: Constitutional Convention, federal spending, elections, and state government. Accessed through PFS: FILE, the databases are accompanied by a comprehensive teacher's guide complete with detailed instructions on how to use the file and related exercises including a role-playing simulation for the Constitutional Convention section.

Scholastic Software also offers CONGRESS IN ACTION for use with APPLEWORKS. This program offers a series of APPLEWORKS Instructional Modules (AIMs), so that students are able to organize information related to current members of Congress. The "Legislative Process" section presents some of the procedural debate on the issue gun control. The user is able to view the range of legislative proposals, existing federal laws related to the issue, and basic statistics on firearm ownership and crime. Students are exposed to a series of well-designed activities such as "conducting an opinion poll" and "lobbying." A major advantage of this particular database is its link with APPLEWORKS. Because many schools already use the word processing portion of the program, students are familiar with its operation. Also, where written reports are needed, a word processor is readily available. CONGRESS STACK (Highlighted Data) provides similar data on the Macintosh computer with a HYPERCARD interface.

There are some intriguing developments in political science simulations. Tom Snyder Productions' DECISIONS DECISIONS: ON THE CAMPAIGN TRAIL places students in the position of a third-party candidate in a presidential election. They are challenged to formulate a platform after exploring questions about the economy, social reform, and foreign policy. Then they must conduct a cross-country campaign tour in order to convey their message to the voters. In the process, economic, political, and social consequences of their positions must be weighed carefully. This is an excellent interactive program. It may be used very effectively with a single computer and LCD-projection system, as much of the actual work is done away from the computer. AND IF RE-ELECTED (Focus Media) offers another approach to a simulation of a presidential election.

Another Tom Snyder program, OUR TOWN MEETING, makes similar use of the computer as a catalyst to promote group interaction. In this instance, students are placed in the position of a typical village board faced with the prospect of needing various civic projects and yet forced to work within budget limitations. Again, the computer acts only as a backdrop, with the real work accomplished by students interacting with one another and with the acting mayor. This program promotes problem-solving and organizational skills. Even speech arts skills are sharpened in presenting oral project reports to the rest of the board for consideration.

In each of these programs, students are learning political science and government by experiencing some of the successes and frustrations of participation. But more importantly, from an educational standpoint they are an active part of the learning process, rather than a passive observer. The computer is used merely to focus attention on the task—not to spoonfeed information to the student.

International relations is a topic in various courses, including American history and government. THE OTHER SIDE (Tom Snyder Productions) is a program designed to present students with the problems of establishing peaceful coexistence in a world where interests and values conflict. Like many of the other programs from the same company, this one is designed to promote discussion in large or small groups. Students work together to try to develop strategies for attaining such goals as a stable economy and national security. With an optional cable, students are able to play the game with other students at another computer or in another room. Accompanying guidelines suggest strategies for even more remote cooperative learning—as via modem with students in another school or even in another country. Similar programs that focus on international relations include BALANCE OF POWER (Mindscape) and POWER OF NATION STATES (Data Disc International).

PSYCHOLOGY AND SOCIOLOGY

For high school psychology teachers, there is an outstanding package of psychology experiments available from Conduit Software. The package is entitled START (Stimulus and Response Tools for Experiments in Memory, Learning, Cognition, and Perception), and consists of a series of four disks capable of running 15 experiments. The sequence makes clever use of the computer's inherent ability to create displays, to generate tones, and to time responses in order to achieve its results. In the "Reaction Time" experiment, reaction times are clocked by having the computer flash an "x" in the middle of the screen, while the volunteer strikes the space bar as soon as possible after observing the symbol. Reaction times are monitored and recorded automatically by the computer. Accompanying documentation offers background information as well as analytical tools. Other experiments include "Precognition," "Prototype Formation," "Pitch Memory," "Probability Learning," and "Dot Enumeration." Each experiment is well conceived and thought out. In general, they demonstrate important psychological principles by exemplifying major experiments conducted over the history of psychology. Documentation adds a great deal to the understanding and use of this package.

Sociology is to a great extent an undeveloped area as far as computer usage is concerned. Conduit Software offers some programs that may prove helpful. DEMO-GRAPHICS uses 1980 statistics on the mortality, population, fertility, and cereal production of 40 countries to help demonstrate the impact of both real and simulated factors on the growth of world population.

DIFFUSION GAME is intended to help students understand the diffusion of innovations and the value of the management approach to effecting a desired behavior change. In this simulation a "management group" has the responsibility of convincing a group of "rural villagers" that innovations should be adopted. Various strategies are available, including diffusion methods.

Conduit also offers SAMP: SURVEY SAMPLING, a program that permits the survey of populations in four different formats: simple random sampling, cluster sampling, stratified sampling, and quota sampling. With each sampling strategy, students simulate an interview of the selected respondents, and a summary of statistics is reported back with response distributions recorded on a five-point scale. This program permits the use of standard statistical analysis including mean, median, standard deviation, and standard error of the responses. After finishing their surveys, students can compare their sample results with the true result obtained from a population-wide census. The less biased procedures are likely to produce sample results closest to these true results.

A somewhat less sophisticated but equally effective tool is Scholastic Software's SURVEY TAKER. It permits the construction of basic surveys, but lacks some of the analytical tools of SAMP. SURVEY TAKER allows students to conduct real, rather than simulated, surveys. It provides easy, menu-driven survey development and includes brief graphical analysis. Both table results and corresponding graphs can be printed out, although user choice of what is printed out is somewhat limited.

Either survey program would make an excellent tool for testing sociological norms. Figure 4.10 shows an example of a survey about family dynamics. Using this kind of survey, sociology classes could draw conclusions about the changing nature of families as a societal institution. As long as the surveys were kept fairly short, a typical class might do one per week. A minor drawback is manual input of response data, but on limited samples this should not pose much of an inconvenience. Ideally, optical character recognition (OCR) equipment could be utilized; eventually programs will be written that will accept this type of input. In any event, these programs enable sociology students to more easily assess and analyze data, and to field test hypotheses about societal norms.

ECONOMICS

A recent resurgence of interest in economics is prompting some vendors to increase publication of programs related to that field. For example, Merrill's ECONOMICS PRINCIPLES AND PRACTICES is a tutorial and simulation

Figure 4.10 Output from Scholastic Software's SURVEY TAKER, which permits students to conduct real, rather than simulated, surveys. It provides easy, menu-driven construction of surveys and includes brief graphical analysis.

```
                         Family Survey

1. Including your parent(s), how large is your family?

        A. 2
        B. 3-4
        C. 5-6
        D. > or = 7

2. During a normal week, how many activities do you do with
   one or both parents?

        A. <3
        B. 3-5
        C. 5-7
        D. > or = 8

3. During the past week, how many meals has your family had
   together as a unit with all family members present?

        A. None
        B. 1-3
        C. 3-6
        D. 7-10
        E. >10

4. During the past week, how many meals have you eaten at a
   fast-food restaurant?

        A. None
        B. 1-3
        C. 3-6
        D. 7-10
        E. >10

5. How many members of your family work a full or part-time
   job?

        A. 1
        B. 2
        C. 3
        D. 4
        E. all
```

disk that offers the following topics: Law of Demand, Law of Supply, price adjustment process, fractional reserves, amortization tables, stock market simulation, and rate of growth triangle. Although the simulations are somewhat simplified, this program works very well when used as a demonstration with an LCD projection system. It has the ability to produce tables and graphs that are fairly impressive in a whole-class environment (see Figure 4.11).

(a)

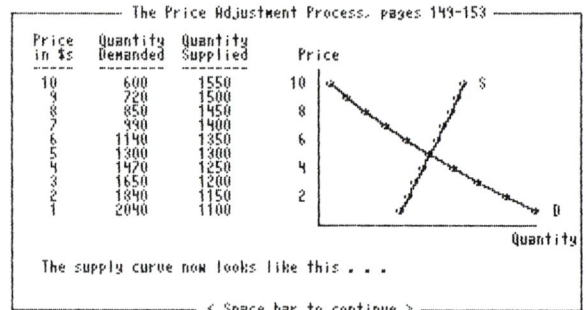

(b)

Figure 4.11 Screens from Merrill's ECONOMICS PRINCIPLES AND PRACTICES, a tutorial and simulation disk that discusses several topics related to economics.

For economics classes interested in supportive data, many of the Scholastic and Sunburst databases offer ample demographic information for case studies of underdeveloped and developing nations. If the instructor desires a simulated study of these topics, SIMPOLICON by Cross Cultural Software offers some interesting opportunities. In this simulation, students are asked to make a variety of decisions regarding the production of goods and services for a hypothetical developing country. Production ranges from manufacturing and industrial to agricultural, so that decisions directly affect the allocation of resources for the production of food, machinery, schools, factories, and other uses. Twelve socio-economic goals can be weighted as to their degree of importance. Disasters (climatic, natural, medical, and so on) and military problems may be introduced at various points. This program does a good job of demonstrating the complexity of the decisions facing the leaders of developing nations. The only drawback is the 10 hours of class time required to complete this simulation and the accompanying follow-up analysis. Otherwise, it provides some excellent exposure to economic concepts such as absolute and comparative advantage, balance of trade, command economy, consumer good, producer good, factors of production, and national wealth.

One of the most useful types of utility program now available are those that take data in table or spreadsheet form and permit the user to construct a variety of graphs and charts. More advanced students will use spreadsheets not only to examine and graph current economic conditions, but also to forecast future economic trends and even to test economic theories by projecting future conditions based on mathematical models arising from these theories. For younger students, EXPLORING TABLES AND GRAPHS by Weekly Reader Family Software is a menu-driven program that allows for limited data entry. It has the versatility of representing the data as a line graph, vertical or horizontal bar graph, pie chart, or pictograph, without having to reconfigure the data (see Figure 4.12). The Beagle Brothers TIME OUT series also contains a graphing module, activated from within APPLEWORKS, which allows data in the spreadsheet mode to be used to construct graphs. For applications where such data is to be used in the preparation of reports, this is the graphing program of choice because word processing is readily available without leaving the program. Both programs offer economics students the ability to organize data and represent it in a more readily usable fashion for visual comparisons. Of course, resulting graphs can be printed out for use in written reports. Instructors can then use the printed graphs to make thermofax

---

Computers in Action

Miss Warren purchased a large number of pretzel rods. She obtained permission for her students to sell them in the school cafeteria. Since the school had several lunch periods, she had them sell the product in successive periods with progressively higher prices at each period. They kept track of the quantity sold during each session. Once the pretzels were all sold, the resulting data was used to verify the Law of Demand. The students graphed their data using the APPLEWORKS program and TIMEOUT: GRAPH. They modified the graphs several times to get the right layout to give the correct impression of their data. The students appreciated this experiment, because it made a tangible connection between the economic theory from their textbooks and a part of the real world with which they are closely connected.

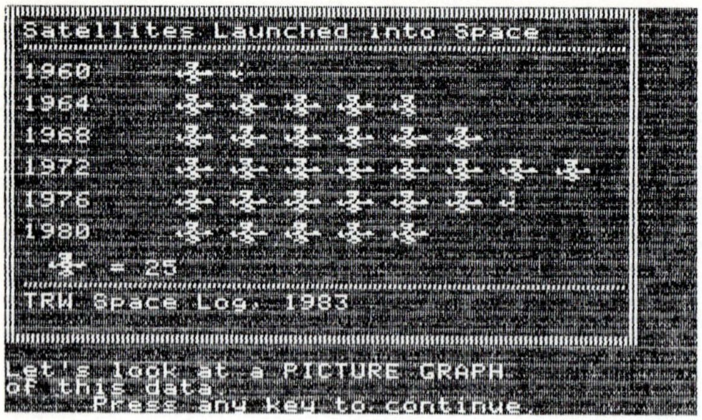

(a)

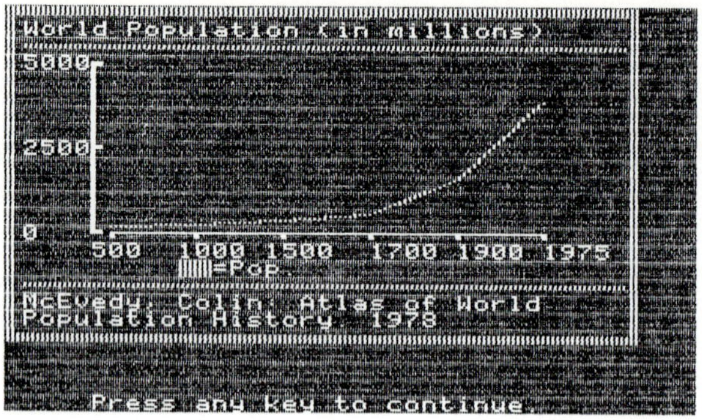

(b)

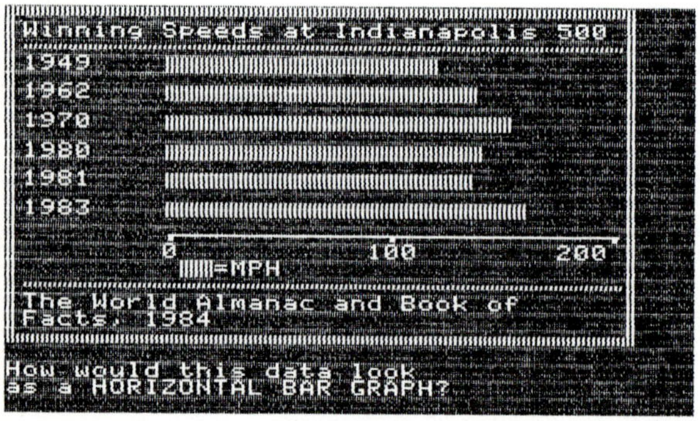

(c)

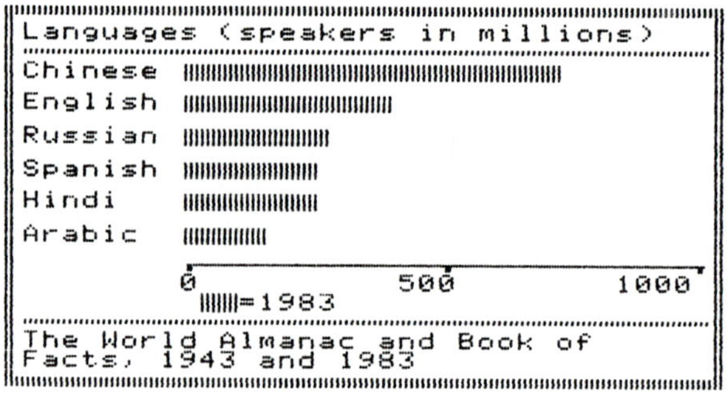

(d)

Figure 4.12 Screens from EXPLORING TABLES AND GRAPHS by Weekly Reader Family Software, which offers a series of menu-driven programs that allow limited data entry. It has the advantage of representing the data as line graphs, vertical and horizontal bar graphs, pie charts, or pictographs without having to reconfigure the data.

(a)

```
039--join(pwolf,pdeer)
         23    1500
        121    1958
          7     112
         10     170
         15     249
         22     350
         28     463
         35     572
------------------------PACIFIC CREST SOFTWARE--PC:SOLVE--------------------
026| wolf and deer populations taking into account the predator relationship.
027| Deer deaths from wolves are taken into account.  The model now
028| does take into account the maintenance level of wolves.  Also, the
029| deer population is unrealistically allowed to go below zero.
030| years=20
031| pmead=.008
032| deerbr=.6  ? wolfbr=.6
033| pwolf=fill(?,years)  ? pdeer=fill(?,years)
034| pwolf[1]=23  ? pdeer[1]=1500
035| maintlev=26
036| for i=2 to years do population
037|
038|
039| join(pwolf,pdeer)
```

(b)

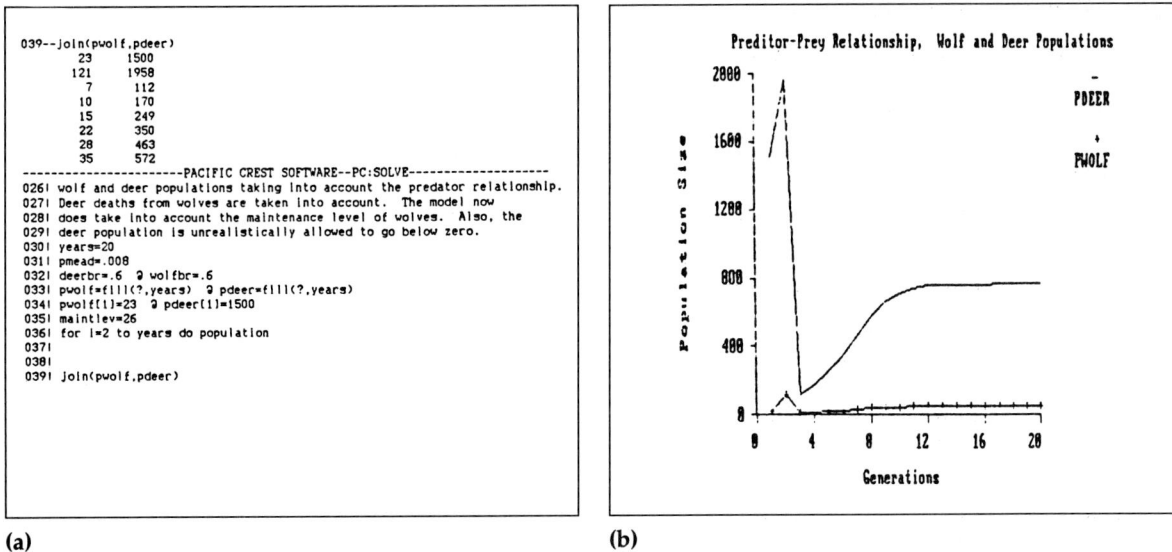

Figure 4.13 Screens from PC: SOLVE, a sophisticated tool that permits the user to access a large number of computerized tools to tabulate and graph data, make projections, and test theoretical models.

transparencies. However, where available, LCD projection systems have a more immediate impact on class presentations.

A sophisticated program for more advanced economics classes is PC:SOLVE, which permits the user to access a large number of computerized tools to tabulate and graph data, make projections, and test theoretical models. Although the example shown in Figure 4.13 focuses on ecology, the same program could be used as a tool to teach problem solving and other higher-order thinking skills in any area in which numerical data can be used to test theories. While this kind of program is useful for individuals or small groups of students, it is also extremely useful as an electronic blackboard for large-group lectures and demonstrations. An economics teacher, for example, could easily change factors in Figure 4.13 in response to student questions, and the resulting changes in the graph would answer questions much more effectively than a verbal response by the teacher. Even without the computer, of course, the teacher could redraw the graph by hand on the chalkboard, but this activity is so tedious that it is not often done.

ARCADE AND RECREATIONAL GAMES

In the old days, students typically learned a great deal of accurate but informal history and geography from the movies. Today, arcade games have replaced (or at least supplemented) the movies for many young people. While not many teachers actually brought *The Sands of Iwo Jima* into their classrooms, they were better teachers if they were aware that many of their students found John Wayne's presentation a bit more interesting than their own. By being aware of what the movie industry was doing, teachers could take advantage of and develop their students' interests. A surprising number of computerized arcade games have a similar degree of motivational interest and historical or geographic authenticity. For example, Lucas Film's THEIR FINEST HOUR: THE BATTLE OF BRITAIN permits players to take either side in the Nazi air attack against England during World War II. By playing the roles of pilots, players who run this program become familiar with the comparative characteristics of the Hawker Hurricane Mk I, the Supermarine Spitfire, the Ju 87B Stuka, the BF-109 fighter, and other aircraft. After training their flight crews, players also explore the basic strategies of combat involved in the Battle of Britain by flying 32 carefully simulated flight patterns. Insights attained through this activity can certainly enable students to approach a major aspect of World War II from a different perspective. Even though programs like this probably do not have a place for all students within the actual social studies classroom, teachers should be aware of their existence and encourage students to apply knowledge from these games to appropriate classroom activities—just as in bygone days students could bring their knowledge from John Wayne and Fess Parker into their history classrooms.

Likewise, many social studies teachers are familiar with the board game called Risk from Parker Brothers. In this game, players compete with each other to conquer the entire world. Although some parents and teachers may object to the game's emphasis on militarism and Machiavellian attitudes, it is nevertheless true that avid Risk players do, in fact, learn about some world geography and some simple military principles that are helpful in understanding the modern world. Likewise, although someone may argue that the Monopoly board game may promote greed or other undesirable attitudes and values, enthusiasts of that game do develop an understanding of some concepts and principles important in economics and real estate. Both RISK and MONOPOLY are currently available in computerized versions from Leisure Genius. Teachers should be aware of the instructive potential of these and other "noneducational" computer games.

SUMMARY

The field of social studies has not been inundated with computer software as rapidly as other fields, such as reading and mathematics. However, as this and the previous chapter have shown, there are numerous good programs currently on the market. In addition, many computer tools such as databases, spreadsheets, and word processors can be incorporated into social studies classrooms to enable teachers to employ their traditional methods even more effectively. A major contribution of the computer to the field of social studies is the easy access it gives students to the information they need to study topics in history, geography, economics, and related fields.

Judging from the progress and improvement in computer programs and hardware since the middle of this decade, educators should expect even more creative uses in the near future. With increased equipment availability, teachers and students should anticipate vastly improved methods of data access and instruction, or, perhaps, a successful resurrection of inquiry methods and individualized methods of instruction. Whatever the educational goal, there is no doubt that today's technology can help improve the chance for success.

CHAPTER 5

HELPFUL HARDWARE AND SPECIAL SOFTWARE

THIS CHAPTER INCLUDES A DISCUSSION of hardware and software that is useful across many grade levels and various subject areas in the social sciences. Many of the topics covered in this chapter were cited briefly in Chapters 3 and 4. The present chapter describes these topics in greater detail as they relate to the social studies curriculum.

LARGE SCREENS AND LCD PROJECTION SYSTEMS

When people think of computer-assisted instruction, they often think of a roomful of computers with individual students seated at each terminal, actively and industriously pursuing the objectives of the curriculum. However, individual use of computers is not as common or as necessary in social studies as in areas such as reading and mathematics. Although individuals and small groups will sometimes work at their own computers, social studies teachers often find that one of the best ways to use the computer is to run a single program with a whole class—either having the class participate in a simulation or using the computer as a tool to generate and share information (such as database information, graphs, or maps). When using a computer program with an entire class, it becomes necessary to find a display mechanism that will enable all of the students to view the computer screen.

In some cases, no screen beyond the ordinary monitor may be necessary. For example, if during the course of a discussion it becomes useful to know the names of all the countries with a GNP over a certain limit whose exports exceed their imports, a single student can conduct the search of a database (using parameters designated by the other members) and report the results to the rest of the class—just as a single student could look up information in an almanac and report it to the others. However, in many instances it is useful to have the entire class look at and interact with the output as it is generated by the computer. In these cases it is necessary to use either a large screen monitor or liquid crystal display (LCD) projection system.

A large-screen monitor may be a 25-inch cathode ray tube (CRT) monitor set aside specifically for use with the computer, or it may be the same monitor used with the TV or VCR for showing movies to the class. A major advantage of the large CRT screen is that almost all schools already have one (or more) that can easily be wheeled into the classroom. A further advantage is that a color CRT monitor will preserve the color graphics which are important in some computer programs—especially simulations.

A disadvantage of the large CRT screen is that students seated far from the screen will be unable to see it very well if the information is printed in small letters, as in the typical 80-column format of some database management programs. In addition, the quality of resolution of some older CRT monitors—especially those designed primarily to show movies rather than to serve as computer monitors—will be inadequate to show text and diagrams as clearly as they would appear on the normal computer monitor. Finally, it is often more trouble to set up and use a large CRT screen than to use a more simple LCD projection system.

To use a large CRT screen, the output from the computer must be sent to that screen instead of to the monitor that comes with the computer. In some cases, this may be as simple as removing a wire plugged into the monitor and plugging it into the CRT screen. If the wire is too short, of course, it should be replaced with a longer wire. Ideally, instead of having the information appear on the large screen *instead of* the computer monitor, it would be best to have the output appear on *both* monitors. This is usually accomplished by using a "Y splitter," which takes output from a single source (the computer) and sends it to two display devices (the computer monitor and the large screen). This enables the teacher to watch the computer monitor while the students watch the large screen.

LCD projection systems offer the advantage of permitting an entire class to view the images displayed in a particular program when used in conjunction with a conventional overhead projector (see Figure 5.1). The LCD system has the major advantage of projecting a very large display on an ordinary projection screen. The projection works just like an ordinary overhead projector, so the teacher can make the display larger by simply moving the projector further away from the screen and focusing appropriately. In addition, the teacher can easily point to elements of the output by using a pencil or other pointer on the display device. The teacher can also place a transparency on top of the device and "draw" on the output. LCD devices are usually easy to set up and provide very clear output. A significant drawback is that at the present time only fairly expensive LCD devices project color displays. Using a system without color is not a problem with some applications, but will interfere with others. However, less expensive color LCD devices are currently under development and should be available shortly. See Table 5.1 for a list of vendors who have LCD projection systems available.

With this technology the teacher has the ability to customize screen displays. For example, in geography a teacher could use an LCD in con-

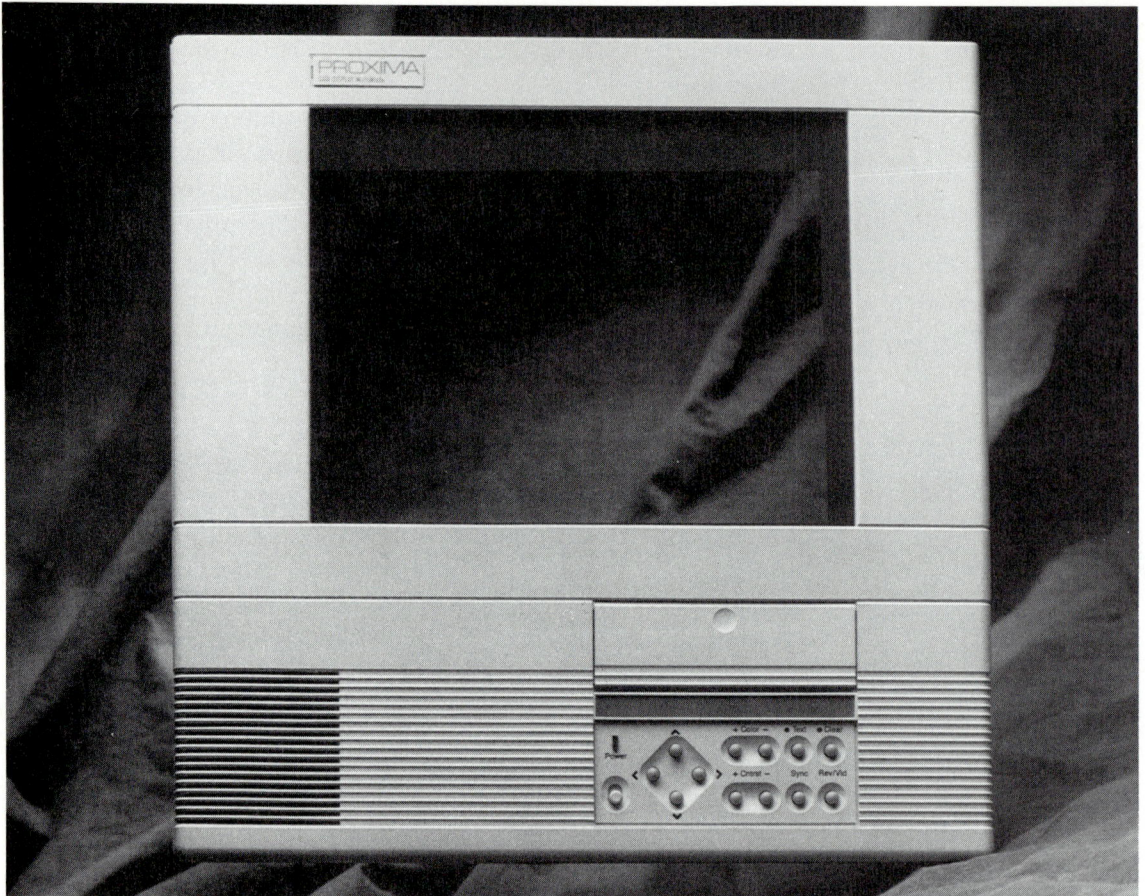

Figure 5.1 An LCD projection screen, which permits a large number of people to view the images displayed in a particular program when used in conjunction with a conventional overhead projector.

junction with a scanner to project local street maps and other incidental displays with great effectiveness for an entire class.

Table 5.1. Liquid Crystal Display (LCD) Panels and their prices. (We have listed the lowest priced models from each of these companies. Prices were effective in early 1991, and they are likely to vary.)

LCD Projection Panel	Vendor	Price
Looking Glass 480A	Chisolm 910 Campisi Way Campbell, CA 95008	$1,295
Magniview	Dukane Corporation 2900 Dukane Dr. St. Charles, IL 60174	$1095
PC Viewer 480GS	In Focus 7770 S.W. Mohawk St. Tualatin, OR 97062	$1,655
Data Display A200SC	Proxima 6610 Nancy Ridge Dr. San Diego, CA 92121	$1,195
QA-25	Sharp Electronics Sharp Plaza Mahwah, NJ 07430	$795
Megabyte 5090	Telex Communications, Inc. 9600 Aldrich Ave., South Minneapolis, MN 55420	$1,795

LOCAL AREA NETWORKS

A network consists of several computers connected in some way so that they can interact with one another. Networks that encompass more than a single site are discussed in the "Computer Modems and Telecommunications" section of this chapter. The term Local Area Network (LAN) refers to a set of computers at a single site that are connected in a way that allows them to work together and share software. At the present time, LANs are most often used as tools that (1) enable students to access programs from a central computer without having to load the disk into each computer and (2) help manage student instruction by assigning programs, keeping scores, and generating progress reports for teachers. For example, the following applications are typical on a LAN:

- A single, licensed copy of OREGON TRAIL (MECC) can be loaded into the LAN's central memory, and students at several different terminals can run the program individually.

- A whole series of programs on American history can be stored on the LAN, and the computer can automatically assign to individual students appropriate programs based on such factors as previous performance, interest, and reading ability.
- Students can access an electronic encyclopedia through the LAN.

A more recent application which is likely to see widespread adoption in coming years is the cooperative use of a single program by several students on the LAN. For example, MECC's WAGON TRAIN 1848 is an updated, networked version of OREGON TRAIL, which was described in Chapter 2. WAGON TRAIN permits students at separate computers to participate as members of a group of pioneers traveling west in 1848. The pioneers select a captain for the wagon train and make various decisions during the simulated trip. Decisions have consequences for both individuals and the group. Programs like this will offer interesting applications of the principles of cooperative learning.

CD-ROM AND LASER VIDEODISCS

A CD-ROM disk is a laser-optical disk which closely resembles its ancestor, the compact music disk (see Figure 5.2). Both technologies were developed by North American Phillips and Sony Corporation during the early 1980s. The CD-ROM disk is virtually indestructible and can store a tremendous amount of material—some 600 megabytes (540 Mb of available user memory), the equivalent to 275,000 pages of text. The contents of the disk can be read by a CD-ROM player (Figure 5.3), which uses a laser to read data. At the present time, the CD-ROM player is not capable of writing to the disk, which means that information can easily be taken from the disk but not saved on the same disk. Libraries are very interested in this technology because a growing number of reference materials including GROLIER'S ENCYCLOPEDIA and ERIC's indexing services are now available on CD-ROM. The computer can search for information on a CD-ROM disk very quickly and accurately. One of the most costly aspects of library operation is the replacement and repair of books in traditional form. Storing books on CD-ROM would eliminate much of this problem and, hence, much of the cost. In addition, CD-ROM references can be updated annually to include new information and thus avoid the relatively disorganized "annuals" now used by most encyclopedia publishers.

Figure 5.2 A CD-ROM disk. The small disk in the girl's hand contains all the information (including pictures and diagrams) from the encyclopedias stacked in front of her.

A CD-ROM workstation consists of a computer, a printer, some type of storage device such as a disk drive or hard disk, and a CD-ROM player. In addition, software is needed to retrieve stored information and to save or print out desired text, graphs, or other information. Because a "search" involves a scan of the entire CD-ROM disk, the user will locate not just one major article, as with the more traditional printed encyclopedia, but all references to the desired topic. (See the discussion of electronic encyclopedias later in this chapter.)

Laser videodiscs have even greater capacity than CD-ROM disks, but they have not become as popular. The strategy of using them is basically the same as that described for CD-ROMs, except that they employ a larger videodisc and player. Although both sides of a laser videodisc will store

Figure 5.3 A CD-ROM player.

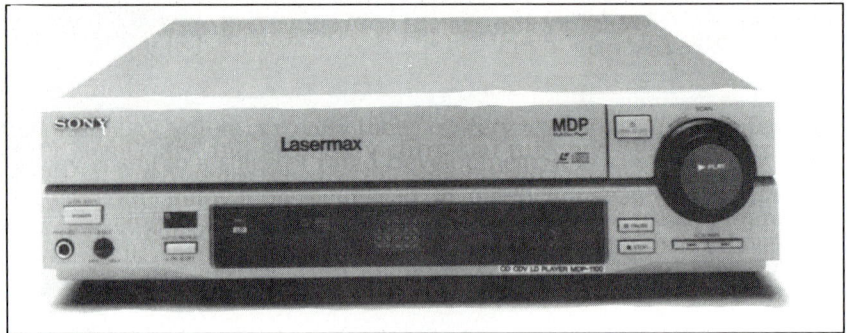

only an hour-long movie, the same disk can store up to 50,000 still pictures or a vast number of words. Because laser videodiscs play and provide instant access to moving pictures, they are particularly useful for interactive video, which is discussed in Chapter 7. In addition, it would be possible to expand CD-ROM applications tenfold by combining them with interactive videodisc applications. For example, COMPTON'S MULTIMEDIA ENCY-CLOPEDIA (discussed later in this chapter and previously in Chapter 4), which is already quite impressive, could provide access to ten times as much information if it were also interfaced with appropriate information on videodisc.

CD-ROM and laserdisc technology applications in the classroom are certain to increase within the next few years. For example, the Bureau of Electronic Publishing has released *U.S. History on CD-ROM*, which includes the full text of 107 books relating to U.S. history, and more than a thousand tables, maps, and photographs. This package includes search and retrieval software, which permits students to examine topics ranging from the Revolutionary War to the Iran-Contra affair.

COMPUTER MODEMS AND TELECOMMUNI-CATIONS

A computer modem is a communication device that permits the transmission of any computer output, including files and programs, via normal phone lines (see Figure 5.4). To set up the system, a phone line must be plugged into the modem and a cable connected from the modem to the communication port in the back of the computer. An RS-232 port is a widely accepted standard for this use, but you do not have to know what RS-232 means in order to use a modem correctly. Once connected, the user can

Figure 5.4 An external modem with an internal modem on top of it. To the right is a pocket modem.

contact any other similarly configured system and communication can be established. Contact could be made with an electronic bulletin board or with a service such as the AppleTalk Network, where educational concepts and ideas can be exchanged among school systems or between school systems and Apple Computer, Incorporated. It could also involve the search for and retrieval of information or data from NASA or from a computerized encyclopedia for use by students in the preparation of projects and other reports. Or school systems could make direct contact with each other to exchange information on their communities, the environment, or other important social or political issues.

Electronic networks can make it possible for students to become actively involved in social issues by communicating and interacting with persons in communities other than their own. Well-designed projects often give students experience in the democratic process.

Telecommunications projects are often nothing more than rapid "pen pal" projects, with students exchanging information almost immediately rather than after the delays typical of mailed letters. The computer can be combined with other current technology, including fax machines and speaker phones, to permit students to communicate effectively with persons who are physically not present. Rather than merely speaking extemporaneously (as in an ordinary telephone conversation) students using the modem have the advantage of being able to think over and revise their ideas ahead of time and send whole passages (textfiles) to their audience via modem. This audience can consist of a single recipient or a whole group of recipients sharing in the communication process. The computer is able to store and retrieve information easily, either in word processing files, in databases, or in other ways.

The values are twofold: (1) students develop communication skills and proficiency in the subject matter by preparing and sending information through the telecommunication system, and (2) students are able to interact with and gain from other persons who would otherwise not be an active part of their environment. With most telecommunications projects, student interest is maintained by the content of the project itself—not by the computer. Students become interested in a national news event, the characteristics of people in a different country, or vacationing in Alaska; and they use the computerized telecommunications system as a tool to pursue their interest more efficiently.

GTE Education Services offers WORLD CLASSROOM, a telecommunications package with curriculum applications in science, social studies, and language arts. Participants include students from all over the world. Classes are organized around clusters of about eight schools that are geographically diverse but similar in age and interests. The activities focus around detailed lesson plans, on-line reference materials, real-life data from around the world, and active interaction with other participants from diverse nations. During the 1990–1991 academic year American students were able to use WORLD CLASSROOM to communicate first-hand with soldiers in the Persian Gulf, to interview East and West German leaders during reunification, to collect data from different locations regarding activity on the New Madrid fault, and to understand the real feelings of Lithuanians and Soviets over independence. In addition, WORLD CLASSROOM participants regularly publish the NewsLink, an international student newsletter, containing news, editorial comments, opinions, poetry, and creative writing.

The NATIONAL GEOGRAPHIC KIDS NETWORK enables students to use a computer to record data and then share their findings via modem with research teammates throughout the United States, Canada, and other countries. At designated times, the NETWORK offers units on such topics as acid rain, trash, and weather; and students collect data at their own schools, which is shared and integrated with information from other schools. A professional scientist examines the data generated by the students and helps them look for patterns in their data. The students gain valuable experience in collecting and analyzing data, critical thinking, drawing conclusions, displaying information in graphs, letter writing, oral and written presentation, and map reading.

The Daedalus Project, operated out of the University of Connecticut, uses telecommunications in a creative manner to stimulate the writing abilities of learning disabled and physically handicapped students. The strategy is amazingly simple. Students were told that a "Mysterious Mel" or someone else at the other end of the modem would answer any letters they would write. With this assurance, students who had never previously shown any interest in writing began communicating and improving their writing skills via modem. Not only did writing skills improve, but students also showed dramatic improvements in self-esteem and in social interaction.

One major use of telecommunications is to conduct surveys on topics of interest to students. However, a caution is in order. Students taking or participating in "surveys" via modem are susceptible to the kind of bias that has become prevalent on some television news programs that encourage viewers to call a "900 number" to "vote" on an important issue. There is absolutely no scientific validity to these "surveys." Presenting these results on a news program is exactly analogous to having the news anchor preface a story with the comment " . . . and this from a completely unreliable source. . . . " Scientific surveys and careful information gathering can be conducted via modem, but it is necessary to take steps beyond the simple computer link-up to verify the validity of the results.

Another valuable service available via modem is the on-line database. Most of these remote database services charge a membership fee and bill the user for on-line time. Outside the field of education, on-line expenses can easily be justified by a law firm needing a quick search for legal precedents; but for a school district strapped for funds, even modest on-line fees can become expensive, especially when the database is searched by students who are inexperienced at using the system. One possible solution is to use a database that charges only a flat *monthly* fee instead of the usual per-minute rates. One such service is called PRODIGY, a joint effort of IBM and Sears. This service is able to provide a high level of consumer and educational information because it sells advertising space, which is transmitted along with the desired information. Table 5.2 shows a sample of some of PRODIGY's services, along with potential classroom and education applications. In many instances, articles from on-line services can be downloaded to a printer, so that important information can be distributed to a class or taken home to create a research paper.

Table 5.2 Some of Prodigy's on-line services and their possible educational applications.

Current Events: Headline News provides an up-to-date capsulized view of the important news of the day. It can be printed out or displayed using an LCD projection system.

Weather: Both national and regional weather maps are displayed, complete with fronts and temperature isobars—ideal for the geography class studying climate.

Consumer Economics/Life Skills: *Consumer Reports*, published by nonprofit Consumers Union, is available complete with product ratings and timely articles on the environment and product safety.

Economics: Business and economic information is available through the Dow Jones News Retrieval service. For high school classes participating in any of the numerous stock market contests, 15-minute delayed stock quotations are available along with company news stories.

Field Trips: The Mobil Travel Guide's historical description of over 80 cities (complete with visitor highlights, special events, economic activities, and points of interest) can enable a class to plan a field trip or write an essay or diary on an imaginary trip.

Research: Over 30,000 entries (updated four times a year) are available from the Academic American Encyclopedia by Grolier. Students can do an on-line search for articles to assist in preparing their report for history, geography, or any of the social sciences. Demographic data is always current.

Student Activities: Articles are available from *Weekly Reader, National Geographic*, and NOVA/WGBH at a variety of reading levels. There is even a student bulletin board to encourage the exchange of ideas with other students.

FAX MACHINES

An alternative to the use of computers and computer modems is the facsimile or "fax" machine. Simply described as a "long-distance photocopy machine," a fax machine scans a document, diagram, drawing, or other written work and sends the digitized signal over normal phone lines to another fax machine, which receives the signal and replicates the document. It is not really set up for interactive exchanges, as in the case of the modem. But, due to the nature of scanned images, it can more easily transmit odd original drawings, diagrams, and graphs (see Figure 5.5). Many fax machines are not even connected to traditional computers, but vendors have started developing the hardware and software to permit students and teachers to transmit faxed information via modem.

SCANNERS

As prices continue to decline and technology continues to improve, school districts across the country will find two pieces of equipment as essential as the photocopy and duplicating machines are now. The first of these is

Figure 5.5 A fax machine.

the scanner. Apple's current suggested retail for the Apple Scanner is around $1500, but discounts in the $200 to $400 range are available. This device allows the classroom teacher to scan any available photograph, map, diagram, or other visual image and save it in digitized format as a file on the computer. Programs like COMPUTEREYES (Digital Vision) permit images to be retrieved, displayed on the screen, printed out, or plugged into a second device—the LCD projection system. IBM has a similar system called LINKWAY.

Scanners come in two general varieties: hand held and desktop. The desktop models are more expensive (over $1000), and they closely resemble some of the personal copiers now available. The hand-held variety are somewhat less expensive ($200–$400), but the quality of the scanned images can sometimes suffer. As in the case of other technologies, as time passes the quality of the product will improve and the price will decline.

Once digitized by the scanner, images may be saved on disk and "brought back" for later use either as classroom presentations on monitors or LCD projection systems or as part of written projects such as a class newspaper using one of the desktop publishing programs. There is one disadvantage: scanned images consume a large amount of computer memory, and in some cases the same results can be achieved using 35 mm. slides or some comparable media. Unfortunately, these other media do not offer the flexibility of scanned images. See Table 5.3 for current suppliers.

DATABASE MANAGEMENT PROGRAMS

A database is simply a collection of related materials arranged in such a way that they can be easily compared and retrieved (Figure 5.6). Database management programs include APPLEWORKS and PFS: FILE for the Apple II series, and Q & A, dBASE, and PARADOX for IBM and compatible computers. Hypermedia programs, such as HYPERCARD on the Macin-

Table 5.3 Scanners for digitizing graphics. (Prices are for Macintosh versions in early 1991, and they are likely to vary.)

Scanner	Address	Price
Handheld Scanners:		
Half-Page Scanner/400	Complete PC 1983 Concourse Drive San Jose, CA 95131	$399
ScanMan Model 32	Logitech 6505 Kaiser Drive Fremont, CA 94555	$499
ClearScan	NCL America 1221 Innsbruck Drive Sunnyvale, CA 94089	$695
LightningScan	Thunderware, Inc. 21 Orinda Way Orinda, CA 94563	$495
Flatbed Scanners:		
MSF=300Z	Microtek Lab 680 Knox St. Torrance, CA 90502	$2695
Focus II 800GSE	Agfa Compugraphic 80 Industrial Way Wilmington, MA 01887	$6,945
Overhead Scanner:		
TZ-3	Truvel 8943 Fullbright Ave. Chatsworth, CA 91311	$6,495

Figure 5.6 Output from APPLEWORKS, a database management program that is integrated with a word processing program and an electronic spreadsheet program.

```
File: Senators                07/26/91  1:53 pm              Escape: Main Menu

Selection: All records


Record 15 of 100  (100 selected)
================================================================================
Last Name: Biden, Jr.              State: -
First Name: Joseph R.              Party: -
Elected: 1972                      Full Terms Complete: -
Term Up: 1990                      Sex: -
Birth Year: 1942                   Place of Birth: -
Home: Wilmington                   Children: -
Marital Status: Married            Military: -
Religion: Roman Catholic           Record Updated: -
Occupation: Lawyer
Education: BA U. of DE; JD Syracuse U.
Previous Office: County Council
Committees: Foreign Rel; Judiciary
Chair Committees: Judiciary
Capitol Address: -
Source: -
--------------------------------------------------------------------------------
Type entry or use @ commands                               @-? for Help
```

tosh and LINKWAY on the IBM, although not strictly database management programs, can perform very similar functions. These programs may vary in the degree of sophistication and difficulty of use, so the classroom teacher should select one carefully. Useful advice regarding the choice of a database management program can be found in Vockell and Kopenec (1989). Inexperienced teachers should consult a reputable software vendor or school lab technician for advice in selecting a good database management program.

Database management programs allow users to "file" and manipulate large amounts of information according to various user-selected classification systems. In a sense, they are analogous to a card catalog system, in which information is accessed first by one of several headings—author, title, subject—and then by reading the file entry itself which contains subsets of information—publisher, summary, and so on. Of course, with such file processing, each card must be created individually. This means repeated entry of identical data. With database processing, however, there is no need for entering duplicate information. Data is entered only once and then integrated by executing the appropriate commands to create the required number of cross-reference files.

Database management programs can be used throughout a school system to automate recordkeeping for virtually any conceivable purpose. Any task that requires access to systematic lists of information is a good choice for entry into a database system. Social studies teachers themselves will find databases useful for a variety of classroom management and other professional tasks, such as keeping up-to-the-minute grade records; creating and altering student discussion, reading, and activity group patterns; cross-referencing assignments by objectives; classifying teaching "idea" files; cataloging handouts, films, and tapes; and organizing notes based on articles read in professional journals and other publications.

Some database management programs are very simple, but others can be complicated to learn and may even require some training. However, they can be extremely useful for handling a wide variety of procedures and problem-solving/decision-making activities efficiently. They are much like word processors, in the sense that novices can easily learn just enough to meet their current needs and then expand to more complex operations as necessity dictates.

Database management software can have instructional applications in social studies, such as those described in Chapters 3 and 4. When learning to use database management programs, students typically go through three steps. First, they learn to use existing databases by retrieving information or generating lists from a database someone else has compiled. Second, they learn to add information to an existing database, where someone else has set up the parameters and they merely have to insert complete data in the proper places. And finally, they learn to create their own databases from scratch, defining categories, collecting complete information, and organizing the files in such a way as to facilitate useful retrieval of the information.

Storing social studies information in a database format offers a number of advantages over more traditional methods of taking notes or doing reports, including the following:

1. Preparing the database offers an opportunity to organize and review the information contained in it. The student entering the information usually notices patterns and is forced to fill in gaps which would otherwise result in a faulty database.
2. Materials prepared in this format can easily be saved, added to, or otherwise retrieved for later use, making it possible to have an ongoing database of an entire semester's work.
3. All or part of a database can be printed out and duplicated for distribution to the class, so that review for final exams becomes an easier task.
4. Databases can be "searched" or cross referenced for specific types of information such as, " . . . all Renaissance artists from Italy born after 1430." This encourages both students and teacher to organize information in a more meaningful way.

COMPUTERIZED ENCYCLOPEDIAS

The Compton subsidiary of Encyclopedia Britannica currently offers an entirely new software product which is likely to revolutionize our methods of gathering information. The COMPTON'S MULTIMEDIA ENCYCLOPEDIA is a complete encyclopedia on a 585-megabyte CD-ROM disk. However, it goes beyond the simplistic approach employed in earlier computerized encyclopedias. Besides its 9 million words of text, the disk includes 15,000 photographs, 60 minutes of audio, a U.S. history timeline, a world atlas, social studies feature articles, an on-line dictionary, and even a built-in notepad so that students may take notes from the articles and print them out for later use. In addition, the program permits the user to access information in several different ways. For example, learners can use an improved keyword strategy, comparable to that available in the earlier computerized encyclopedia, to find all articles in the entire encyclopedia that menion a designated topic or combination of topics. But they can also follow more traditional approaches, such as moving quickly from one topic to another without having to pull another volume off the shelf, or moving from a general topic to a more specific topic as the need and interest naturally dictate. The program provides seven different ways to access the information from the CD-ROM disk and permits the user to move easily from one access method to another.

CD-ROM technology is discussed in greater detail in Chapter 7.

TEST GENERATORS

One of the major responsibilities of social studies teachers is to test their students to see if they have mastered the subject matter covered in their classes. To construct and administer tests, teachers should enter test items into an item bank, store and retrieve these items, and present them to students in an orderly manner. Many teachers have traditionally accomplished these tasks by writing the items on index cards, storing them in file boxes, and then typing them onto stencils from which tests are generated.

The computer can assist teachers in developing good tests. Several companies that publish social studies textbooks currently make available computerized item banks that enable teachers to generate multiple versions of tests and quizzes related to these textbooks. Some packages, like CREATE-A-TEST from Cross Educational Software, include test item banks on various subjects (including social studies) dealing with topics likely to be covered in all major textbooks. In addition, there are computer programs created specifically to help teachers generate their own tests. The ideal test generator should accomplish the tasks listed in Table 5.4.

Unfortunately, at the present time there are no test generating programs we know of that perform all of these tasks. Excelsior's QUIZ meets many of these requirements on MS-DOS computers. TESTWORKS (Milliken) is perhaps one of the most sophisticated computerized test generators. This program comes with both a comprehensive manual and a computerized tutorial to make it easy for teachers to learn how to use the program. In addition, there is a "help disk" that users can access whenever they are confused. Multiple-choice test items can be entered in a normal upper- and lower-case format. The stem can be up to three lines long, and each answer is restricted to a single line. It is possible to highlight words to emphasize them when they appear on the screen. The program serves as a menu-driven database to store and retrieve test items. The computer will generate hardcopy tests, selecting the items according to prescribed rules. When it generates a test, the computer also provides an answer sheet for the teacher. In addition, it is possible for students to take tests interactively while seated at the computer terminal. During interactive testing, the computer can provide feedback for correct and incorrect responses. The computer also records the student's performance, enabling the teacher to examine scores after all students have taken a test at the computer. While

Table 5.4 Tasks that many teachers would like a good test generating program to perform.

1. Allow the teacher to store and retrieve from the computer the same sort of items that the teacher would otherwise store in a test-item bank.
2. Generate tests at random from these electronic item banks, using the same (or better) selection strategies that the teacher would normally use.
3. Permit entry of questions from a normal word processing program (such as APPLE-WORKS).
4. Permit the use of spelling and grammar checking programs.
5. Select items for tests according to prescribed criteria (such as item format, level of difficulty, and instructional objectives).
6. Generate equivalent alternate forms of the same test.
7. Permit the students to take tests interactively at the computer terminal, as well as through the normal printed format.
8. Provide statistical analyses (including item difficulty and item discrimination) that would enable the teacher to improve the quality of the test.

students take the test interactively, the computer stores information about each item's difficulty. The teacher can use this information to revise the curriculum, to decide what items to use on subsequent tests, or to upgrade the quality of the items. The program requires a password to get into the teacher management functions, which makes it unlikely that students can tamper with the test items or with the scores.

However, even this high-quality program has some severe shortcomings. For example, teachers who have grown used to word processing programs will find the editing system to be weak. The program will not provide the automatic wraparound function which enables the typist to enter words into the computer while the machine automatically starts a word on a new line whenever it is appropriate to do so. Nor does it have a "search or replace" capability. Instead, it provides a framework to permit the user to retype a line containing an error once the cursor has been manually moved to the proper location. If the user starts to type a word that will not fit on a line, it permits him to back up and to start the word over on the next line. If the overflow is on the final permissible line of the stem, though, he may need to revise and retype the entire passage.

Some testing programs overcome a few of the shortcomings observed in TESTWORKS, while others have even more severe drawbacks, such as providing only a limited number of options. The important point is that teachers should be aware of both the potential and the limitations of test generators and use them (or ignore them) to suit their own classroom needs.

This chapter cannot summarize all the available test generators. A more complete discussion of test generators that may appeal to social studies teachers can be found in Chapter 8 of *The Computer in the Classroom* (2nd ed.) or in Vockell and Hall (1989).

Teachers sometimes want to use testing occasions to do more than merely quiz students. For example, it may be desirable to have the computer ask questions and then provide detailed remediation when students make mistakes, or branch them ahead when they provide insightful answers. Teachers wishing to do this should use "authoring programs," described in *The Computer in the Classroom*. Authoring programs do much more than test; but they also require considerably more effort on the part of teachers to prepare for student use.

Many teachers find it more efficient to use a simple word processor or database management program to generate their tests. By using a word processor, for example, a teacher can easily store a large number of questions on any subject in an item bank. To put these items onto a test, the teacher would use an appropriate function of the word processor to merge (or "cut and paste") them into a single document. This process is not as automated as would be possible with a test generator, but the advantage is that the teacher can enter the questions much more easily, can use grammar and spelling checkers to improve the quality of the questions, and can make corrections to the questions much more quickly.

GRADEBOOKS

Careful recordkeeping is an important part of the lives of all social studies teachers. Electronic gradebook programs (Table 5.5) can help teachers keep track of student performance. Table 5.6 lists some of the recordkeeping tasks that an effective teacher might want a gradebook program to perform. Different programs perform these tasks to varying degrees. Chapter 8 of *The Computer in the Classroom* and Vockell and Kopenec (1989) discuss the extent to which each specific program listed in Table 5.5 accomplishes the tasks in Table 5.6.

Many teachers refuse to use electronic gradebooks because they get along perfectly well with noncomputerized procedures. Often this is an accurate perception. If all you want is a place to write grades down so that you won't forget what a student did, then entering these grades into a computer may be more trouble than it's worth; use your regular gradebook instead. In addition, some school systems demand that teachers submit their grades in a standard, bound gradebook. Teachers in these systems often shy away from computers because they would have to both enter the information into the computer and copy it into the bound gradebook.

However, most teachers find that there are considerable advantages to using an electronic gradebook. Most significantly, once the scores are correctly entered, additional functions become available with almost no extra effort. For example, assume that you are teaching a class of 25 students and give them 15 weekly quizzes and a final exam. You want the final exam to count for half the grade and the weekly quizzes to count for the rest. With a regular gradebook, you would enter the scores as the students received them and at the end of the semester you would average the weekly quizzes and combine them with the exam score to compute the final grade. You might want two kinds of averages: an average for the entire class for each test, and an average for each individual for the grading period. It would be nice to keep cumulative averages after each quiz, but this would require

Table 5.5 Some gradebook programs for teachers.

Program Title	Company	Format
AEIUS GRADEBOOK	Aeius	MS-DOS, Macintosh
BOBBING SOFTWARE GRADEBOOK	Bobbing Software	Macintosh
CLASS MANAGER	William K. Bradford	Macintosh
CLASS RECORDS PC	Alphatel Computer Prod.	MS-DOS
GRADEBOOK DELUXE	Edusoft	Apple II
GRADE MACHINE	Misty City	MS-DOS, Apple II, Macintosh
GRADE MANAGER	MECC	Apple IIe
GRADE2	Excelsior	MS-DOS
THE GREATER GRADER	Ability Systems	Apple II
KALAMAZOO TEACHER'S RECORD BOOK	Hartley Courseware	Apple II
MASTER GRADES II	Midwest Software	Apple II
MCGUFFY'S GRADER	Midwest Software	MS-DOS
REPORT CARD II	Sensible Software	MS-DOS, Apple II, Macintosh
TEACHER MANAGEMENT TOOLS	Bertamax	MS-DOS

considerable extra work. If you wish to show the students their grades, you would have to make an extra copy of your gradesheet, read it to them from your gradebook, post the gradebook, or require them to keep this information for themselves. At the end of the grading period, of course, you will write the grades down on a report card or some kind of notice to the students and/or school administration. If you make a mistake, if a student takes a retest, or if a grade has to be changed for any reason after averages have been calculated, you must recalculate any averages based on the corrected score.

If you used a computerized gradebook in the preceding example, you would simply have to enter the scores for each student for each weekly quiz

Table 5.6 Tasks that many teachers would like to see a gradebook program perform.

1. Allow the teacher to enter grades for students as easily as would be possible with a normal gradebook.

2. Permit the teacher to make easy alterations of previously recorded scores to correct clerical errors or to accommodate retests or rescoring of previous work.

3. Compute averages for the students' work during an entire grading period.

4. Apply weighting formulas to grade computation (for example, count the exam for half the grade, homework for 10 percent, weekly quizzes for 25 percent, and class participation for the rest).

5. Convert numerical grades to letter grades according to prescribed standards.

6. Provide records of performance (complete with current averages) for students at any time during a grading period.

7. When students are absent for tests or fail to turn in assignments, provide the option of counting this as either a zero, an "F," or "no grade"—and compute averages accordingly.

8. Compute averages for the entire class for any recorded assignment.

9. Compute separate averages requested by the teacher (for example, quiz average, exam average, homework average), as well as record the overall performance of students.

10. Provide hardcopy lists of student performance.

11. Provide anonymous printouts of student performance, so that the teacher can post scores with confidentiality.

12. With large classes (or multiple sections of the same class), provide both combined printouts for the entire class and separate printouts for subgroups.

13. Flag students with designated levels of performance on specific tests (such as students who were absent for a quiz, who scored above 90 percent, or who failed a test).

14. Flag students with designated levels of cumulative performance (for example, students who have been absent for more than two quizzes or whose average is below 70 percent).

15. Generate reports for individual students.

16. Generate reports that include standardized comments (such as how to interpret the grades, how to make an appointment to see the teacher, or whether the subsequent grades will be cumulative).

17. Generate personal letters to individual students, incorporating information about their grades and inserting specific comments based on these grades.

18. Allow the reuse of a set of names during another grading period without retyping all the initial information.

19. Include other information (such as phone numbers, names of parents, and student nicknames) in the same database with the grades.

and for the exam. The computer would take care of weighting the scores (making the exam equal in importance to the combined set of quizzes) and would automatically compute averages for each test and for each individual during the grading period. If a score needed to be altered, you would have to change ("edit") that score; but the computer would instantly perform for you any recalculations in which that score was involved. If you wished to generate a cumulative list of scores each week, the computer would do this for you. If you wished to send each student a personal note describing his or her performance after five weeks, the computer would generate this note for you. And if you wished to deliver a stern warning to all students with an average below 70 percent or praise to everyone over 90 percent, the computer could do this as well. It would even be possible to have the computer feed your grades into a report card program and to generate mailing labels to send report cards home to the students' parents.

The major shortcoming of gradebook programs is that they are often inflexible. They are almost all designed simply to record and average scores and to generate reports. They often come up short if the teacher wishes to do something out of the ordinary, such as base grades on a combination of scores received on tests and points received for additional activities. Teachers using unusual grading systems have three options: (1) continue using noncomputerized gradebook systems; (2) use an appropriate electronic gradebook for part of the record keeping (such as computing averages) and combine this with a noncomputerized method for the unusual aspects; or (3) use a database or spreadsheet program instead of a gradebook program.

Many database programs (discussed earlier in this chapter) have all the computational capabilities needed for keeping track of grades. The major disadvantage of database programs compared to electronic gradebooks is that the user of the database must invent her own instructions to tell the computer how to accept scores, perform the calculations, and generate reports. However, this task needs to be performed only once, and thereafter this set of instructions ("template") can be reused as often as necessary. The major advantage is that the database program is much more flexible. It can store not only grades, but any other information that can be organized in a structured manner. For example, the same database that stores students' test scores can also store information regarding extra credit activities, the titles of students' reports, students' addresses and phone numbers, absences from school, reading preferences, and nicknames. In addition, database and word processing programs are often "integrated," which means that the information from the database can be transferred directly into the word processor. This makes it possible to generate more personalized feedback letters to students than would be possible with most gradebook programs.

Electronic gradebook programs provide a pre-designed recordkeeping service for teachers. Database programs perform many operations in addition to keeping grades. If you can learn how to use a gradebook program in an hour, it may take you three hours to gain equal proficiency on the database program. In addition, the database program will probably be more expensive. However, once you have learned to use the database program, you will be able to use it for the wide variety of recordkeeping and instructional purposes described in this and the previous chapters. Once you've mastered an electronic gradebook, all you can do with it is keep track of grades. The gradebook is tailored to a specific need at the expense of generalizability.

Computerized gradebooks are much more refined and effective than the test-generating programs described in the preceding section of this chapter. Most teachers would benefit from using either a gradebook program or a database management program to keep their grades and other records.

DESKTOP PUBLISHING

Desktop publishing has made its way out of the business world and into elementary classrooms. These sophisticated graphics/word processing programs are used to generate newsletters and newspapers. These programs can play an important role in the social studies curriculum. Desktop publishing programs are definitely worth considering for teacher tasks as well. Because of the combination of graphics and text, these programs can create masters for overhead transparencies and printed worksheets. They can be used in place of a regular word processing program for any task that requires the addition of graphics. PUBLISH IT! by Timeworks, QUARK XPRESS by Quark, and THE CHILDREN'S WRITING AND PUBLISHING CENTER by The Learning Company are used successfully by teachers to complete tasks like those described in the previous sentences.

One middle school teacher has her students create an historical newspaper in conjunction with studying American history. In small groups students not only write stories incorporating events from various historical periods into their versions of the "Historical Times," but they also conduct research into the life and times of each period and use this information to write news and feature articles, obituaries, advertisements, and the like. In pre-computer days this teacher had conducted a similar project; but the computer greatly simplifies the task—enabling the students to focus on history rather than on peripheral, mundane tasks unrelated to educational objectives. Instead of retyping text to delete and insert material, readjusting the layout by hand, and redrawing graphics and headlines to fit, they now use PUBLISH IT! (Timeworks)—a fairly sophisticated desktop publishing program that the students were easily able to master—to produce much more sophisticated newspapers in about the same time or less. The students can write articles on their word processor and feed them into PUBLISH IT!, create headlines using various fonts, draw or scan graphics for insertion, lay out pages in multiple columns, and revise and edit all phases of the project, as needed.

Across the curriculum teachers have found numerous ways to incorporate the versatility of desktop publishing into their courses. Some typical applications for both students and teachers include the following:

- Producing newspapers and newsletters
- Producing literary magazines
- Creating brochures
- Creating advertisements
- Creating handouts
- Writing illustrated reports
- Writing illustrated stories and poems
- Creating overhead transparencies to accompany oral presentations
- Creating instructional manuals for using computer software and other technology

Good desktop programs are both powerful and easy to use. For all their power, the intuitive interfaces of many of these programs make it relatively simple for users to get up and running quickly. In fact, it is possible for students to desktop publish a simple document with very little instruction from the teacher. PUBLISH IT!, for example, contains many of the features usually found only in high-end programs designed for use in the business world. Users can create master pages that repeat the same margins and other layout features on each page, link frames to jump text from one page to another, use a wide range of fonts, create or import graphics, create or import text files from word processors (such as MICROSOFT WORD), and use style sheets to make global formatting changes and save the styles for use on other documents.

HYPERMEDIA

Occasionally, a new medium encourages entirely new ways of thinking. A concept called "hypertext" is likely to have this kind of impact on communication processes. Hypertext is exemplified in a program called HYPERCARD (Claris), which is shown in Figure 5.7. The basic idea behind hypertext is that a reader is presented with a segment of text or graphic information and then can branch immediately to any other segment as needed. For example, a person reading an instruction booklet on how to use a computer usually reads it from beginning to end. With hypertext, however, the user would read the first screen and then go wherever interest or need suggested. This might mean going to the second screen, or it might mean going into a more detailed explanation of a term mentioned on the first screen. A reader branching to a screen providing a detailed explanation might go to another screen that furthers this explanation, to a screen that defines or diagrams a term on this explanation page, back to the first screen of the original text, or to the second screen of the original text.

Perhaps the best way to envision the operation of a hypertext application is to think of it as a collection of electronic index cards, each containing

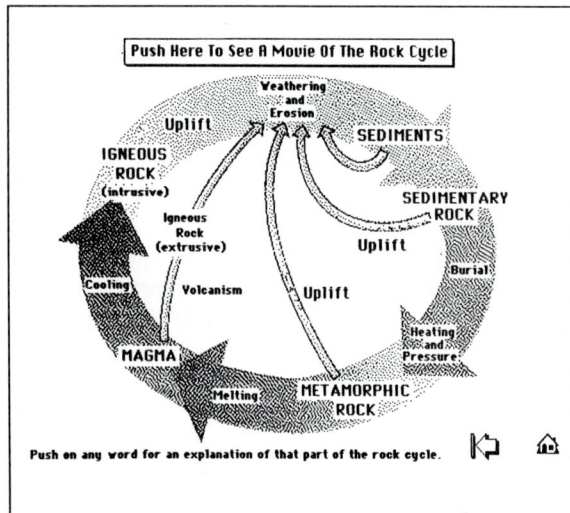

(a)

(b)

Figure 5.7 Screens from HYPERCARD by Claris.

encoded information and references. Each card in this "stack" may contain printed information, data, pictures, and sound, some of which may be stored on a CD-ROM or laserdisc. The creator of a stack is free to include a variety of different media (hence, the term "hypermedia"), and is also able to pursue branches or subtopics of the original. This "nested topic" effect is one of the major advantages that hypermedia has over conventional databases. The user merely locates and clicks the mouse on the picture or icon representing the desired topic, and information stored in the computer's memory, on CD-ROM, on laserdisc, or floppy disc will be retrieved and displayed. If CD-ROM text or sound is sought, the host computer will direct the appropriate search, locate the data, and display or play it. If photographs or video segments are needed, the host computer will locate these on the laserdisc and play or display them. Hypermedia takes advantage of current technology to create the maximum impact for its user.

It may have occurred to you by now that hypermedia, when used in education, is often really nothing more than sophisticated branching-programmed instruction. It also closely resembles the way a person browses through an interesting book—or the way a good researcher tracks down useful information on a topic of interest. What is unique about programs like HYPERCARD is that they provide an *interface* that makes it *easily possible* for the designer to program this degree of branching and *easily possible* for the user to move through the text. The strategy described in the preceding paragraph can be easily be applied to a textbook, to a computerized almanac or encyclopedia, to a database, to a collection of pictures, to a map or diagram, or to almost any topic imaginable.

Figure 5.8 shows a screen from EARTHQUEST (Earthquest). Its creators refer to this program as a "knowledge navigator" because it enables users to explore places and ideas from all over our planet. The main menu offers a choice of major topics, and the user is easily able to branch off into specific areas of interest. For example, a person choosing "North America" from the main menu would next see the screen shown in Figure 5.9, which presents a collage of images related to North America. By clicking on many of the objects on the screen, the user activates hidden "buttons," which immediately branch to more specific topics, such as birds, animals, Native Americans, agriculture, or tourist attractions of North America. After branching to one of these, the user can either go back to the North America screen, to the main menu screen, to an even more specific

Computers in Action

Sandra Smith was a student in a seventh-grade history class. As part of its study of local history, the class was investigating its home state of Indiana. After she booted HYPERCARD on the Macintosh computer in her bedroom, a title screen appeared on her monitor showing a series of symbolic icons. From this "home card" she selected the map icon and clicked the mouse once. After a few seconds, a map of the United States appeared. She centered the mouse over Indiana and clicked again. A large map of her state appeared with small stars highlighting locations of its major cities and an accompanying menu, giving her the following choices:

STATE FLOWER

STATE SONG

EARLY HISTORY

STATE BIRD

STATE TREE

MAJOR RIVERS

CURRENT ECONOMICS

DEMOGRAPHICS

CURRENT STATE OFFICIALS

FAMOUS HOOSIERS

A quick look at actual pictures of the official state flower, bird, and tree was made possible by the interactive laserdisc attached to her computer system. A video photograph of each was flashed on the screen. As she clicked on "State Song," a digitized version of "Back Home Again in Indiana" was retrieved from the CD-ROM and a few bars of the refrain were played back through the system. After taking down the names of the current state officers from the captioned video photographs, her assignment was now complete. As Sandra was about to turn off the equipment, she noticed the category "Famous Hoosiers." Because the rest of her homework had already been completed, there was time to "browse" through the biography section. She had read Booth Tarkington's *Seventeen* and some poetry by James Whitcomb Riley, but it was fascinating to gain some perspective on their lives and to see photographs of each. As her mother called upstairs for "lights out," she heard lingering refrains of Hoagy Carmichael's *Stardust* drifting out from Sandra's room.

Figure 5.8 A screen from EARTHQUEST (Earthquest, Inc.), which is referred to as a "knowledge navigator," because it enables users to explore places and ideas from all over our planet.

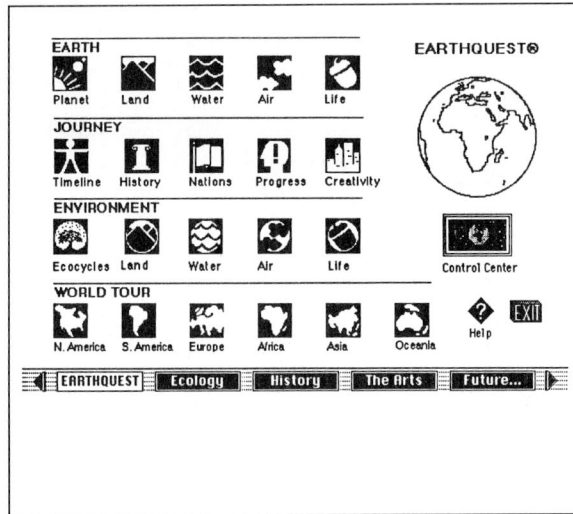

screen (such as information about a specific bird or about Niagara Falls), or to another appropriate screen. In addition to branching by selecting hidden buttons, the user can also choose the rectangles at the bottom of the screen. For example, the index rectangle enables the user to select from a list of 75 topics addressed in the stack, and the info rectangle provides a list of topics related to the one shown on the screen. A user might start in North America,

Figure 5.9 A screen from EARTHQUEST (Earthquest, Inc.). A person choosing "Planets" from the main menu would next see this screen, which presents an option to obtain information about specific planets.

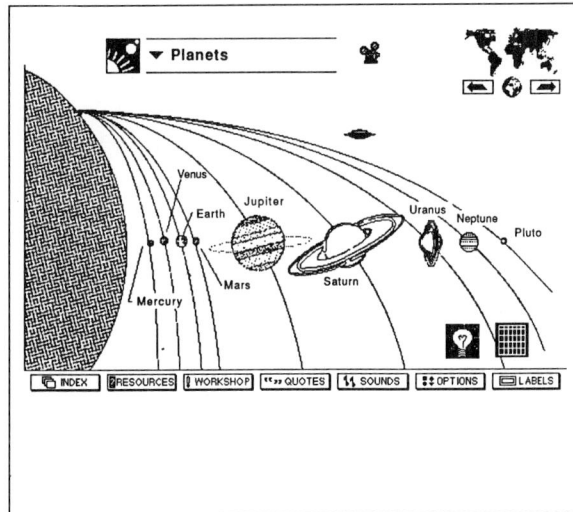

Common Hypertext Terms

As hypertext becomes more popular, it will become more important to understand terms related to it.

Hypertext refers to the overall strategy described in this chapter of letting users move through structured text in an efficient, orderly manner. *HYPERCARD* is a specific program from Claris that runs hypertext applications on the Macintosh computer. IBM's LINKWAY provides a similar service on MS-DOS computers. Programs with hypertext features available for the Apple II series of computers include HYPERSTUDIO (Roger Wagner Publishing), TUTORTECH (Techware), and HYPERSCREEN (Scholastic).

A *stack* is the term applied to a typical hypertext program. The metaphor is that the program consists of a collection of index cards, each containing systematic information, including words, pictures, animated sequences, and sound or a combination of these. These cards are imagined to be arranged in a stack, and the hypertext program enables the user to go almost instantly from any point on one card to a related point on another card in the stack. Synonyms for stack include "file," "story," and "set."

A *card* usually refers to a single screen in the stack. This is sometimes referred to as a "page" or "segment."

The *home card* is the starting point in the stack. From this point the user can most efficiently branch to any other point in the stack.

Links among cards are referred to as *buttons*. Selecting a button enables the user to branch to another card. Some buttons go forward to new text, some go backward to previous text, some ask questions, some play music,

---

notice an animal, recall a similarity to an animal in Africa, switch to Africa to make the comparison, and come back to North America. The developers have designed this as an open-ended stack, and they are already planning add-on stacks with more detailed information on topics such as rain forests and Native Americans. It is also possible for students to add their own contributions to the program. A program like this can serve as a useful resource for numerous units.

Hypermedia also makes possible the incorporation of dictionaries or glossaries directly into social studies lessons. COMPTON'S MULTIMEDIA ENCYCLOPEDIA (discussed earlier in this chapter) is an excellent example of a large-scale application of hypermedia strategies. The dictionary com-

and so on. Sometimes the buttons look like actual buttons. Sometimes they are covered by icons that identify functions (for example, a right arrow to go to the next page). And sometimes they are invisible: a halloween screen may have invisible buttons hidden inside the ghost, the witch, or the pumpkin. When the user selects a button, the program branches according to programmed instructions.

Clicking refers to the act of selecting a button, and thereby making a choice telling the computer where to branch. Clicking usually involves moving a cursor to where the button is located and then pressing a key on the keyboard or pressing a button on a mouse.

The term *hypermedia* usually refers to the process of integrating several different media, with a hypertext program coordinating them all. For example, a good hypertext program can present text, sound, pictures, and animation—all accessible at the push of a button. COMPTON'S MULTIMEDIA ENCYCLOPEDIA is a good example of using hypertext to provide easy access to an encyclopedia supplemented by sound and animation.

Interest in hypermedia is expanding rapidly, and new developments and peripherals constantly improve its flexibility. For example, the Apple II Video Overlay Card is a useful circuit board that permits a single video monitor to show both the computer text and the visual presentation from a VCR or videodisc player.

The *HyperStudio Forum* newsletter from the HyperStudio Network, *Stack Central* from A2-Central, and *The Stack Exchange* from Techware offer information about existing stacks for teachers and students. Hypermedia stacks will undoubtedly proliferate in coming years.

ponent of MULTIMEDIA ENCYCLOPEDIA exemplifies part of the value of hypertext. Although physical dictionaries provide a very useful means for learning words in context, few persons using an ordinary encyclopedia actually look up words as the need arises, largely because it is a disruptive process. That is, it would be inconvenient to move back and forth between the encyclopedia and the dictionary every time a need arises. However, the hypermedia capability of the MULTIMEDIA ENCYCLOPEDIA makes it easy for readers to obtain definitions of words at the moment when these definitions are most valuable—when the reader is reading the words in context. The user simply uses the mouse to move the cursor on top of the unusual word and clicks a button: the definition almost instantly appears on the screen. If a word in the definition needs further defining, the user can click again for another definition; otherwise the program returns to the original encyclopedia entry.

Hypertext strategies can make it reasonable and easy to integrate many of the strategies and components discussed earlier in this chapter and throughout this book. For example, hypertext interfaces will soon enable a student running a simulation to move from that simulation to a series of CD-ROM reference sources. These sources provide information that will be helpful in running the simulation. The student then moves from the reference sources to a database in order to retrieve and restore information, and then back to the simulation. Not only can students do this at their own computers, but the simulation, CD-ROM, and database could also be on separate computers in separate countries and linked by modem.

SUMMARY

This chapter has described hardware and software that are useful across many grade levels and various subject areas in the social sciences. Large screens and LCD projection systems are hardware options that enable the teacher to share output from a single computer with an entire classroom of students. CD-ROM and laser videodiscs increase the memory capacity of the computer by providing immediate access to large amounts of information stored on disk, often permitting sound, graphics, or animated presentations that would be impossible with simpler floppy disk storage.

Computer modems and telecommunications systems make it possible to extend the classroom beyond its walls by accessing computers at remote locations—in other classrooms and even in other countries. Computerized scanners enable teachers to convert graphic information into a digitized format, which means that any sort of picture can be stored, projected onto a large screen, or printed in a newsletter or other print format.

This chapter has also examined several general types of software. Database management programs enable teachers and students to store and retrieve any information that can be organized into categories or lists. Test generators allow teachers to store test items and to generate tests and quizzes from these item banks. Electronic gradebooks help teachers keep accurate records of student performance, tabulate grades, and communicate feedback to parents and students. Hypermedia strategies provide an interface that makes it easy for users to move freely within a program, directing their attention exactly where their needs and interests guide them.

REFERENCES

Vockell, E. L., and J. Hall. "Computerized Test Construction." *Clearing House* 62 (1989): 113–123.

Vockell, E. L., and D. Kopenec. "Record Keeping Without Tears." *Clearing House* 62 (1989): 355–359.

SELECTING
AND USING
COMPUTERS
AND SOFTWARE

SOME PRACTICAL PROBLEMS may arise when teachers try to introduce the computer into their social studies classrooms. This chapter identifies some of these problems and suggests solutions.

SOFTWARE SELECTION

The key point in software selection is to identify software that actually fits the needs of your students. Resist the temptation to use a piece of software just because it's "a great program." A program is a good program for your students if it helps them attain the desired objectives they need to attain. A program that is good for one class or for one student may be no good at all for other students.

The Computer in the Classroom provides detailed guidelines for selecting drills, tutorials, and simulations. This section summarizes just a few guidelines of particular importance in selecting social studies software:

1. Select software that is compatible with your overall approach to social studies instruction or that supplements your major approach.
2. Select software that teaches skills that are not easily taught through other media.
3. Select software that compensates for weaknesses in your curriculum or teaching style. For example, if your curriculum is heavy on verbal presentations, provide some programs emphasizing graphics for students who learn more easily through that method. If you have a rapid-fire mode of presentation, provide some programs that teach the same skills at a slower pace.
4. Select programs that promote cooperative learning. (See the "Important Principles of Instruction" section of Chapter 2.)
5. When selecting programs for higher-level objectives, look for those that can be used effectively with large groups during the learning phase of instruction. (See the "Teacher-Directed Use of Computers" section later in this chapter.)

It is impossible to select appropriate software without considering the situation in which it will be used. The best way to evaluate the potential usefulness of a piece of software is to perform a task analysis of the instructional activity for which it will be used and then check to see how well the computerized material fits into this instructional unit. For example, the lesson analyses on the following pages present several educational goals and evaluate the usefulness of specific pieces of software for attaining these goals.

Lesson Analysis 1 shows that if the goal is to help the student come to a better understanding of what it would be like to travel the Oregon Trail in pioneer days, then MECC's OREGON TRAIL is a very good program to help students attain this goal. On the other hand, Lesson Analysis 2 shows that if the goal is to help the student identify the important routes that pioneers traveled when moving west, the major cities along these routes, the dates of the major migrations, the numbers of people involved in these migrations, and the names of people involved in these pioneering trips, the same program is not very useful at all. Our point is this: We resist saying that OREGON TRAIL is a "good" or a "bad" program. It is more useful to determine exactly what we need and then decide whether or not OREGON TRAIL will help us meet that goal.

Before selecting a software package, therefore, the teacher should ask, "What do I actually want to *do* with the program? Why do I need a computer program at all?" Let's assume that the answer to this question is that the teacher wants to give a good introduction to a skill, provide opportunities to apply that skill, and let students interact with the computer program to verify that they have understood and can apply the skill before moving on to a more complex activity. In the preceding description, the teacher is actually using the computer as a "surrogate tutor." In selecting software for this purpose, therefore, it is appropriate to list the tasks that the teacher would ask the tutor to perform, and then see how well the computer performs these same tasks. Lesson Analysis 3 lists the tasks that a good tutor would perform for individual students being tutored on interpreting graphs, if an individual tutor were available. (Note that the same lists of tasks could be used for verifying the mastery of almost any noncomplex social studies concept or skill.)

Finally, Lesson Analysis 4 evaluates software designed to be a *tool* in a unit which is primarily a noncomputerized activity. In this case, the goal is to help the student learn to obtain information to test a hypothesis in social studies. If the teacher is aware that most of the activity will be performed away from MECC's WORLD GEOGRAPH and that the program will merely provide a more efficient tool for accomplishing Steps 4 and 5, then this is a good program for that purpose. On the other hand, if the teacher wants help with other steps in the task analysis, it will be necessary to look elsewhere.

In addition to the steps that appear in a task analysis, there are other considerations in effective software selection. For example, when selecting computer simulations to demonstrate social studies phenomena, the soundness of the model underlying the simulation must certainly be examined. If students running OREGON TRAIL succeeded or failed without regard to the soundness of their understanding of pioneer life, that program would be worthless. Likewise, if one of the graphing programs drew faulty line graphs or if WORLD GEOGRAPH contained inaccurate information, these programs would be rendered ineffective. In addition, as discussed

---

Lesson Analysis 1

Educational Goal: The learner will come to a better understanding and appreciation of what it would be like to travel the Oregon Trail in pioneer days.

Activity: The student will take a simulated trip to Oregon.

Effective, Noncomputerized Strategy:
1. Present the learner with an interesting situation and a problem requiring a decision by the learner.
2. Provide access to information necessary for the learner to make the decision.
3. Accept input (the decision) from the learner.
4. Give realistic feedback, based on a sound model.

   A teacher could say, "When travelers left Missouri for Oregon, they had to decide what to take with them. Here is a list of possible items. What would you take, if you were a pioneer?" If the student made a bad decision, the teacher could say so, or the other members of the group could discuss it, or in some other way the learner could conclude that it was a bad decision. Or the learner could be permitted to make more decisions until the ill effects of the first decision became obvious, although this latter course of action would be very difficult for the teacher to manage effectively. The same strategy could be applied to correct decisions.

   Another strategy would be for the teacher to show a movie in which pioneers encountered difficulties and ask, "What could they have brought along that would have helped them solve these problems?" Discussion and feedback would be similar to that in the previous strategy.

What the Computer Program Does: OREGON TRAIL performs all four of the steps stated in the activity description. Moreover, the program does this in a way that is probably more interesting than could be accomplished by a teacher either with verbal descriptions alone or with the help of a good film. In addition, the program keeps track of the activities and provides feedback more effectively than would probably be possible without the computer. However, the program does not focus on *why* things happen. (If someone dies, the computer does not indicate that the person died because the learner forgot to bring medicine.)

Conclusion: OREGON TRAIL would probably be a good program for this purpose, provided the teacher is willing to integrate it with some sort of discussion focusing on *why* the various outcomes occurred.

later in this chapter, if software is to be used for group instruction, the "friendliness" of the user interface must be considered.

Social studies software continues to proliferate rapidly. Many teachers acquire software by looking for titles that sound like they fit their needs. This is not a wise strategy. Shelves and file cabinets in schools are filled with programs that "sounded good" but have never been used at all. The task analysis strategy suggested on the preceding pages may take more time, but it is much more likely to lead to the selection of good software.

Choose software that meets your real needs.

Lesson Analysis 2

Educational Goal: The learner will identify the important routes that pioneers traveled when moving west, the major cities along these routes, the dates of the major migrations, the numbers of people involved in these migrations, and the names of people involved in these pioneering trips.

Activity: The student will take a simulated trip to Oregon.

Effective, Noncomputerized Strategy:
1. Present the learner with an interesting description of the items covered in the stated educational goal.
2. Ask the learner questions to determine whether he/she understands or can recall the designated information.
3. If the learner gives a correct answer, provide positive feedback and move on to the next question.
4. If the learner gives an incorrect answer, provide corrective feedback, further hints, and/or remediation and return to Step 2.
5. When the learner has amply demonstrated learning, give final positive feedback, stop asking questions, and move on to another activity.

A teacher could show a movie, have the students read a good book, have them read a chapter in the textbook, conduct a discussion, or coordinate a combination of these activities. Afterwards, either the teacher or the students themselves would engage in some sort of formative and eventual summative evaluation to verify that the information has been understood and retained.

What the Computer Program Does: OREGON TRAIL performs none of the steps stated in the activity description. The program could be a partial presentation of Step 1, but it covers only one of the possible routes traveled by pioneers, and learners can easily complete the program without focusing on the specific pieces of information stated in the educational goal. The program makes no attempt to accomplish Steps 2–5.

Conclusion: OREGON TRAIL would probably *not* be a good program for this purpose. The accomplishment of this goal requires a drill or tutorial rather than a simulation.

HARDWARE SELECTION

The key point in hardware selection is to identify your software first, and then select hardware that will run this software. At the present time, a very large amount of the very good social studies software (and software for other elementary and secondary curricula) runs on Apple II computers. This is a good reason to purchase Apple II computers for your social studies program. However, some programs initially written for the Apple are later converted to run on other computers, and some extremely effective social studies programs are designed for other computers. This is especially true of many of the tool programs, such as database management programs,

---

Lesson Analysis 3

Educational Goal: The learner will interpret line graphs correctly in social studies presentations.

Activity: The student will be shown a series of graphs and will interpret them accurately. Two computer programs that enable students to perform this activity are MECC's GRAPHING PRIMER and Sunburst's INTERPRETING GRAPHS.

Effective, Noncomputerized Strategy: The following nine steps would typically be performed by a good tutor to verify that a student has demonstrated mastery of the skill "interpreting graphs accurately." These steps assume that initial learning of graph interpretation has taken place earlier—perhaps in the textbook or even in a different course several years previously. The same set of nine steps could be used to teach any social studies skill, such as reference book usage or database management. Note that this task analysis is offered purely as an *example*. We are by no means suggesting that all social studies units should focus on skills that follow these steps.

1. Give a verbal summary (if necessary) of how to read a graph. Or have the student give a verbal summary of the skill. (This step may often be skipped, and the tutorial sequence may begin with Step 2.)

2. Ask a question requiring the student to interpret a graph.
3. If the student answers the question correctly, give positive feedback, and then ask additional questions, if more are necessary to verify ability to apply the skill.
4. If the student answers the question incorrectly, provide a verbal restatement of how to read a graph, a physical demonstration of the skill, or both. This should paraphrase the original summary from Step 1, focusing as specifically as possible on the misunderstanding that led to the incorrect answer.
5. Instead of Step 4, the tutor could offer prompts to stimulate the student to think more carefully and thereby generate the correct answer. This is often a better idea than Step 4, especially if the tutor is able to focus on a specific shortcoming or a misconception held by the student.
6. If the student continues to make errors, repeat Steps 4 and 5. If the student seems to be getting closer to the right answer, it may be appropriate to repeat these steps even more often. If the student is making no progress, move on to Step 8.
7. If the student gives the right answer after Step 4 or 5, ask another question to verify that

CD-ROM and laserdisc materials, and hypertext applications, which are often designed for MS-DOS or Macintosh computers. However, the distinction is not clear-cut: the Apple II does run many excellent tool applications, and outstanding instructional programs are becoming increasingly available on MS-DOS and Macintosh computers. Also note that with extra boards and disk drives, the Macintosh LC computer can run a large amount of Apple II software.

When purchasing computers, the key point is to first decide what you want to do. Then look for software that will accomplish your goals. And finally, select computers that will run that software. This is the ideal

---

the student is really able to interpret the graph (rather than just guessing). Eventually ask questions that will apply the skill in settings that require generalization of the skill; that is, have the student perform a task not exactly parallel to those she has been performing. Repeat Steps 4 through 6 as necessary.

8. If the student shows a persistent inability to interpret graphs, move back to an earlier phase of instruction, perhaps providing concrete experience with graphs of easily observed objects or familiar information. When the student is ready, return to Step 1 of this tutorial sequence.

9. When the student has answered sufficient questions to demonstrate mastery of graph interpretation, certify that she is ready for the next step in the learning sequence. This might mean interpreting more complex graphs or using graph interpretation as part of a more complex activity.

What the Computer Programs Do: INTERPRETING GRAPHS (screens (a) and (b), next page) presents three line graphs and a statement that relates two variables. The student is asked to select which graph matches the statement. If the student gives the right answer, the computer approves and moves on to the

next question. If the student gives a wrong answer, the computer paraphrases the meaning of the graph selected by the student and then repeats the question. This process continues until the student gives the right answer, and then the computer moves on to another question. The program continues to run until the learner decides to quit or it runs out of questions.

GRAPHING PRIMER (screens (c) and (d) next page) performs exactly the same activities as INTERPRETING GRAPHS, except that it stops and gives feedback (percentage correct) after 10 questions. The GRAPHING PRIMER disk also contains several additional programs on line graphs, such as a tutorial review of their meaning and a drill requiring the learner to read exact data from a line graph. The same disk has comparable programs for bar graphs and pie graphs.

Conclusion: As long as "interpreting a line graph" refers to activities comparable to those in screens (a)–(d), then both programs perform tasks 2 and 3 very well. Neither performs Step 4, and both perform Step 5 only to a very limited extent—by explaining the wrongly chosen line graph when a student makes an error. A different program on the GRAPHING PRIMER disk provides Step 1, but INTERPRETING GRAPHS makes no attempt at Step 1. Neither program attempts Steps 7 through 9. INTERPRET-

(continued on next page)

procedure to apply whenever a school is purchasing new hardware. In reality, however, schools already own computers, and teachers are often forced to purchase software that is compatible with the existing hardware. Because a proliferation of computer brands breeds confusion, school systems are understandably interested in committing their resources to a single brand, so that teachers can learn to run the machines and so that the computers can be maintained more easily. However, it should be noted that some of the examples described in this book indicate specialized applications of the computer and might therefore provide a good reason to deviate from a system's "one brand of hardware" rule. For instance, using a Macintosh or IBM to run COMPTON'S MULTIMEDIA ENCYCLOPEDIA

Lesson Analysis 3 (continued)

ING GRAPHS has the advantage of a larger pool of questions.

What this all means is that either program would be useful for students who already understand the information fairly well and merely need to brush up or verify their mastery—Steps 2, 3, and part of 5 would serve these students very well. For students with minimal difficulties, GRAPHING PRIMER would be better, because that program offers Step 1; whereas users of INTERPRETING GRAPHS would have to consult another source (such as a textbook, peer, or teacher) for the review. However, if these additional sources are easily available, then the two programs are equally beneficial.

On the other hand, for weaker students neither program is very useful. These students would need

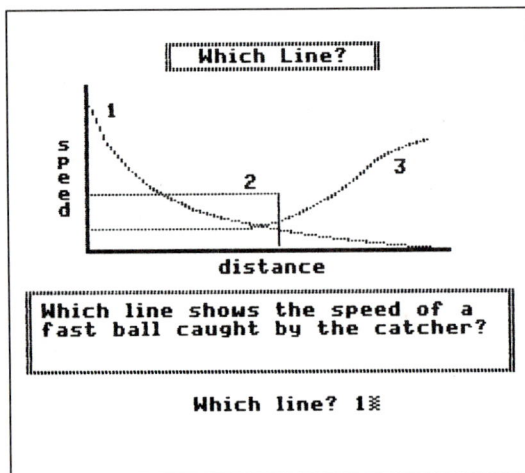

(a)

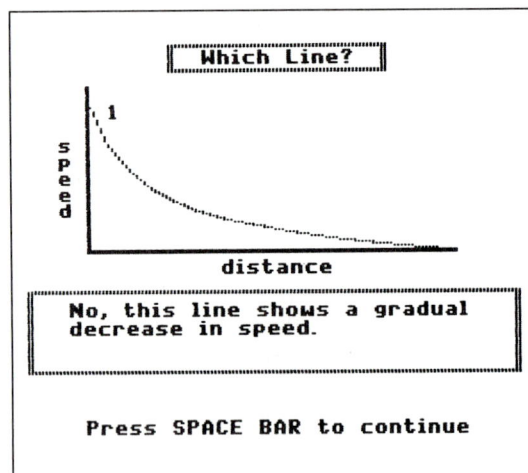

(b)

in the library or media center would not interfere with the overall integration of Apple II software elsewhere in a school building. The major instructional advantage of using a single brand of computer is that software purchased for use on one computer can easily be used on other computers of the same type. When this portability is not a factor, then the reasons to stay with a single brand become less compelling.

Besides computers, certain peripheral devices are important for computerized social studies instruction. For example, some software requires a speech synthesizer. It is important to ascertain what kind of speech synthesizer your software requires before you commit yourself to the purchase of incorrect hardware and software. The Apple IIGS has a built-in

---

Steps 4 through 9, where both programs are notably lacking. However, this extreme deficiency is negated if Steps 4 through 9 can be provided from some other source. For example, in a classroom employing peer tutoring, the computer could provide Steps 2, 3, and part of 5, while the peer tutor could provide the other steps as needed.

Finally, GRAPHING PRIMER has additional programs on the same disk. Because social studies students need to interpret bar and pie graphs as well as line graphs, this greater variety may give an advantage to that program. However, if a teacher wanted her students to have access to a large number of review activities on this important skill, it would be useful to make available *both* of the programs—under the constraints described in this analysis.

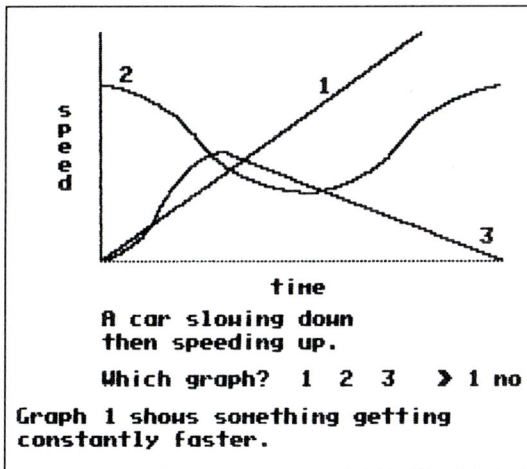

(c)

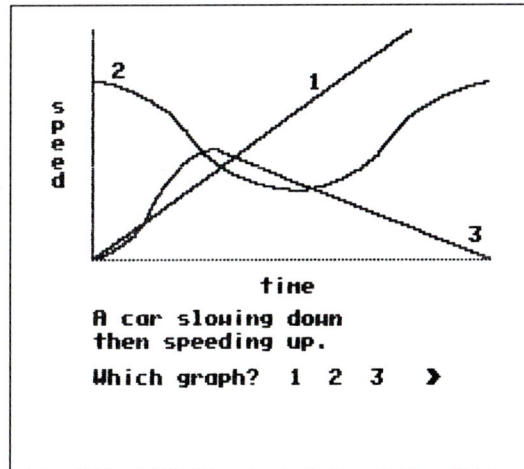

(d)

speech synthesizer, but there are several "talking" programs on the market that require an additional "Echo" speech synthesizer to work correctly on this computer. Others do not have this requirement. In addition, some programs that require an "Echo+" synthesizer will not work with a standard "Echo" synthesizer. Unless you ascertain requirements of this kind ahead of time, you are likely to purchase software that will not run on your hardware.

Lesson Analysis 4

Educational Goal: The learner will obtain information to test a hypothesis in social studies.

Activity: The student will use WORLD GEOGRAPH to determine whether the birth rate of a nation is strongly related to its gross national product.

Effective, Noncomputerized Strategy:
1. The student selects a hypothesis and formulates it correctly. (This is actually a very complex process, which could be broken down into further substeps.)
2. The student decides what information is needed to test this hypothesis.
3. The student identifies appropriate sources from which to find this information.
4. The student finds the needed information.
5. The student tabulates the desired information in a form useful for interpretation.
6. The student performs whatever analysis is necessary to evaluate whether a "strong relationship" exists.
7. The student makes a judgment regarding whether the hypothesis has been confirmed or rejected.
   Note: At each step, a good teacher or tutor would provide appropriate guidance and feedback.

A teacher could provide an initial stimulus, such as a chapter in the textbook, and follow this with a discussion. Students would then either select or receive an assigned hypothesis.

Alternatively, the teacher could be more directive, assigning a specific hypothesis, or breaking the task into smaller components by going directly to one of the higher steps and either beginning the sequence there or teaching that specific skill in isolation.

What the Computer Program Does: WORLD GEOGRAPH enables students to zero in on a particular region or specific country and find the statistical information stored in the database. It also presents this information in a limited number of appropriate graphic formats. In other words, the program serves as a useful tool to perform Steps 4 and 5.

Conclusion: WORLD GEOGRAPH would probably be a good program to serve as a tool in accomplishing this educational goal. It would enable students to accomplish Steps 4 and 5 more efficiently than would be possible with nonelectronic media. (However, even at these steps, feedback and guidance—whenever necessary—would have to come from a source other than the computer.) To accomplish the overall goal, the program would have to be integrated with other instructional activities—such as traditional teacher- or textbook-directed strategies or additional computerized tools. If what the teacher needs is a good tool for Steps 4 and 5, then this is a good program.

Some apparently convenient programs become impractical when you carefully examine the hardware requirements. For example, a $50 program might require the addition of a $200 device to each of 25 computers before you can run it. If this device serves no other useful purpose and will become outdated within two years, it may be better to select a different piece of software.

Other chapters of this book present information regarding LCD projection systems, CD-ROMs, and laserdisc systems. The important point to remember is that before you commit yourself to any of these materials, you should make sure that the peripherals are compatible with your computer. To prevent wasteful expenditures, the best strategy is to ask vendors very specific questions regarding the hardware needed to run the material you are purchasing:

- "I have an Apple IIE computer with two disk drives, a color monitor, and 128K of memory. Will this program run on that configuration?"
- "I would like a list of exactly what equipment is needed to run this CD-ROM application. Your list says that I need a VGA monitor. What does that mean? If I try to run it without a VGA monitor, what will happen?"

Specific questions can avoid future frustrations.

More detailed guidelines for hardware selection are found in *The Computer in the Classroom*.

TEACHER-DIRECTED USE OF COMPUTERS

Much social studies software is designed so that students can sit directly at the keyboard and run the program themselves. This is not necessarily a good idea. During successful instruction, students must pass through both a learning phase and a practice phase. As the name indicates, during the *learning* phase students have not yet mastered the concept or skill under consideration; therefore, guidance, corrective feedback, and reinforcement are important. On the other hand, once students have initially mastered the concept or skill, they need to *practice* it beyond initial mastery; during this phase feedback or supervision from an outside source is often unnecessary. With factually oriented software and simple skills (such as recognition of states), there is often sufficient guidance within the computer program itself to enable students to profit from working alone or in small groups without teacher interaction even during the learning phase. However, with higher-order programs, the software is rarely designed to provide effective guidance, feedback, and reinforcement; therefore the presence of a competent teacher as a facilitator and coordinator during the learning phase of instruction is crucial. Even excellent software is often trivialized by students trying to guess the right answer rather than working to understand the thinking strategy under consideration.

We are not suggesting that if you encounter students who are effectively learning a new thinking skill by themselves you should tell them to stop. There is nothing inherently wrong with students running thinking skill programs in small groups or even individually. Such groupings may be especially desirable under circumstances such as the following:

- After students possess a sound initial understanding of the thinking skills involved in the program, they may need to pursue additional practice to make the skills part of their automatic, individual repertoires.
- After students have initially learned a thinking skill, there may be four or five good programs that provide additional practice. It may be better to let students choose one or two of these programs that interest them rather than forcing the whole class to run a single program.
- When cluster grouping is used for gifted students, there may be times when they should work together on a project while the rest of the class pursues tasks that these gifted students have already thoroughly mastered. (The term cluster grouping refers to the strategy of putting "clusters" of gifted students in heterogeneous classrooms with a trained teacher who will stimulate them intellectually and encourage them to interact with one another. This is a soundly based alternative to putting them in special classes for gifted students.)
- When slower students need additional practice to master skills for which faster students need no more practice, they can often benefit from working privately or in small groups. This allows the slower students the time to practice skills they have initially learned but which have not yet become automatic.
- When specifically structured peer tutoring programs have been established, tutors and tutees can often work effectively together at their computers. (Just telling students to "work together at the computer" usually does not qualify as structured peer tutoring.)

However, we urge teachers to be cautious and to avoid the overuse of individualistic learning with social studies programs. Students are likely to waste a great deal of time by using these programs when they cannot guide themselves and have no skilled teacher to guide them.

During the learning phase of instruction, software designed to teach higher-order thinking skills is best utilized in an environment where persons (such as a teacher) with a true understanding of the concept or thinking strategy can pose problems and ask questions that cause students to stretch their understanding. A good way for teachers to provide this guidance is often to run computer programs with a large group of students, employing either a large monitor or an overhead display device, and lead the students in a group-interactive use of the software. Students cannot, will not, and do not automatically ask these same questions of themselves or each other. Even the most experienced educators often find this type of teaching challenging: asking students to learn to pose problems, react nonevaluatively, and question each other critically seems unfair. If teaching thinking skills is difficult (and it is), how can we assume that two or three students will teach each other or themselves effectively? Students can (and should) practice together—and sometimes students can help other students understand and master thinking skills—but this is comparatively rare.

Peer tutoring of factual information is extremely effective, as is peer modeling of process skills. But peer teaching of process skills is not likely to have good results; the teacher should maintain responsibility for monitoring progress in thinking skills and prompting their development through effective discourse.

Teachers often assume that it is appropriate for students to go to the lab to practice their skills after they have been introduced to the software. Because they can become more actively involved in more problems, it is probably true that students can greatly benefit from *practicing* thinking skills alone or in small groups. But there is a crucial distinction between learning and practicing a skill. To repeat: Our belief is that many teachers make the mistake of sending students off to practice skills that they have not yet learned. This is almost certain to be counter-productive. Thinking is best produced and challenged with discourse. Effective discourse requires a teacher's knowledge, not only of the software and its mechanisms, but also of how students learn, how groups interact, and how responses affect process.

For example, students who learn to conduct an effective database search have developed important research skills. The correct use of search strategies will enable students to think more carefully in social studies as well as in many other areas, and the skills will be useful both on and off the computer. A computerized lesson can help students learn to use these strategies correctly. However, students who receive minimal instruction and then go off to practice on their own have little chance of realizing when their strategy is imperfect and no good way of improving that strategy. An experienced teacher, on the other hand, can tell when students are using an imperfect strategy and prod them to improve their thinking. While such improvements *could* occur when students are working alone, they are much more likely to happen under teacher guidance and stimulation.

Before sending students to work alone or in groups, the teacher should have ascertained that this relatively unsupervised approach is the best way to produce the kind of learning that is desired. In other words, assume first that the lesson should be teacher-directed, and then grant independence as it becomes obvious that independent work will provide a better use of academic learning time.

USING THE COMPUTER WITH LARGE GROUPS

With higher-level software it is often a good idea to work with the whole class or at least a large group during the learning phase of instruction. This does not necessarily eliminate the use of the computer; some programs are easily adapted to large group instruction. Effective lesson plans for using the computer along with teacher-facilitated discourse to teach higher-order thinking skills to large groups are contained in Chapter 8 of *The Computer and Higher-Order Thinking Skills* (Vockell and van Deusen, 1989). Because social studies often applies higher-order thinking skills, readers of this book would benefit from examining and applying those lesson plans.

An exciting classroom atmosphere often arises when the teacher projects a thinking skills program onto a 25-inch monitor for the entire class to view. The teacher changes from evaluator to facilitator, from the person who knows answers to the person who asks questions. The computer can be thought of as another teacher from down the hall who has come into the classroom to assist in teaching the lesson. This "other teacher" poses the problem and provides feedback for the students. The original teacher has the task of helping the students by asking questions and posing problems to challenge them to fully develop their ideas and hypotheses, as well as by responding to them in a way that keeps them involved in the process.

The teacher should project such programs onto a large screen so that all the students in the group can see it. The group can be either the entire class or a group designated by the teacher. In addition, it is important that the teacher should run the program ahead of time and be thoroughly prepared for situations that are likely to arise.

Unfortunately, not many current social studies programs can easily be used in the way demonstrated in the lesson plan. The software must have a simple user interface, so the allotted time is spent thinking, hypothesizing, conjecturing, inferring, analyzing, and testing rather than typing, becoming frustrated, and swearing. The program should allow for collaborative learning so that small groups can attack the problem as a way of collecting input for the whole class. It should allow for modeling of the thinking process by the teacher; if the program is timed or uses an invariant process, the teacher cannot model the thinking process appropriately. For example, MECC's program OREGON TRAIL is superbly done with one major flaw— aspects of it employ an invariant process. For example, if the class makes a mistake by not acquiring proper supplies at Fort Kearney, it would be pedagogically useful to back up and restart from the fort; but this is impossible. This lack of versatility makes it very difficult to adapt to the needs of a large group of students to whom the teacher must respond flexibly.

USING THE COMPUTER WITH SMALL GROUPS

The previous sections discussed advantages of large-group use of computers under fairly direct teacher supervision during the learning phase of instruction. During the practice phase of instruction, students can use computers more efficiently alone or in small groups, relatively unsupervised by the teacher. While working alone is sometimes desirable, solitary work also has its shortcomings. When students work alone at computers, the following disadvantages are likely to occur: (1) the social isolation involved can create mood states (such as loneliness, boredom, frustration, and fear of failure) that interfere with sustained effort to complete learning tasks; (2) students are denied the opportunity to summarize orally and explain what they are learning; and (3) computers cannot provide social models to be imitated and used for social comparisons (Johnson and Johnson, 1986).

The cooperative learning and peer tutoring literature suggests that small groups can overcome these difficulties. Students can work in groups in many different ways at the computer. For example, they can work individually and take turns using the computer, they can compete, or they can cooperate. Current research (Slavin et al., 1985; Slavin, 1983, 1986) suggests that the cooperative approach is usually the best. The key components of effective cooperative learning are positive interdependence, individual accountability, and shared responsibility for one another. This means that the success of the group requires that each person have a role, be accountable for that role, and be interested in helping the other members attain important goals.

Closely related to the concept of cooperative learning is that of peer tutoring. Research on this topic (Cohen et al., 1982) indicates that when students tutor their peers, both the tutor and the tutee benefit from the process. Furthermore, rarely in real-life settings do individuals perform or solve problems in isolation. In today's world, we are required more than ever before to interact with others. Therefore, it is often highly desirable, during the practice phase of instruction, to have students work cooperatively in small groups rather than alone. (A remarkable technological innovation would be to place two or three chairs, instead of just one, at every computer station.)

What this all amounts to is that small groups at the computer are very often a preferable scenario to students working alone on programs that teach thinking skills. In some cases, large-group (whole-class) presentations may even work best, especially when new material is being introduced and guidance or feedback from a knowledgeable person (teacher) is essential. Once important skills have been thoroughly learned by some members of the class and at least partially mastered by everyone, then small groups may provide a better use of academic learning time than a continued large-group session.

In addition, small-group activities at the computer will support the learning of social studies and other skills only if the group sessions are structured in a way to promote them. Usually, this means (1) incorporating the direct instruction approach described in Chapter 2; (2) assigning group activities only after the unit has been appropriately introduced to a large group; (3) ascertaining that group members have actual roles that they understand and objectives that they can meet; and (4) teaching students to interact properly with the program and with one another.

| TRANSFER OF THINKING SKILLS | To be useful, what is learned on the computer must be transferred beyond the computerized setting. The principles of generalization are no different for computerized instruction than for any other type of instruction. When the computer is used as a tool to support a good social studies curriculum, learning can be expected to transfer beyond the original setting in exactly the same ways that it would after any effective instruction. In some cases, however, computer programs present self-contained units of instruction; here it would be useful to focus specifically on the transfer of learning. The following brief discussion focusing on the transfer of thinking skills is pertinent for both highly integrated and relatively isolated units of instruction. |

The most important principle in promoting transfer is to have students focus their attention on what they did that was successful. The teacher needs to ask questions that cause students to label the processes used in their thinking: "How did you figure it out?" Concept development depends on language development. Until the student knows a name (label) for a concept, it is practically impossible to utilize or transfer the concept to a new environment. Therefore the teacher should always ask students to reflect on what they have constructed. If necessary, the teacher should provide prompts to help students realize what they have done and to put their insight into words.

The teacher needs to ask reflective questions at the end of the lesson, prompting students to classify the strategies learned in the lesson and to predict in what other situations they might use those same strategies. For instance, after a lesson using WORLD GEOGRAPH or any other computerized database, the teacher might ask the students to come up with other times in school that they are asked to think as they did while conducting the database search. Likewise, if a group of students using OREGON TRAIL first fail to make the trip successfully, the teacher might help them analyze their mistakes and change one variable at a time on subsequent trips in order to determine what factors *cause* success on the simulated trip. The teacher could then focus attention on the fact that this is an application of the scientific method that they have been studying in their science class and encourage them to identify other areas in the social studies curriculum or elsewhere in which the same experimental methodology can usefully be employed. Thoughtful students might think of numerous applications.

When teaching a content lesson requiring one of the previously taught thinking processes, teachers can get the students to look back by asking "What kind of processes did we use when we solved the problem in . . . ?" By teaching the process in isolation and asking the students to predict when they will use it (anticipation of transfer), and by applying the process to content by asking students to look back at the processes used previously (reflection to engender transfer), the teacher can move into and out of context transferring the processes as necessary. The teacher should constantly look for opportunities to encourage transfer by using the "Remember when . . . ? Now let's . . . " rule: *"Remember when* we used careful observation and predicted outcomes to sequence events in _____? *Now let's* see how we can use that same strategy with this story. . . . "

As we have stated, the principles described in this section are not unique to computerized instruction: they are simply good pedagogy. We have focused specific attention on them to promote the widest possible generalization of skills learned at the computer.

COMPUTERIZED DRILLS ON FACTUAL INFORMATION

Different social studies teachers have different feelings about "memory work." Some teachers believe that "drills" over important facts are important, while others adamantly maintain that drills are demeaning and useless. But the fact remains that social studies programs are often criticized for permitting students to graduate from them without knowing "basic facts"—unable to recognize, define, or interpret information about key dates, persons, and concepts important to their society.

Perhaps the objections arise from associating drills with rote memory, as when we "drill" information into a child's head by repeating it over and over in monotonous fashion. However, if a drill is defined as an exercise that provides repeated practice and feedback regarding a designated objective, it becomes obvious that they play an important role in social studies education. In fact, drills are probably essential in such areas as geography and history. Both Figure 6.1 and Figure 6.2 provide examples of drills, although the first emphasizes simple rote memory and the second calls for application of fairly complex understanding.

Figure 6.1 A screen showing a portion of the drill section from ROCK CYCLE (Ward's Natural Science).

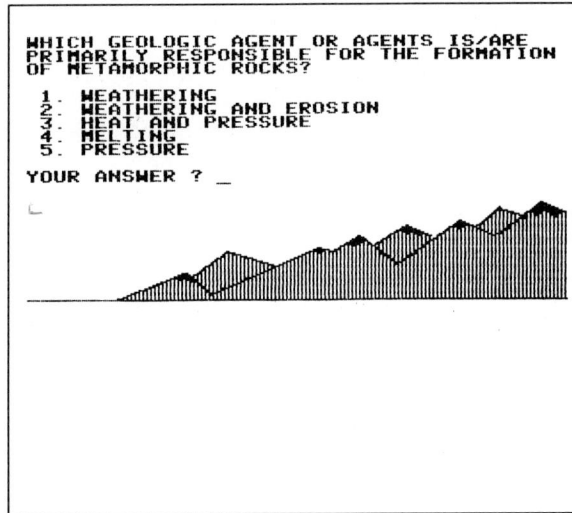

```
WHICH GEOLOGIC AGENT OR AGENTS IS/ARE
PRIMARILY RESPONSIBLE FOR THE FORMATION
OF METAMORPHIC ROCKS?
   1.  WEATHERING
   2.  WEATHERING AND EROSION
   3.  HEAT AND PRESSURE
   4.  MELTING
   5.  PRESSURE
YOUR ANSWER ?  _
```

The important point is that many objectives can be reached only if the learner is given abundant opportunities to give a response and to receive feedback for that response. Sometimes this practice is devoted to attaining a "lower-level" objective, such as recalling a simple fact. It is important to note, however, that these lower-level facts may in themselves be very important. These skills are low level only in the sense that they call for little prerequisite knowledge (that is, they are at the lower level of Bloom's

Figure 6.2 A screen from *A Tale of Two Cities*, from Hartley's HARPER & SELLER'S GUIDE TO THE CLASSICS, showing part of a unit on symbolism.

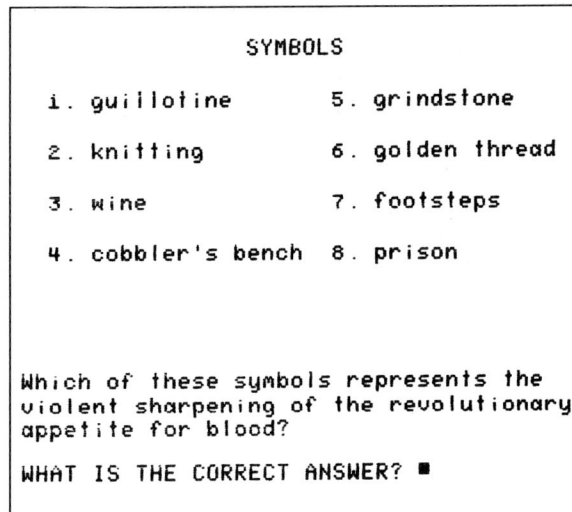

```
             SYMBOLS

   1.  guillotine      5.  grindstone

   2.  knitting        6.  golden thread

   3.  wine            7.  footsteps

   4.  cobbler's bench 8.  prison



Which of these symbols represents the
violent sharpening of the revolutionary
appetite for blood?

WHAT IS THE CORRECT ANSWER? ■
```

Taxonomy of Educational Objectives). In addition, it is important to note that these lower-level objectives are important prerequisites for higher-level activities, and the lower objectives must often become automatic before the learner can accomplish the higher objectives. One of the serious problems in group instruction is that the group "moves on" immediately after the slowest students have shown even a tentative mastery of the information under study. These slowest students are the very ones who most need to "overlearn" the material; that is, they need to practice it to the degree where it becomes automatic (as it already has for the fastest students in the same group). When slow students do not receive an opportunity to overlearn basic concepts, they are almost certainly doomed to difficulty and failure when they approach more complex concepts building upon an automatic knowledge of these basics.

Drill and practice activities are not limited to lower-level objectives. The only way a learner can become proficient at some higher-level activities (such as applying principles or solving problems) is to have frequent opportunities to practice the skills involved in those activities and to receive feedback regarding the correctness of performance.

Drills sometimes get a bad reputation because different learners need different amounts of practice while pursuing a designated objective. In the typical classroom, the teacher must focus on middle-ability students, with the result that slow learners need more practice than the teacher can provide and fast learners are bored because they have to continue practicing what they have already learned. This is where the computer can provide an immense advantage in arranging for effective use of academic learning time. By working at computer terminals, students can pursue objectives by getting practice tailored to their own needs. In addition, the learner must respond to each problem presented by the computer (not just when she is called on by the teacher), and feedback is immediate.

A good drill program supervises or conducts what traditional methods textbooks refer to as "recitation" or "seatwork activity." A computerized drill will be effective to the extent that it imitates this type of a one-on-one contact between a teacher and student. This means that a good program should (1) focus clearly on appropriate instructional objectives; (2) state the problem or question so that the student knows what to do; (3) refrain from giving irrelevant clues; (4) provide appropriate advice, tools, or prerequisite information needed to give the response; (5) give immediate feedback from the learner's response; (6) provide remedial information if necessary; (7) move to easier or more difficult levels of questions as the learner's responses indicate; and (8) provide continued practice until the learner shows mastery of the objectives under consideration. Some drills can carry out all of these instructional activities, although this is not always necessary or even desirable. For example, in some cases, the teacher may wish to determine when the student is ready to move to a more difficult level of instruction instead of letting the computer do this. Likewise, if a program does not keep careful records on disk of the student's performance, the teacher can often compensate for this by merely having the students record their scores on a sheet of paper as they complete their session at the computer.

Figure 6.3 shows a very simple example of useful feedback supplied by the computer. The learner has demonstrated confusion by indicating that he thinks Abraham Lincoln was the first president of the United States. The computer has responded by stating that George Washington was the answer it was seeking. Moreover, the computer goes on to show that Abraham Lincoln was actually the sixteenth president of the United States, during the time of the Civil War. A confused student could carefully read this screen to come to an understanding of the difference between Washington and Lincoln. This is a simple but important strategy. If the learner has confused two persons or concepts, the best time to point out the distinction is immediately after the mistake has occurred.

INTEGRATING SOFTWARE INTO THE CLASSROOM

When deciding when and where to teach a piece of social studies software, the teacher needs to anticipate where the concept, process, or social studies skill is going to be applied to content. A social studies teacher may choose to use a history simulation *after* his students have read a passage from a book on the simulated topic. In this case, part of his goal would be to use context clues to *reconstruct* the lesson or to recall information that has been partially forgotten. Another teacher may use the same program for a topic that her students are not going to read about at all. Her goal would be to use context clues and general principles to explore a completely novel situation. There would be considerable overlap between the two applications, but the teachers would focus their goals and discussions differently, depending on the role the program is supposed to play in the curriculum.

It is *not* a good idea to buy and use a program simply because it is considered a good program. A good program is one that helps students use their academic learning time more effectively to reach an important goal.

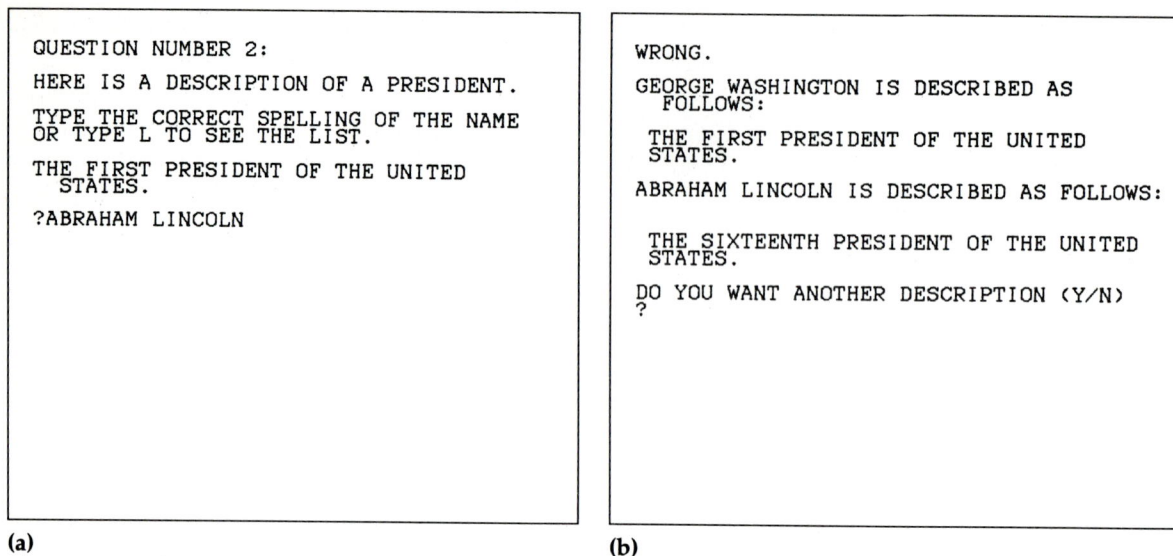

```
QUESTION NUMBER 2:

HERE IS A DESCRIPTION OF A PRESIDENT.

TYPE THE CORRECT SPELLING OF THE NAME
OR TYPE L TO SEE THE LIST.

THE FIRST PRESIDENT OF THE UNITED
   STATES.

?ABRAHAM LINCOLN
```

```
WRONG.

GEORGE WASHINGTON IS DESCRIBED AS
   FOLLOWS:

THE FIRST PRESIDENT OF THE UNITED
STATES.

ABRAHAM LINCOLN IS DESCRIBED AS FOLLOWS:

THE SIXTEENTH PRESIDENT OF THE UNITED
STATES.

DO YOU WANT ANOTHER DESCRIPTION (Y/N)
?
```

(a)   (b)

Figure 6.3 Screens from CONCEPT MASTERY, which shows a very simple example of useful feedback supplied by the computer.

Always have a goal in mind when you direct your students to use a piece of instructional software.

SUMMARY

Software should be selected in such a way as to help students attain the goals of a school's social studies curriculum. This chapter has described some guidelines for selecting social studies software, and has examined some software designed to help teachers with classroom management tasks. This chapter has also discussed the importance of selecting hardware that will run the designated software most effectively.

When organizing students for using computers, teachers often assume that each student should work at a separate machine. Although individual use of the computer can be a wise use of resources, it is often better to have students work in groups at the computer. Especially during the learning phase of instruction, it is usually beneficial to have a whole class work with the teacher on a single large screen connected to the computer. This chapter has offered guidelines for grouping students at the computer.

Finally, this chapter has presented strategies for transferring skills learned in computerized social studies lessons and for integrating these skills throughout the curriculum.

REFERENCES

Cohen, P. A., J. A. Kulik, and C. C. Kulik. "Educational Outcomes of Tutoring: A Meta-Analysis of Findings." *American Educational Research Journal* 19 (1982): 237–248.

Johnson, D. W., and R. T. Johnson. *Learning Together and Alone: Cooperative, Competitive, and Individualistic Learning.* Englewood Cliffs, N.J.: Prentice-Hall, 1986.

Slavin, R. E. *Cooperative Learning.* New York: Longman, 1983.

Slavin, R. E. *Educational Psychology: Theory into Practice.* Englewood Cliffs, N.J.: Prentice-Hall, 1986.

Slavin, R. E., S. Sharan, S. Kagan, R. Hertz-Lazarowitz, C. Webb, and R. Schmuck. (Eds.). *Learning to Cooperate, Cooperating to Learn.* New York: Plenum, 1985.

Vockell, E. L., and E. Schwartz. *The Computer in the Classroom* (2nd Ed.). Watsonville, CA.: Mitchell **McGRAW-HILL**, 1992.

Vockell, E. L., and R. van Deusen. *The Computer and Higher-Order Thinking Skills.* Watsonville, CA.: Mitchell **McGRAW-HILL**, 1989.

CHAPTER 7

WHAT THE FUTURE OFFERS

TECHNOLOGICAL ADVANCES will make possible new applications in social studies instruction. The following sections describe some of these potential innovations. This chapter contains no science fiction: We are nearly 100 percent certain that all of technology described here will be available for classroom use within the next few years. The only doubt is whether schools will actually implement the technology and, if so, whether teachers and students will use the technology to its maximum benefit. As indicated in Chapter 1, in the past 10 years computers have not had a significant impact on social studies education. In our opinion, a major difference between then and the years ahead is that forthcoming technological advances will offer benefits that are more obviously applicable to social studies programs, and therefore implementation of the new technology may be expedited. At the same time, however, we are aware that the application of this technology will not be fruitful unless teachers integrate these innovations with effective, noncomputerized strategies that will make teachers and students want to use them. This chapter is intended to help you become a more competent consumer of these technological innovations as they become available.

HYPERMEDIA

Hypertext was introduced in Chapter 5. The term "hypermedia" refers to the integration of hypertext strategies with other media, such as electronic visual and auditory presentations. Hypermedia technology is rapidly expanding, and future years will certainly witness an increase in the number of hypermedia "stacks" designed for the social studies. There are only a small number of commercially prepared stacks currently available, but a growing number of companies and universities are working to increase this supply. Because using hypermedia is easy enough that a person with high interest and expertise in social studies but limited computer experience can create or add to a stack, good materials are likely to proliferate rapidly. Much of the hardware and software discussed earlier in this text can be used very effectively with hypermedia, and the products currently under development will introduce even greater possibilities. For example, scanners can be used to introduce maps, diagrams, graphs, and even photographs into a hypermedia stack. If sound is an important element of the presentation, sound digitizers can permit digitized speeches or music to be included.

Several programs have begun to appear as add-ons or expansions of HYPERCARD. MIND MAP from William K. Bradford Publishing Company is a good example of a program that gives students in grades 6 through 12 a framework to use multimedia skills to solve problems (Figure 7.1). The program employs clustering—a widely used problem-solving and creativity strategy that facilitates the free flow of ideas and then allows students to intelligently organize, manage, and recall these ideas through the use of visual metaphors. The program enables students to generate and revise printed or multimedia reports in which they can take significant pride. It is especially suited to cooperative learning efforts in language arts, science, and social studies. Teachers who have fostered creative writing across the curriculum will find that programs like this enable their students to express themselves in ways previously considered to be reserved to universities and corporations.

Hypermedia also makes possible the smooth incorporation of dictionaries or glossaries directly into social studies lessons. COMPTON'S MULTIMEDIA ENCYCLOPEDIA (discussed earlier in Chapter 5) is an excellent example of a large-scale application of hypermedia strategies. The dictionary component of the MULTIMEDIA ENCYCLOPEDIA exemplifies part of the value of hypertext. Although physical dictionaries provide a very useful means for learning words in context, few persons using an ordinary encyclopedia actually look up words as the need arises, largely because this is a disruptive process. That is, it would be inconvenient to move back and forth between the encyclopedia and the dictionary every time a need arises. However, the hypermedia capability of the MULTI-MEDIA ENCYCLOPEDIA makes it easily possible for readers to obtain definitions of words at the moment when these definitions are most valuable—when the reader is reading the words in context. The user simply uses the mouse to move the cursor on top of the unfamiliar word and clicks a button—and the definition almost instantly appears on the screen. If a word in the definition needs further defining, the user can click again for another definition; otherwise the program returns to the original encyclopedia entry.

In addition to stacks designed specifically for use with hypermedia programs like HYPERCARD (Claris) or LINKWAY (IBM), we can expect to see the basic hypermedia concept applied to all kinds of software. Independent applications of hypermedia have already started to appear. For example, although COMPTON'S MULTIMEDIA ENCYCLOPEDIA does not employ a commercial hypertext program, it certainly uses the hypermedia

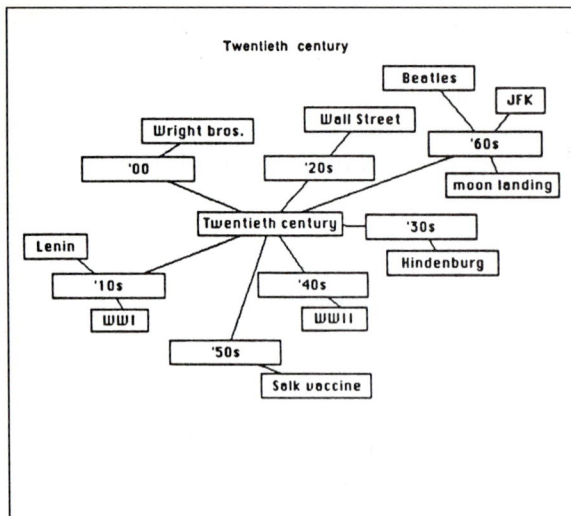

(a)

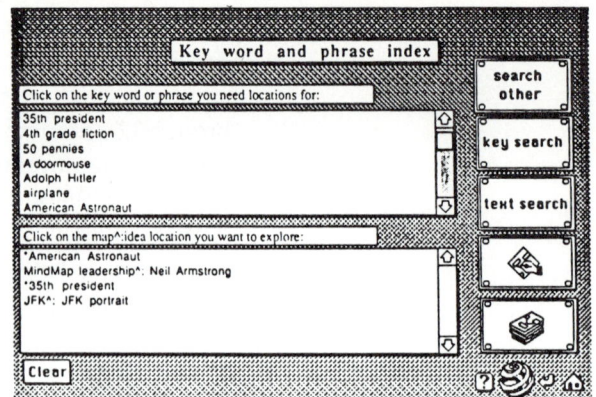

(b)

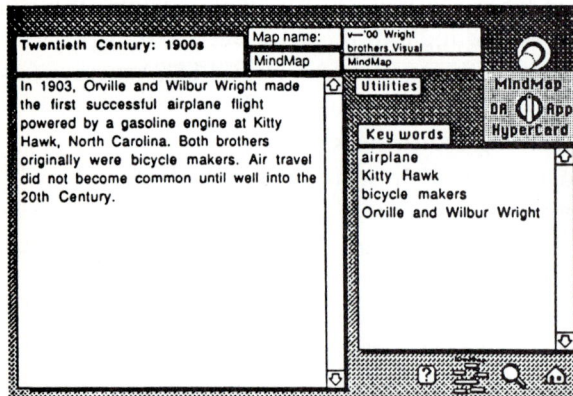

(c)

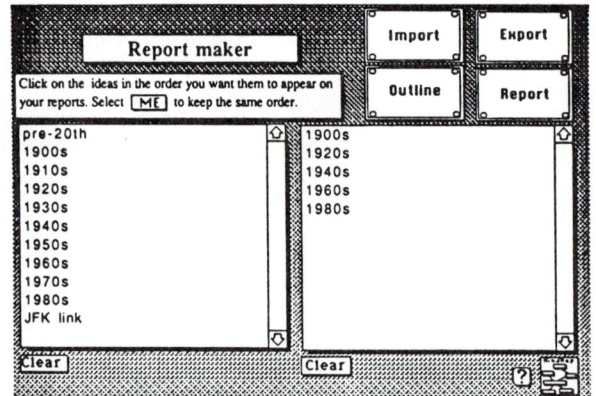

(d)

Figure 7.1 Screens from MIND MAP (William K. Bradford Publishing Company), a program that gives students in grades 6–12 a framework to use multimedia skills to solve problems: (a) The students first brainstorm and cluster ideas; (b) then expand them briefly; (c) then develop the ideas further; and (d) finally organize a composition that can include multimedia elements.

concept as the major interface permitting users to move easily into and throughout the encyclopedia.

At a much simpler level, teachers and students who are running a program might wish to move somewhere else within that program (or temporarily into another program); but the way most software is now designed makes this impossible. With hypermedia strategies, users will easily be able to move wherever instructional needs call them, instead of being limited to a predetermined sequence. This free and spontaneous access will greatly enhance the value of a very large number of social studies programs. As pointed out in Chapter 6, the invariant sequence or other unfriendly user interfaces often make it difficult to use a program on a large screen for an entire class. Hypermedia will often provide an interface that makes a single, good program usable by either a large group, a small group, or an individual student.

As hypermedia becomes more common, it is likely that users will get accustomed to the idea of nonlinear thinking. This could be perceived as a problem by teachers who invest huge amounts of energy in getting students to follow a clear, systematic line of thought: Why encourage them to jump around in their thinking? However, the nonlinear thinking of hypertext is by no means haphazard. Because hypermedia requires careful planning and complete sets of information, hypermedia programmers and users will learn to incorporate and expect these characteristics in their own thinking and presentations.

INTERACTIVE VIDEO TECHNOLOGY

When using present technology, teachers often enhance social studies lessons with films or videotapes. Interactive video technology—the combination of a laser videodisc and a computer—is likely to make these enhancements even more effective. This technology, still in its developmental stages, makes it possible to access various combinations of moving pictures, still pictures, text, and sound almost instantaneously. For example, a student might be reading a passage on the computer screen about the knights of the Round Table. She might call up the map of England at the time of the Arthurian legends, and then request a more detailed map of Nottingham or a map of the same area in 1990. After returning to and finishing reading the passage, the learner might request a video presentation of the same story, with the written text appearing at the bottom of the screen. She would be able to stop the video presentation at any time, and then a menu would appear, asking if the computer should move back to an earlier part, skip ahead, provide a definition, simply pause, or exercise some other option. This is just one example of what can be done with interactive video. Numerous applications are likely to become available as the technology develops and becomes less expensive and more widely used.

By interfacing laserdisc technology with a program like HYPERCARD, it will soon become convenient to develop and use really first-class databases that include still and moving pictures as well as written text. For example, students will be able to answer questions and solve problems by browsing through a well-prepared and interesting laserdisc devoted to a specific topic. They might watch a video segment that presents a problem in economics, quickly move to a combination of several still diagrams with accompanying text that provide information to help solve the problem, develop a hypothesis, move to another segment of the laserdisc that shows the results of testing that hypothesis, go back for another look at the problem, go to slow motion or stop action to examine certain aspects more closely, look for additional information on another laserdisc, state a new hypothesis . . . and continue until they have satisfactorily resolved the problem. During this process, of course, students would not be obligated to work solely or even predominantly with the interactive laserdisc. Rather, like other good resources, the laserdisc materials simply serve as a vital tool that is available to provide useful information to individuals, small groups, or entire classes.

Interactive video technology is currently available even without HYPERCARD; however, it is expensive and somewhat difficult to program for specific applications. At present there are relatively few useful videodiscs for educational topics. Just within the past year, good disks have become more common and prices have begun to drop. We foresee programs like HYPERCARD helping solve the programming problem. This is because HYPERCARD programmers will simply concentrate on organizing the laserdisc into a useful database from which information can be easily accessed, without consideration of the specific questions users will want to answer. Teachers and students will be able to use the resulting comprehensive series of databases as a flexible tool for answering questions and solving problems.

The National Geographic Society, Lucasfilm, Apple Computer, and the California State Department of Education have combined their efforts to produce an interactive social studies program for grades 5–12. The program

is called GTV: A GEOGRAPHIC PERSPECTIVE ON AMERICAN HIS-
TORY. It combines laserdiscs with the Apple IIGS computer to give the user
complete control over visual, auditory, and textual information providing
an overview of American history. The first videodisc in the series holds two
hours of moving pictures, divided into three 40-minute segments. The
advantage of the package over simple videotape is that the individual
teacher or student can rearrange various sequences to create a lesson or a
student report. This first disk also includes 1600 still images and 200 maps,
with a computer-accessed index that permits the student or teacher to
search for a particular image.

ABC News Interactive and Optical Data Corporation have combined
forces to produce an instructional package called MARTIN LUTHER
KING, JR.: INSTANT REPLAY OF HISTORY. Consisting of a well-designed
videodisc and a set of HYPERCARD stacks, the program permits students
and teachers to access information about Martin Luther King and the Civil
Rights movement in ways that will lead to insightful analysis of important
historical problems. The videodisc includes full-motion clips, photographs,
maps, graphs, biographies, newspaper articles, and an on-line glossary of
important terms. The subject matter includes not only important information about King himself, but also such wide-ranging related information as
details on the Montgomery bus boycott, the text of the 14th Amendment to
the U.S. Constitution and the 1956 Federal Court decision, and interviews
with children on the state of racism today. Users can employ a series of
HYPERCARD buttons to move throughout the text, usually with the
assistance of a well-designed index.

There are many ways in which a product like this can be used. Students
or teachers can thoroughly research important topics; teachers can prepare
and present uniquely tailored lessons; and students can use the package to
present equally interesting reports on subjects that would otherwise be
difficult to research. The same companies have produced THE '88 VOTE
and IN THE HOLY LAND.

Recent developments in multimedia have presented logistics
problems that have required ingenious solutions. For example, as laserdiscs
have proliferated, it has sometimes become necessary to change disks
during the running of a program to access the correct information. "Laserdisc jukeboxes" have begun to appear for this purpose, designed to stand
alone in a library or other relatively unsupervised area and permit users to
access interactive laserdisc information. The user selects a program, and
while the software is booting up and giving instructions, the machine

automatically loads the laserdisc required for that application. The durable structure of the unit protects the laserdisc and software from damage or theft.

Finally, it is possible to combine the worlds of the video*disc* and the more common but less flexible video*tape* in creative ways. The ELEC-TRONIC ENCYCLOPEDIA OF AMERICAN HISTORY (Warner) is a set of over 40 laserdiscs containing film segments relating to American history since the very early 1900s. Teachers can preview these segments covering a vast amount of history, select the segments that relate to their courses, and copy these segments to videotape to show to their classes. These tailor-made videotapes can then be integrated into carefully prepared lectures and discussions.

CD-ROM

CD-ROM technology has barely begun to have its impact on social studies education. Electronic encyclopedias (such as COMPTON'S MULTIMEDIA ENCYCLOPEDIA) will be found in most school libraries, and students will use these to access information much more efficiently than has traditionally been possible. However, simple logistics will make it unlikely that the electronic encyclopedias will replace hardcopy versions. If a school has just a single copy of an electronic encyclopedia, only one student (or small group of students) can use it at any time. This may be much less efficient than having several students use separate volumes of a hardcopy encyclopedia. The encyclopedia can be put onto a local area network (LAN), enabling several computers to access the same CD-ROM disk, but when this is done the entire LAN must often be dedicated to the single purpose of using that one CD-ROM disk. In actual practice, schools are likely to retain the traditional hardcopy version of the encyclopedia, so that students will start a search at the computer and then continue at a more leisurely pace at the hardcopy encyclopedia. In fact, as CD-ROM encyclopedias become more popular, it is likely that students will become more enthusiastic about the use of encyclopedias in general, and schools may need two or three hardcopy versions of the encyclopedia to satisfy the insatiable needs of their eager learners.

CD-ROM technology is rapidly becoming easily accessible to both students and teachers. Optical Data's VISUAL ALMANAC is an interactive multimedia kit that uses the HYPERCARD format to provide a large number of pictures, graphs, tables, ideas, and concepts related to many topics, including geography and history. Users can easily browse through this "sampler" and use appropriate materials for reports and presentations. CD-ROM packages related more specifically to social studies have already begun to appear. *The Great Books of the Western World* and *The Library of American Civilization* both contain vast quantities of ideas that would be of interest to social studies students, but at present they are difficult to access. Note, however, that in order for these reference materials to become truly accessible, they not only must be entered onto CD-ROM disks, but they also need to be integrated with useful access systems (perhaps employing a hypermedia format) to enable students to find information as their needs and interests dictate.

The TIME MAGAZINE COMPACT ALMANAC from Compact Publishing presents a huge compendium of news-related information. The 1991 edition includes the full text of *Time* magazine from 1989 through April 1, 1991. In addition, the CD-ROM disk includes articles on important topics likely to be of interest to students, ranging from Henry Ford and Adolf Hitler to the Women's Movement, as well as more than 400 tables of vital statistics and other information commonly associated with almanacs. While the ALMANAC does not include all the pictures that appeared in *Time* during the designated period, it does include over 200 pictures illustrating the major events covered on the disk. To stimulate interest, the accompanying software provides a NewsQuest quiz that encourages users to search articles for answers to questions. The software enables users to browse with simple pull-down menus to find any article, picture, essay, chart, table, or map as well as to search the disk for pertinent articles by using up to six key words. Students can also use icons associated with various articles to move quickly to related articles, images, charts, maps, and tables on the same topic. While using the almanac, students are able to use the software to make notes, which they can save or print. It is a safe bet that numerous magazines will soon be available in this kind of hypertext, easily accessed format and that it will soon be possible to search more than one journal at a time using this browse and search format.

Applications of CD-ROM and laserdisc technology to the classroom are certain to increase within the next few years. These applications will make it possible for both student and teacher to have access to a wider range of information than has ever been easily available in social studies classrooms. In addition, the mechanisms for accessing this information will improve, so that previously unavailable information will be easily incorporated into both student and teacher presentation.

A Modest but Grandiose Prediction

At this point, we will go out on a limb and make a specific prediction about a package that we think will be developed in the near future. While this book was being written, the Public Broadcasting System (PBS) presented on television a series entitled "The Civil War." The series met with popular acclaim, and videocassettes are already available for the general public. Our bet is that someone will package the following materials.

1. A laserdisc version of this series.
2. A CD-ROM disk containing (a) textbook-style treatments of the Civil War geared toward several different age levels, (b) several popular treatments of the Civil War that have already been published elsewhere, (c) a large amount of primary source material related to that conflict, and (d) timelines related both to the Civil War and to other time periods.
3. A hypermedia interface that will permit students to move freely throughout the materials described above.

We have certainly not thought of all the information the package will contain. The following are some examples of how this package will be used:

- A student who knows that her great grandfather died at the Battle of Gettysburg will sit at a single work station and do all the research for a written term paper integrating huge amounts of interesting information about this topic.

TELECOMMUNICATIONS

Future years will offer improved quality and faster speeds in modems. The number of classrooms that provide access via modem to computers beyond the school's walls will greatly increase as teachers and students begin to see the value of "what's out there." And many more states and regional organizations will provide electronic bulletin boards, informational databases, and other valuable resources that students can access via modem.

ICAI

Tutorials providing branching programmed instruction as a form of computer-assisted instruction are covered at length in Chapter 1 of *The Computer in the Classroom*. It is possible to combine branching tutorials with artificial

- Another student will present a visual report of the same battle by integrating into his own videotape scenes from the PBS series, maps from different time periods taken from the CD-ROM disk, and personal videotapes that he made while visiting the battlefield and interviewing a guide there.
- A social studies teacher will prepare a one-hour introductory presentation on the Civil War by choosing from a hypertext menu that selects a predetermined shorter sequence from the lengthier original set of laserdiscs.
- An English teacher in the same school will prepare an entirely different introductory presentation for *The Red Badge of Courage* by making a different selection from the same hypertext menu.
- A media specialist will sit at the side of a classroom while the teacher leads a discussion on the Civil War. As the needs demand, the specialist calls up sequences from the PBS series, maps, statistics, and other information needed to enhance the discussion.

The above implementations will indeed be possible. Will they actually occur? Our belief is that events very much like each of these implementations will happen. Will these events occur in your school? That depends on your interest in and eagerness to obtain materials of this kind and in your ability to convince others of the usefulness of such activities.

intelligence to provide a strategy called Intelligent Computer-Assisted Instruction (ICAI). Like a good human tutor, an ICAI program monitors student responses and tries to determine the reasons behind student errors. The computer then provides tutorial or remedial information specifically designed to overcome these errors.

A good example of this strategy is a program called MENDEL, which tutors high school and college students on various aspects of genetics. MENDEL is both a problem-solving simulation and an intelligent tutorial. In the first of MENDEL's roles, the program presents the learner with problems to solve while he uses the computer as a tool to conduct experiments and collect or interpret data. In its second role, MENDEL assumes the role of a human tutor. This program is described in detail in Vockell and Schwartz (1992) and in Streibel and colleagues (1987). Applied to a social

Computers in Action

Miss McCabe's fifth-grade U.S. history class was preparing reports on "20th-Century Presidents." While one group prepared the biographical descriptions of Presidents McKinley, Roosevelt, Wilson, Harding, and the others, another group used scanners to digitize photographs of the presidents and a desktop publishing program to integrate the text and photographs. Yet another group busily assembled sound bytes taken from actual presidential speeches. The end product—a multimedia presentation—was more impressive than the traditional projects from past years, when students had looked up information in books and encyclopedias and had stood in front of the classroom to read their reports. The school's principal asked that the entire project be presented to the parents using an LCD projection system in the cafeteria during the annual open house.

studies unit, such a program could perform the following tasks for a student:

1. It could make inferences about the answers made by the student, drawing conclusions about what skills the student possesses or still needs to develop.
2. It could maintain a history of a student's actions (including the strategies the student tried and the results of these strategies).
3. It could make inferences about the reasons for the student's problem-solving actions. These would be drawn from a combination of what the student has done and said. (In doing this, a human tutor is building a model or representation of each student's or group of students' comprehension abilities.)
4. It could compare a model of a student's knowledge with the tutor's understanding of the problem.
5. It could make a decision on the form of tutorial advice and the timing of this advice.
6. It could evaluate whether or not the student has benefitted from the advice.

Students running such a program would have an experience much the same as if they were studying a unit with a human tutor seated beside them, a tutor with a knowledge of social studies skills and a willingness to offer help whenever it is needed. The development of this type of program is described in greater detail in Streibel and colleagues (1987). Although a social studies program like this does not exist, the technology is already available. Programs of this kind can be developed in areas where the computer can be programmed to solve a problem and then check to see how closely its solution compares to that of a human learner.

Within the next few years we expect to see software and book publishers expand their offerings that take advantage of the full strengths of the computer to teach social studies skills. Specifically, we expect to see more programs that integrate multimedia and database applications into the social studies curriculum.

In this book we have taken the position that computers don't teach complex skills; teachers teach these skills, using the computer as a tool. As artificial intelligence and intelligent computer-assisted instruction evolve, the roles of the teacher and the computer may shift. It is possible that within the next 10 years *some* social studies skills may be most effectively taught by having students interact directly with computers without teacher mediation. However, the overall guiding principle for teaching social studies skills in the classroom will continue to be that a knowledgeable teacher should stimulate a motivated group of students to pursue these skills, using computers or other materials as appropriate tools.

SUMMARY

As technology advances, the future is likely to see expanded and innovative applications of the computer in the field of social studies instruction. Interactive video will integrate textual and visual presentations, and allow learners to move easily backward and forward within a software package. Developments in the use of CD-ROM will make it possible for social studies students to access huge amounts of information at a single work station. Intelligent Computer-Assisted Instruction will give the computer more precision when responding to the specific needs of individual learners as they are experiencing computerized social studies instruction. Hypermedia will provide information (such as definitions of words) at the time when it is really needed, and will let students and teachers branch through programs in the instructionally most desirable manner.

Publishers are likely to extend their efforts in producing materials for specific topics within the general area of world history. In addition, we expect to see more good programs in the areas of economics, psychology, and sociology, where currently there are very few. Because computer technology is still in a stage of rapid development, it is also likely that other technological innovations will lead to instructional developments that cannot be predicted at the present time.

REFERENCES

Streibel, M. J., J. Stewart, K. Koedinger, A. Collins, and J. P. Jungck. "MENDEL: An Intelligent Tutoring System for Genetics Problem-Solving, Conjecturing, and Understanding." *Machine-Mediated Learning* 2 (1987): 129–159.

Vockell, E. L., and E. Schwartz. *The Computer in the Classroom* (2nd Ed.). Watsonville, CA.: Mitchell **McGRAW-HILL**, 1992.

CHAPTER 8

SOFTWARE REVIEWS

THIS CHAPTER PROVIDES fairly detailed reviews of 25 software packages available for the social studies curriculum. Appendix B provides less detailed summaries of a much larger number of programs. The goal of the present chapter is to briefly discuss these 25 programs which are typical of the kinds of help teachers can expect from the computer in their social studies classrooms. Some of these programs have been discussed in previous chapters, and crossreferences can easily be found in the index.

TITLE: ANASAZI

Producer: Harcourt, Brace, Jovanovich (part of the HBJ Historian series)
Grade Level: 7–12
Suggested Retail: $16.00
Required Memory: 64K/256K
Available for: Apple II series, IBM
Subject Area: U.S. history
Copy-Protected: Yes
Type: Simulation

DESCRIPTION

This is one of a series of 7 programs dealing with problems that occurred in U.S. history. Others include 1865: SHOULD THE SOUTHERN STATES BE READMITTED TO THE UNION? and JUNE–DECEMBER 1894: WHAT ACTION SHOULD THE PRESIDENT TAKE CONCERNING THE PULLMAN STRIKE AND ITS AFTERMATH? This one deals with the mysterious disappearance of the Anasazi Indian tribe. The first part of the program presents historical background data related to the problem. Students are then left to resolve the problem in small committees. These results are then compared to current historical thinking on the problem. Accompanying documentation provides handouts, suggestions for time management and teaching strategies, and a complete printout of source documents.

EVALUATION

Students are placed in a position to organize ideas and draw conclusions based on real historical data. Thus, the computer merely provides a forum and acts as a catalyst in allowing students to draw their own conclusions. However, with the exception of the title screen, this program is heavily dominated by on-screen text. Use of graphics is very limited. Operation of the program is slowed by the requirement to access the disk after each screen. Overall, this is an intellectually stimulating program that is perhaps better used at the high school level. It offers a good look at the research techniques and some insight into the process of developing historical conclusions.

TITLE: APPLEWORKS

Producer: Claris
Grade Level: 5–12
Suggested Retail: $249.00
Required Memory: 128K
Available for: Apple II series
Subject Areas: All
Copy-Protected: No
Type: Utility

DESCRIPTION

APPLEWORKS is an integrated program that includes a word processor, database, and spreadsheet components. Two disks that provide the new user with background information (APPLE PRESENTS APPLEWORKS) and practice (APPLEWORKS TUTORIAL) are enclosed in the package. The word processor is an easy-to-use 80-column program with both basic and fairly advanced editing features. The database allows for a maximum of 1350 records with a maximum of 1024 characters per record. The spreadsheet offers room for 6000 filled cells (128K) with a maximum of 127 columns and 999 rows. The beauty of APPLEWORKS is its ease of use and the integration of information among the three applications. The "Copy" and "Move" options make it simple to use information from the spreadsheet or database in a word processing document. Keystroke cues are common to all three applications, which makes switching from one function to another easily accomplished. Supplementary programs from the TIMEOUT series by Beagle Brothers offer additional options such as spelling correction and an on-line thesaurus.

EVALUATION

This program can support teacher tasks such as grade management, student information management, and test design, as well as student tasks. Teachers who themselves have become educated without the use of an integrated program like APPLEWORKS are sometimes unaware of the tremendous advantages a program like this can confer for gathering, organizing, and presenting information. Other word processors are available for young learners, including BANK STREET WRITER, MAGIC SLATE, and FREDWRITER; but these are not as easily integrated with the database and spreadsheet as is APPLEWORKS.

TITLE: ATLAS EXPLORER

Producer: Springboard
Grade Level: 4–12
Suggested Retail: $79.00
Required Memory: 128 K
Available for: Apple II series (available in 5¼-inch and 3½-inch disks)
Subject Area: Geography
Copy-Protected: No
Type: Tutorial, game, tool, database

DESCRIPTION

This program uses maps and pull-down menus to review world geography. It also provides demographic information on countries and poses questions based on this information. Student recordkeeping is provided. The user can "zero-in" on the area of the world in question by using a screen-defined box, eventually focusing on the desired region of study. The documentation is well written, providing helpful screen inserts to keep the user properly oriented.

EVALUATION

This program makes excellent use of graphics. It is much easier to use when a mouse is available, rather than the keyboard. The scope of questions is limited to population, capitals, area, and language. Questions tend to be repeated even if answered correctly. Disk swapping in the 5¼-inch format becomes cumbersome. Program use without a mouse is very tedious. This is a good resource program. It has good potential as a reference tool, perhaps used in conjunction with an LCD projection system to introduce a new area of study.

TITLE: CHILDREN'S WRITING AND PUBLISHING CENTER

Producer: Learning Company
Grade Level: 2–Adult
Suggested Retail: $89.95
Required Memory: 128K
Available for: Apple II series
Subject Areas: All
Copy-Protected: Yes
Type: Desktop publishing

DESCRIPTION

THE CHILDREN'S WRITING AND PUBLISHING CENTER is an entry-level desktop publishing program. It combines a word processor with graphics and layout design capabilities. The student has the choice of a one- or two-column layout, eight font styles, and 140 graphics. The teacher's guide contains lesson ideas and activities. A data disk of templates is included. This desktop publishing program introduces primary-aged children to the skills involved in creating and printing a newsletter.

EVALUATION

While this is a truly impressive program, teachers should also consider the possibility of using a more sophisticated desktop publishing program, such as PUBLISH IT! Although the more advanced programs are probably prohibitively complex for young children to use without adult guidance, teachers often discover that they themselves benefit from the desktop publishing opportunities of a program like PUBLISH IT! If a teacher is adept at using these more sophisticated programs, then it is relatively easy to introduce the desktop publishing process to young learners and guide them in its use.

TITLE: CONGRESS IN ACTION

Producer: Scholastic
Grade Level: 6–12
Suggested Retail: $59.95
Required Memory: 128K
Available for: Apple II series
Subject Areas: Government, political science
Copy-Protected: No
Type: Database

DESCRIPTION

This three-disk set contains information on current members of Congress as well as important legislation. The legislation sections focus on important—and somewhat controversial—issues, often presenting articles with opposing opinions. Databases are accessed using APPLEWORKS. The documentation provides a good overview of these databases as well as a basic primer on the use of APPLEWORKS, including reference sheets for frequently used commands. It also contains sample lesson plans.

EVALUATION

The program makes good use of a powerful integrated program (APPLEWORKS)—counting somewhat on teacher familiarity with its use. In so doing, CONGRESS IN ACTION utilizes preset templates. Since APPLEWORKS is an integrated program, students can search the database for information, then incorporate it into the word processor to make reports. Also, materials can easily be printed out to generate hardcopies. This program presents an excellent opportunity for increasing study and research skills using an electronic database.

TITLE: CROSSWORD MAGIC

Producer: Mindscape
Grade Level: 3–Adult
Suggested Retail: $49.95
Required Memory: 128K
Available for: Apple II series, MS-DOS, Commodore, Macintosh
Subject Areas: All
Copy-Protected: Yes
Type: Utility

DESCRIPTION

CROSSWORD MAGIC allows teachers and students to easily create crossword puzzles that are professionally formatted. The teacher or student enters words that are arranged on the screen in a crossword design. Then definitions of clues are entered, and once again the computer handles the formatting. After the puzzle is complete, it can be printed out to be used in paper form or it can be saved to disk to use at the computer keyboard. In either case, original puzzles can be designed to meet individual or group needs. Motivating puzzles can easily be generated for any area of social studies.

EVALUATION

Other companies also publish programs that generate crossword puzzles, but we have seen none as easy to use or with output as attractive as CROSSWORD MAGIC. However, MECC'S PUZZLES AND POSTERS has the advantage of generating "wordsearch" activities from the words used in a crossword puzzle, without requiring the teacher to enter the words a second time to generate the wordsearch.

TITLE: DECISIONS, DECISIONS: ON THE CAMPAIGN TRAIL

Producer: Tom Snyder Productions
Grade Level: 7–12
Suggested Retail: $119.95
Required Memory: 64K
Available for: Apple II series, IBM
Subject Areas: Political science, civics, current events
Copy-Protected: Yes (backup disk included)
Type: Simulation, game

DESCRIPTION

Students are asked to participate in a simulated general election as a third-party candidate. In order to influence the outcome and, perhaps, win the election, priorities must be set, with a point system used to keep track of progress. Pregame preparation is necessary for effective participation, and a postgame follow-up and evaluation are recommended. Results may be printed out. The package provides sample lesson plans, questions, and activities. Also included are reproducible worksheets on the economy, energy, social reform, the environment, foreign policy, and crime.

EVALUATION

This package does a fine job of teaching the meaning of positions such as conservative, liberal, and independent. It also demonstrates the connection between the political arena of an election and important issues such as the environment and crime. Positions on these issues, however, are often generalized. The program suffers from a limited use of graphics and limited responses to decisions made by the participants. There are too many written screen responses, with positions often being overly simplistic. The program can be used to effectively cover the election process. Research and reference materials (included with the package) should be made available to students while participating, since some screens do not show what choices mean or represent.

TITLE: EXPLORING TABLES AND GRAPHS

Producer: Weekly Reader Family Software
Grade Level: Level I (7–10), Level II (10 and up)
Suggested Retail: $39.95
Required Memory: 48K
Available for: Apple II series
Subject Areas: Math, social studies
Copy-Protected: Yes (backup disk available for $10)
Type: Tutorial, game, tool, utility

DESCRIPTION

This program allows the user to input data in a two-variable format. It then uses the data to create graphs in various forms, including picture graphs, vertical bar graphs, horizontal bar graphs, line graphs, and pie charts. A tutorial section explains the use and application of the various graphs. A game section then uses student accuracy (or lack of it) to create data, which is incorporated into a variety of graphs.

EVALUATION

This program is very easy to use. Teachers who wish to make it part of a math or social studies unit will find it requires little previous knowledge of computers. For grades 3, 4, 5, and 6, written worksheets are included. A weakness is that the game and demonstration portions of the program should permit more "escape" opportunities, so that one does not have to complete an entire section before going on to the next section. This is a good utility program for general classroom use. It works especially well with LCD projection systems.

TITLE: GEOWORLD

> Producer: Tom Snyder Productions
> Grade Level: 6–12
> Suggested Retail: $79.95
> Required Memory: 64K
> Available for: Apple, IBM
> Subject Areas: Earth science, geography, geology
> Copy-Protected: Yes (backup disk included)
> Type: Simulation, database

DESCRIPTION

With GEOWORLD students explore for and test for valuable mineral resources, as well as engage in the mining of these resources. In the process, they select a geographic area, obtain strata diagrams, obtain core samples, and perform geochemical tests on these samples. If the first of these operations show some promise of success, they can spend an additional portion of their budget on mining operations. During the program students have access to instructional materials. The object of the simulation is to produce a profit. The package contains lesson plans, game sheets, resource information sheets, strata diagrams, and maps. References are made to appropriate chapter and page numbers of related textbooks. Future revisions might include a section or an addition on ecological responsibility.

EVALUATION

GEOWORLD makes excellent use of graphics to show test results and cross sections of strata. Students are encouraged to keep track of results on accompanying worksheets. Results may be saved for future reference in either report or database form on APPLEWORKS. A weakness is that limited "escape" key availability inhibits the ability to move around the program. In order to change menu selection, sometimes arrow keys are used and at other times the spacebar is used. Although this is a minor irritation, it will interfere with large-group presentation of the program. This program is highly engaging. Students can work as individuals or as teams in a cooperative learning environment. As a byproduct of their exploration for world resources, users will gain increased map skills.

TITLE: HIDDEN AGENDA

Producer: Springboard
Grade Level: 6–12
Suggested Retail: $79.00
Required Memory: 128K
Available for: Apple II series
Subject Area: Political science, geography, economics
Copy-Protected: Yes
Type: Simulation, game

DESCRIPTION

This program challenges students to be the president of a Central American nation that has just rid itself of a cruel, despotic dictator. In order to successfully direct this nation, one must make a series of decisions regarding cabinet members, advisors, the economy, and sudden "emergencies." As time passes, these decisions become more difficult and hectic. Ultimately, the user faces the "verdict of history," which judges the level of accomplishment.

EVALUATION

The program makes good use of graphics, and it forces either single users or teams to interact with the screen action. Unfinished games can be saved. In preparation for the simulation, teachers should familiarize students with terms such as "junta" to avoid confusion or misunderstandings during the game.

TITLE: HYPERATLAS

Producer: Micro Maps Software, Inc.
Grade Level: 6–12
Suggested Retail: $99.95
Required Memory: 1MB
Available for: Macintosh
Subject Area: Geography
Copy-Protected: No
Type: Tool, utility, database

DESCRIPTION

HYPERATLAS is a two-disk set containing a series of HYPERCARD stacks. The "World" disk contains the following stacks: World Economic Info, World Population Info, User's World Info, and Import World Info. The "USA" disk contains these stacks: USA Political Info, User's USA Info, User's City Info, Import, U.S. State Info, and Import U.S. City Info. This program takes advantage of the HYPERCARD ability to sort through, connect, and otherwise process data; and thus it becomes a powerful tool to search databases of geographic, economic, and demographic information. Both maps and data can be printed out for classroom use. They can also be displayed using an LCD projection system. The documentation for HYPERATLAS is minimal, considering the great potential it offers the educational system, especially the social science area. The publishers offer a 31-page pamphlet, which highlights the operation of the program.

EVALUATION

This program gives immediate access to a variety of information important to many social studies classes. It should be a vital part of any social science reference area. However, since the documentation offers very few user suggestions and gives very little instruction on the use and operation of HYPERCARD, unless the user has prior knowledge of the proper use of HYPERCARD, some of this potential is lost. Until more schools invest in Macintosh equipment and provide teacher training, its vast potential may not be fully realized. This is one of the best of a new generation of programs that promises to drastically change methods of teaching and research in the decade ahead.

TITLE: MAPS WORLD, MAPS USA, and MAPS EUROPE

Producer: Adam Cobb and King, San Francisco, Calif.
Grade Level: Elementary
Suggested Retail: $19.95
Required Memory: 128K
Available for: Apple II series, Commodore 128
Subject Area: Geography
Copy-Protected: Yes
Type: Game, database

DESCRIPTION

These programs let the learner fly a helicopter to locate specific places, including countries, major cities, and bodies of water. The computer selects a random starting location. MAPS USA and MAPS EUROPE have a removable boundary option. MAPS USA can be set for the student to identify a randomly selected state. Use of a joystick is required.

EVALUATION

The program is a good source of information on demographics such as population, capitals, and so on. However, on maps without political boundaries, locations are difficult to ascertain from the one shade of green. Overall, the program has merit as an enrichment exercise.

TITLE: NATIONAL INSPIRER

Producer: Tom Snyder Productions
Grade Level: 3–6
Suggested Retail: $69.95
Required Memory: 64K
Available for: Apple, IBM
Subject Area: Geography
Copy-Protected: Yes (backup disk included)
Type: Game

DESCRIPTION

This menu-driven game allows individuals, teams, or an entire class to try to "discover" resources, current population, and elevation associated with various states. The program establishes variables and awards points for successful discoveries. It motivates students to do research. The package comes with lesson plans, resource sheets, and reproducible masters.

EVALUATION

NATIONAL INSPIRER allows for variation in reading speeds. It locks out wrong team numbers so that one cannot accidentally go out of turn. The program can be used as an individual, team, or class exercise. It would work well with an LCD projection system. However, there are sometimes delays between screens with no intermediate information. Annoying buzzer sounds become a distraction. Some screens cycle automatically without any keystrokes. Overall, this program is a good addition to any unit in which U.S. resources and demographics are being studied.

TITLE: THE OTHER SIDE

Producer: Tom Snyder Productions
Grade Level: 5–12
Suggested Retail: $69.95
Required Memory: 64K
Available for: Apple, IBM
Subject Areas: Geography, political science
Copy-Protected: Yes (backup disk included)
Type: Simulation, game

DESCRIPTION

This is an interactive game/simulation in which two sides on one or two computers work collaboratively or competitively to construct a bridge. If two computers are used they must be connected by a cable or modem. CAD (computer-assisted defense) can enter the game to ensure the survival of one side or to change the game. It is possible to turn off this device if the correct code is discovered. The documentation is well written and easy to follow. The package includes two equally well-prepared student guides.

EVALUATION

This package encourages strong interactive involvement. Teams must work together to arrive at a successful strategy. The program may also be used as a political science simulation to teach diplomacy. However, games will take a long time to complete. The games are automatically saved after each turn so that they may be resumed later. This program has been on the market since 1985 and has a proven track record. It is also used in foreign countries: Japan, China, Great Britain, Austria, and the Union of Soviet Socialist Republics.

TITLE: OUR TOWN MEETING

Producer: Tom Snyder Productions
Grade Level: 5–12
Suggested Retail: $99.95
Required Memory: 64K
Available for: Apple II series, IBM
Subject Areas: Civics, government
Copy-Protected: Yes (backup disk included)
Type: Simulation, game

DESCRIPTION

OUR TOWN MEETING simulates a meeting of a local town or village board, complete with agencies and projects. The agencies, consisting of one to four persons, are in charge of preparing reports in order to convince the board (or computer) of the wisdom of funding these projects with a limited budget. The game may be played by as many as 15 students per computer, with students playing various roles. Because the type of decisions facing the students often mimic real-life dilemmas facing local boards, this program fosters an atmosphere of cooperation among the participants.

EVALUATION

This is an excellent program to use in conjunction with a study of local government. It is especially strong in promoting good group interaction. It accurately represents the dynamics of a village board decision process. One problem is that there seems to be little noticeable difference among the three levels of difficulty. In addition, the dollar levels of the projects are often unrealistically low. As a convenience, more "escape" opportunities should have been added to allow agencies to redo decisions. Overall, this is an excellent government simulation. Part of the program requires oral presentations made to the hypothetical board, as well as preparation of reports in smaller groups. As a result, the learning process is centered on group interaction—not interaction with the computer.

TITLE: PC GLOBE, PC USA, and PC NATIONS

Producer: PC Globe, Inc.
Grade Level: K–12
Suggested Retail: $69.95
Required Memory: 128K
Available for: IBM, Apple IIGS
Subject Area: Geography, economics
Copy-Protected: Yes
Type: Tool, database

DESCRIPTION

These programs offer IBM-compatible users a clear and convenient method of obtaining physical and demographic information about the United States and other countries. Pull-down menus give the user quick access to both maps and database information. Additionally, the "Point-and-Shoot" option allows the student to use a mouse to focus the pointer on a specific region or country and obtain immediate map retrieval. Maps can be screen altered to show not only political features, such as major cities and boundaries, but also major topographic features or population densities. The PC GLOBE database contains information on a variety of topics including population, age distribution, language, ethnic groups, health, gross national product, resources, imports and exports, government, culture, and tourism. Data can be displayed in bar graph format. Maps can be printed out. PC USA contains similar information for each of the 50 states. PC NATIONS has information on flags, currency, time zones, health and trade data, tourist attractions, and even national anthems for over 175 countries.

EVALUATION

These programs are part of a new generation of software that will dramatically change the nature of library/classroom research. Administrators will appreciate the economy of a research instrument that does not have to be replaced because of student damage or missing pages. Teachers will appreciate the immediate access to useful information, much of which can be displayed using LCD projection systems. Finally, students will appreciate the availability of fresh, regularly updated information and maps, which can easily be reprinted for inclusion in reports. Except for the spartan nature of the documentation, there are very few weaknesses in these programs. Programs like these will eventually be part of the reference area of nearly all libraries—school and public. Their relative low cost also makes them suitable for home use.

TITLE: POINT OF VIEW

Producer: Scholastic
Grade Level: 7–12
Suggested Retail: $249.95
Required Memory: 1MB
Available for: Apple IIGS
Subject Area: U.S. history
Copy-Protected: Yes
Type: Tool, database

DESCRIPTION

This CD-ROM-based package gives students and teachers very rapid access to a huge assemblage of information consisting of milestones in U.S. history, dynamic charts and maps, graphics, essays, documents, and audio and visual presentation. Students or teachers can move through the data as their interests dictate or to pursue specific hypotheses. In addition to serving as a valuable research tool, the program makes it easy for users to add to the database and to devise their own presentations.

The person entering POINT OF VIEW begins with a "Milestone View," which can easily be changed to any other time from 1756 to 1990. The categories and topics listed on the milestone screens can be controlled by the student or teacher. The user simply clicks on a topic, and information becomes immediately available on the screen. In many cases, it is also easily possible to obtain more detailed or cross-referenced information.

Users can expand the database by adding supplementary information on existing topics or by adding new topics. For example, students of American literature could add literature categories, or students could add information about their own family histories. Users can digitize pictures and add them to the database. It is also possible to interface this program with laserdiscs or other media. For example, a student researching the American civil rights movement might use POINT OF VIEW in combination with Optical Data's MARTIN LUTHER KING to access vast amounts of information integrated with the full range of American history.

EVALUATION

The charts and maps offer an especially useful tool. The user can follow prompts and select a map to research a topic or to demonstrate a point. By following further prompts, the user can obtain charted data focusing on specific areas of the map. Even more dramatically, the user can scroll along the timeline, and the appropriate changes will instantly appear on both the map and the chart—giving the appearance of animation. This dynamic presentation of information is impossible in a textbook format.

Version 1.1 runs faster than the old version, but there are still delays. Good teachers can fill the time lags with useful activities, such as predicting what will appear on the screen after the delay.

TITLE: PRINT SHOP

Producer: Broderbund
Grade Level: 3–Adult
Suggested Retail: $49.95
Required Memory: 128K
Available for: Apple II family, MS-DOS, Macintosh
Subject Areas: All
Copy-Protected: Yes (backup disk available)
Type: Utility

DESCRIPTION

PRINT SHOP is a popular graphics and text generator that can be used to design posters, banners, greeting cards, and letterheads. Choices for borders, fonts, and graphics are made with simple keystrokes using the arrow keys and the return key. A preview option allows the user to see the final product before it is printed. The popularity of this program has spawned many companion programs and imitators. The color version of PRINT SHOP takes advantage of 3- and 4-color ribbons in generating colorful posters, banners, and so on. PRINT SHOP COMPANION and GRAPHICS LIBRARY 1, 2, and 3 plus HOLIDAY EDITION, PARTY EDITION, and SAMPLER EDITION provide added graphics, fonts, or borders to complement those on the original disk. PRINT SHOP's Teacher's Guide shares ideas to expand the use of the program beyond merely "decorating" the classroom. Typical social studies applications of the program involve making posters, banners, or cover sheets for reports. PRINT SHOP COMPANION also includes a calendar option that enables students to create calendars focusing on such topics as historical events and the customs of various cultures.

EVALUATION

In the hands of a creative teacher, PRINT SHOP and its companion programs can be used effectively in the social studies classroom. Similar programs include the GARFIELD series by Random House, BANNER MANIA by Broderbund, PROFESSIONAL SIGN MAKER and SUPER SIGN MAKER by Sunburst, STICKYBEAR PRINTER by Weekly Reader Software, and the WALT DISNEY series by Walt Disney.

TITLE: REVOLUTIONS: PAST, PRESENT, AND FUTURE

Producer: Focus Media, Inc.
Grade Level: 7–12
Suggested Retail: $159 ($477 for network version)
Required Memory: 48K
Available for: Apple II family, TRS 80
Subject Area: World history
Copy-Protected: Yes (backup available)
Type: Tutorial

DESCRIPTION

This package teaches students by taking them step by step through the historical analysis surrounding several revolutions. Based on these descriptions, students can form conclusions about the causes and effects of such events.

The program itself consists of five parts:

Part I: Presents a tutorial on the definition of revolution.
Part II: Reviews the American, French, and Russian Revolutions in terms of chronology of events and their social, political, and economic impact.
Part III: Teaches "how to analyze a revolution."
Parts IV and V: Generate graphs from data created, and help measure instability and "revolutionary potential."

EVALUATION

The program organizes this unit of study in a logical fashion using valuable thinking and analysis skills. It encourages research. However, because it lacks graphics, much of the program is presented using a descriptive format that lacks visual appeal. Overall, it offers a good basis for unit research projects on revolutions.

TITLE: THE RIPPLE THAT CHANGED AMERICAN HISTORY

Producer: Tom Snyder Productions
Grade Level: 5–12
Suggested Retail: $69.95 lab pack; $225.00 includes 10 disks
Required Memory: 64K
Available for: Apple, IBM
Subject Area: American history
Copy-Protected: Yes (backup disk included)
Type: Game

DESCRIPTION

This program challenges users to locate a destructive "ripple" by listening to conversations from the past and doing "ripscans" over a U.S. map to find the location of the problem. Once learners believe they are "on top of" the ripple, they can attempt to "unrip" it. If they are wrong, the game is over. Otherwise, they get another problem. Students practice thinking skills in addition to learning historical information.

EVALUATION

The program promotes the use of textbooks and reference books. It gives a sense of logical sequence and timelines. This is a good program for small-group activity. The limited graphics, however, reduce motivation. Learners' ability to "tunnel" forward and backward in time is somewhat obscured because they are not told the current year, which can lead to confusion and disorientation. A "year meter" of some sort would be an improvement. This program provides a reasonably good exercise for small groups if they have some previous, overall knowledge of American history. However, as we indicated in Chapter 4, a major problem is that students often have not covered all the historical facts in RIPPLE until the end of the course—this reduces its usefulness as a review mechanism until the very end of the semester.

TITLE: SIMPOLICON

Producer: Cross Cultural Software
Grade Level: 6–12
Suggested Retail: $120.00
Required Memory: 48K
Available for: Apple II series
Subject Areas: Economics, political science
Copy-Protected: Yes
Type: Simulation

DESCRIPTION

SIMPOLICON challenges the user to make decisions regarding the allocation of various resources. Their goal is to create and maintain a stable, secure country with a well-balanced economy in order to achieve personal, group, and national success. Diversion of resources to military uses for "invasion" purposes is part of the simulation.

EVALUATION

Students are offered realistically simulated decision-making situations faced by nations at various stages of economic development. However, no graphics are used in this program, and it may tend to become too statistic-oriented with all decision outcomes connected to dollar values. That is, success or failure of students' decisions is measured strictly in economic terms. The program requires 10 or more hours for completion, including periodic debriefings. If a curriculum has an economic component, SIMPOLICON may prove valuable.

TITLE: START (Stimulus and Response Tools for Experiments in Memory, Learning, Cognition, and Perception)

Producer: Conduit
Grade Level: 11–12, college
Suggested Retail: $150.00
Required Memory: 48K/192K
Available for: Apple II series, IBM
Subject Area: Psychology
Copy-Protected: Yes (backup disk included)
Type: Simulation, tool

DESCRIPTION

START provides a series of 15 experiments in psychology including reaction time, precognition, prototype formation, problem solving, pitch memory, dot enumeration, probability learning, and same/different distinctions (pitch, color, shape). It makes excellent use of the characteristics of the computer keyboard and monitor to provide a setting for these experiments. For example, to test reaction time, the participant is asked to stare at the center of the monitor, wait for a dot to flash, and then strike a key as soon as possible after viewing the flash. The program measures reaction time in hundredths of a second. Each experiment is set up as a lesson, complete with descriptions of current, major theories and laws in the field of psychology. In addition, results of these experiments can be compared to existing norms and expected outcomes.

EVALUATION

The documentation for START is both sophisticated and well written. The program is menu driven. Very little set-up time is required. It makes good use of computer equipment. This is an excellent tool for a high school or early college psychology course. Student interest is greatly enhanced by performing experiments either in a computer lab or, in some cases, as part of a classroom demonstration with an LCD projection system. This is a great opportunity for the classroom teacher to add a "scientific" aspect to a psychology course that is routinely oriented toward the textbook and "selected readings."

TITLE: STICKYBEAR TOWN BUILDER

Producer: Weekly Reader
Grade Level: 1–3
Suggested Retail: $39.95
Required Memory: 48K
Available for: Apple II series
Subject Area: Geography, social studies
Copy-Protected: Yes
Type: Simulation, game

DESCRIPTION

This program allows the user to construct a sample town on the screen using either a mouse or keyboard commands. Once the town is completed, the user can then "take a drive" around this new community or play a hide-and-seek game locating 12 items hidden at random in the town.

EVALUATION

This is an excellent program for teaching the concept of neighborhood and community to very young learners. Towns can be "saved" and "loaded" for later use. The program permits ample "escape" opportunities. It would work better if it provided a brief tutorial on directions, and some aerial views of buildings are difficult to distinguish. This program lends itself well to any primary curriculum that has a unit on map directions or neighborhood services.

TITLE: SURVEY TAKER

Producer: Scholastic Software
Grade Level: 5–12
Suggested Retail: $29.95
Required Memory: 64K
Available for: Apple II series
Subject Areas: All
Copy-Protected: Yes
Type: Tool, utility

DESCRIPTION

This useful utility permits the user to construct a survey in the multiple-choice format. The completed survey may be printed out. Once the survey has been completed, the user may compile the results and present them in either graph or data form.

EVALUATION

The program provides a very effective way of constructing a questionnaire for a class or an organization. It also gives some insight into organizing and presenting information. A problem is that use of SURVEY TAKER may become tedious: going from one section of the program to another requires some loading time and the user must access the disk on each occasion. However, with a few reservations, this is an excellent tool for political science and government classes, where taking a poll of student or community feelings is a useful exercise. It could also be used as an election analysis tool, and poses interesting possibilities for checking societal norms against local norms for a sociology class.

TITLE: TIMELINER

Producer: Tom Snyder Productions
Grade Level: K–12
Suggested Retail: $59.95; lab pack $180; 10 data disks $140; combination $245
Required Memory: 64K
Available for: Apple, IBM
Subject Area: History, social studies
Copy-Protected: Yes (backup disk included)
Type: Tool, utility

DESCRIPTION

TIMELINER permits the user to create timeline diagrams and print out the result in a "sideways" fashion suitable for wall display or bulletin boards. These diagrams may be created from scratch or downloaded from any of several available data disks (American History, World History, Pre-American History, Science and Technology, The Arts, Events of the '70s and '80s, A Day in the Life of . . . , Everything is Relative, and Fun with Facts and Figures). Preset timelines can then be used "as is" or altered or merged to fit a specific application. The clear documentation makes extensive use of mock-ups of actual screens.

EVALUATION

The program is easy to use. All screens are menu driven. It could be used with an LCD-display system to introduce a unit of study, but the limitations of the screen would reduce the visual perspective. The program allows for the expansion and compression of timelines as needed. This is an excellent utility program for use at many grade levels.

APPENDIX A

Glossary of Important Terms

Academic Learning Time (ALT). The amount of time a student spends attending to relevant academic tasks while performing those tasks at a high rate of success.

ALT. See *Academic Learning Time.*

Artificial Intelligence. The use of computers to imitate or expand human intelligence. Computers that play chess usually employ artificial intelligence. Another example is found in "expert systems" being developed to offer doctors "second opinions" on their diagnoses of patients.

Authoring Language. A computer program that enables the user to enter commands that instruct the computer to carry out various tasks, such as the presentation of a drill or tutorial. An authoring language is usually easier to learn but less flexible than a programming language.

Auxiliary Storage Device. Any device (such as a tape or a floppy disk) on which programs and other computer data can be stored in order to be transferred into the computer's memory.

BASIC. One of the most commonly used programming languages for microcomputers.

Branching Programmed Instruction. A form of programmed instruction in which the nature of each step in a learning sequence is determined by the student's response at the previous step.

Byte. A character stored in the computer's memory.

CAI. See *Computer-Assisted Instruction.*

Cathode-Ray Tube (CRT). The "television" screen that displays output from the computer.

CBE. See *Computer-Based Education.*

CD-ROM Disk. A laser-optical disk that closely resembles a compact music disk and holds much more information than can be stored on an ordinary floppy disk. At the present time, it is possible for ordinary users to read data from these disks but not to store information on them.

CMI. See *Computer-Managed Instruction.*

Computer-Assisted Instruction (CAI). The use of the computer to provide instruction directly to the learner. When students run a drill, tutorial, or simulation, they are engaged in CAI.

Computer-Based Education (CBE). A synonym for computer-managed instruction.

Computer-Managed Instruction (CMI). The use of the computer to coordinate instructional activities. CMI may be used in conjunction with

CAI, but it may also be used to coordinate noncomputerized modes of instruction.

Computer Program. A set of instructions that make the computer carry out specified operations.

Corrective Feedback. Information that explains to the learner the nature of a mistake or suggests ways to move from the incorrect answer to a correct answer.

Courseware. Computer software designed for instructional purposes.

CRT. See *Cathode-Ray Tube*.

Cursor. The "prompt" (often a flashing box or a flashing line) that indicates where the next entry will take place on the CRT screen.

Database. An organized set of information. A database management program provides electronic access to a set of information by permitting entry, storage, sorting, and retrieval of data.

Disk Drive. A mechanism into which floppy disks are inserted in order to transfer information to and from the computer's random-access memory.

Diskette. See *Floppy Disk*.

Documentation. Hardcopy or electronic information that describes how to use a piece of hardware or software.

Drill. A program that provides repeated practice and feedback regarding a skill or concept.

Electronic Bulletin Board. An electronic communication system, usually accessed via modem, that enables users to share information about topics of common interest.

Fax Machine. A machine that scans a document, diagram, drawing, or other written work and sends the digitized signal over normal phone lines to another machine, which receives the signal and replicates the document.

Feedback. Information indicating that a response is right or wrong. Feedback may be either positive or negative.

Floppy Disk. A small and compact auxiliary storage device on which information can be kept for subsequent transfer to the computer's random-access memory.

Gradebook. A program designed to keep records and generate reports on student performance.

Graphics. Diagrams and pictures drawn with the aid of the computer.

Hardcopy. Output that is printed on a permanent surface (such as paper) instead of merely appearing on a temporary surface (such as a CRT screen).

Hardware. The physical equipment that comprises a computer system. It is differentiated from the software, which runs on this physical equipment.

Help Screen. A screenful of information that provides instructions on a specific topic or answers to a question that the learner asks. Help screens usually appear in response to a request initiated by the learner.

Hypermedia. A programming strategy that permits a user to examine a segment of text or graphic information and then branch immediately to any other segment as needed.

Hypertext. See *Hypermedia*.

ICAI. See *Intelligent Computer-Assisted Instruction*.

Input. Information that is sent into the computer's memory, usually from a keyboard, from an auxiliary storage device, or through a modem.

Intelligent Computer-Assisted Instruction (ICAI). The application of principles of artificial intelligence to computer-assisted instruction, which enables the computer to analyze learner characteristics and to adjust its presentation of information in response to these characteristics.

Interactive Videodisc System. A combination of a computer and a videodisc that displays visual and auditory sequences in response to input provided by the learner.

Interface Card. An electronic connection device that fits inside the computer to add additional elements (such as disk drives, printers, and modems) to a computer system.

Joystick. An instrument that permits the user to move the cursor or in some other way control movement on the CRT screen.

Keyboard. The "typewriter" portion of the computer, which permits entry of various characters into the computer's memory.

Kilobyte (K). One thousand bytes. The computer's memory size is normally indicated in kilobytes. (Note that a thousand kilobytes comprise a megabyte, abbreviated as "MB.")

LCD (Liquid Crystal Display) Projection System. A mechanism that can be attached to a computer to project its output onto a large movie screen, instead of (or in addition to) the regular computer monitor.

Light Pen. A device, similar to a pen, that permits input into the computer when it is held near the CRT screen and its button is pushed.

Linear Programmed Instruction. A form of programmed teaching in which all learners go through the lesson from beginning to end in exactly the same sequence.

Memory Expansion Card. A device with memory chips which when inserted into the computer increases its random-access memory.

Memory Size. The number of bytes of random-access memory that the computer makes available to the user. In general, computers with greater memory sizes can run more complex programs and store larger amounts of data than those with smaller memories.

Menu. A screenful of information and prompts that enable the learner to choose from a list of activities that the computer may perform.

Microcomputer. A relatively small computer that employs a microprocessor. Microcomputers are also referred to as "personal computers." They are smaller than mini-computers, which in turn are smaller than mainframe computers.

Modem. A device for transferring information from one computer to another, usually across telephone lines.

Monitor. A CRT or LCD screen that is connected to a computer system and displays the input going into the system and the output coming from it.

Monochrome Monitor. A monitor that displays output in a single color on a background of another single color (for example, black on white). It is distinguished from a color monitor, which will generate a wide variety of background and foreground colors.

Mouse. A device for moving the cursor or in some other way controlling movement on the CRT screen. A mouse differs from a joystick in that it controls movement more precisely but is less suited to many gamelike activities.

Negative Feedback. Information indicating that the learner's response was incorrect. If negative feedback also explains to the learner the nature of the mistake, it becomes corrective feedback.

Network. A series of computers that are connected in some way. Some networks are permanent (the computers always work together), whereas others are temporary (the computers may be joined together for particular operations).

Output. The information provided by the computer in response to instructions or input from a user. The output usually appears on the CRT or on a sheet of paper, but it may be sent directly to an auxiliary storage device or to another computer.

Paddles. Tools for moving the cursor or for producing some other kind of movement on the CRT screen. Like the joystick, paddles are used mostly in gamelike applications of the computer.

Peripheral Devices. Any of the devices that are added on to the main computer system. Peripherals include disk drives, printers, joysticks, and modems.

Port. An external point of connection for the peripheral devices associated with a computer system, such as a printer or modem. Ports often come built into the computer and serve the same functions as interface cards, which often must be added to the system.

Positive Feedback. Information indicating that the learner gave the correct response. Positive feedback is usually considered to be a form of reinforcement.

Printer. A mechanism for generating hardcopy, printed output from a computer.

Programming Language. A set of rules and commands that instruct the computer to carry out various tasks. A programming language is usually more difficult to learn but also more flexible than an authoring language.

Prompt. This term has two separate meanings in instructional computing. First, the cursor or some other symbol is referred to as a "prompt" when the computer is waiting for the learner to make a response. Second, a clue that stimulates the learner to give a correct answer is also called a prompt. Prompts of this second type usually appear when the learner has made a mistake or requested help.

Public Domain Software. Software that is not protected by copyright restrictions. It is legal to make copies of public domain software.

RAM. See *Random-Access Memory*.

Random-Access Memory (RAM). The temporary portion of the computer's memory. All information in RAM is erased the moment the computer is turned off. Information is loaded into RAM through the keyboard, from a floppy disk or another auxiliary storage device, or through some other input device.

Read-Only Memory (ROM). The permanent portion of the computer's memory. ROM is not erased when the computer is turned off. Part of the ROM includes instructions to automatically transfer information into RAM. Information available in ROM is immediately available as soon as the computer is turned on, but ROM cannot be easily modified.

Reinforcement. The strengthening of a behavior by providing pleasant consequences. In computer-assisted instruction, reinforcement usually consists of either positive feedback, some sort of pleasant visual or auditory display, or the opportunity to engage in a pleasant activity (such as an electronic game).

Resolution. The degree of precision or clarity produced in graphic displays. High-resolution graphics are created with a large number of tiny dots on the screen. Low-resolution graphics are created with small squares. Pictures drawn with higher resolution look much more realistic.

ROM. See *Read-Only Memory*.

Scanner. A machine that takes a picture, map, diagram, or other visual input and stores it in digitized form for later reproduction on a computer screen or in printed format.

Shell Program. A computerized drill program into which users can easily insert their own instructional material. For example, a vocabulary shell program might permit the teacher or student to insert words or definitions, and then the computer would provide a drill on those terms.

Simulation. A program that imitates realistic events that would otherwise be impossible or difficult to incorporate into the classroom because the presentation would be expensive, dangerous, time-consuming, unethical, or otherwise impractical.

Software. The instructions and information (program and data) given to the computer to make it perform designated activities. The software is the set of instructions that makes the hardware carry out its appropriate functions.

Spreadsheet. A program that permits the organized entry and tabulation of numerical data in such a way as to provide automatic recalculation of formulas programmed by the user.

Telecommunications. The process of communicating between computers via modem.

Test Generator. A program that automatically generates tests or quizzes, using items and guidelines entered by the instructor.

Tutorial. A program that provides instruction on a topic. A tutorial is usually a computerized presentation of branching programmed instruction.

User Friendliness. The ability of a program to accept and respond to input in such a way that the user can easily interpret and make use of the computer's response.

Videodisc. An auxiliary storage device that employs laser technology to present audio and video displays. Videodiscs can be used in combination with a microcomputer for interactive instruction.

Word Processor. A computer program that enables the computer to be used to type and edit documents.

APPENDIX B

Software Summaries

The following table contains information pertaining to the software programs mentioned in this book and additional software of interest to social studies teachers.

The first two columns give the *Title* and the *Vendor* of each program. Addresses for vendors may be found in Appendix D. The third column designates the *Category* of each program. *General* software includes programs that fit into many subject areas. If there were very few programs available in a field of study, these were also lumped into the General category. *Elementary* refers to programs specifically useful to children in early elementary grades. Programs in this category usually cover general, basic topics, like community, friendship, and basic map reading skills. The categories *Geography, History, Government* and *Economics* are obvious.

The *Computer* column describes computer brands for which the software is available. Abbreviations are as follows: *II* stands for the Apple II series and compatibles. *IIGS* means that the program is designed specially for the Apple IIGS. (Nearly all programs labeled for the Apple II will also run on the GS, and several programs designated in the table for the Apple II have a separate version that takes advantage of the full capabilities of the GS.) Programs labeled *II* (but not *IIGS*) will run with the Macintosh LC's adapter card. *MS* is an abbreviation for MS-DOS, which refers to IBM and compatibles (Tandy 1000 and others). The label *64* stands for the Commodore 64 computer. *Mac* refers to the Macintosh computer. Note that new releases will sometimes render these descriptions outdated.

Grade refers to grade level based on the publisher's identification. K is kindergarten, the numbers 1–12 correspond to grade levels.

Finally, the *Comment* column briefly describes the topics covered in the program. Many of these programs are described in greater detail elsewhere in this book, and cross references can easily be found in the index.

TITLE	VENDOR	TOPIC
1865	Harcourt Brace Jovanovich	History
20TH-CENTURY AMERICA	Educational Activities	History
49'ers	Hartley	History
88 VOTE	Optical Data	History
<in COMMON> GEOGRAPHY	Sunburst	Geography
<in COMMON> PEOPLE, PLACES, & THINGS	Sunburst	History, Geography
AD GAME	MicroEd	General
ADVENTURE ISLAND	Queue	General
ADVENTURES WITH CHARTS AND GRAPHS: PROJECT ZOO	National Geographic Society	Elementary
AFRICA	Educational Activities	Geography
AFRICAN GEOGRAPHY	Sunshine Computer Software	Geography
AGENT USA	Scholastic	Geography
AIR POLLUTION	EME Corporation	Geography
ALEXANDER THE GREAT	MicroEd	History
ALL ABOUT AMERICA	Unicorn	Geography, History
AMENDMENTS TO THE CONSTITUTION	Classroom Consortia Media	History, Government
AMERICA COAST TO COAST	Mindscape	Geography

COMPUTER	GRADES	COMMENT
II, MS	7–12	Simulation dealing with reconstruction after the Civil War.
II	7–12	Database tool for solving problems about American history.
II	5–10	Simulation of California gold rush.
Mac	9–12	Interactive videodisc developed by ABC News.
MS	6–Adult	Students use inference skills to categorize geographical facts.
MS	4–6	Students categorize people and places from history and geography.
64	5–10	Tutorial and practice on reading and interpreting bar graphs.
II	3–10	Simulation (stranded on island) social studies, and decision making.
II	4–8	Students practice activities related to charts and graphs.
II	7–12	Clarification of misconceptions—drill on geography of Africa.
MS	7–12	Drill based on map of Africa.
II, MS	4–10	Simulation of agent traveling U.S. trying to disarm a bomb.
II, MS	9–12	Simulation of carbon monoxide poisoning in urban environment.
64	5–9	Facts about Alexander the Great.
II	2–6	Quizzes and games on American facts for young people.
II, MS	8–12	Factual treatment of amendments—includes crossword puzzles.
II	4–9	Facts about the states.

TITLE	VENDOR	TOPIC
AMERICA MOVES WEST	Orange Cherry	History
AMERICAN DISCOVERY	Great Wave	Geography
AMERICAN EXPLORERS	Aquarius	History
AMERICAN FOREIGN POLICY	Focus Media	History
AMERICAN GOVERNMENT	Queue	Government
AMERICAN GOVERNMENT I–IV	Intellectual Software	Government
AMERICAN HISTORY	Learning Arts	History
AMERICAN HISTORY: 1865–1912	Queue	History
AMERICAN HISTORY ACHIEVEMENT I: TO 1860	Microcomputer Workshops Courses	History
AMERICAN HISTORY ACHIEVEMENT II: 1860–1890	Microcomputer Workshops Courses	History
AMERICAN HISTORY ADVENTURE	Queue	History
AMERICAN HISTORY ADVENTURES	Learning Arts	History
AMERICAN HISTORY GAMES	Queue	History
AMERICAN HISTORY KEYWORD SERIES	Focus Media	History
AMERICAN INDIANS	Right On	History
AMERICAN INVENTIONS	Right On	History
AMERICAN PEOPLE	Focus Media	History

COMPUTER	GRADES	COMMENT
II, 64	4–10	Facts about history of western U.S.
Mac	4–12	Games and activities to explore American geographical concepts.
II, MS	7–12	Facts about early explorers.
II	9–12	Factual focus on post–Civil War American history.
II, Mac, MS	7–12	Tutorial covers wide range of topics—good interaction.
II, MS	9–12	Five separate programs on key concepts of government.
II	4–8	Factual treatment of America 1607–1810.
II, MS	7–12	Comprehensive tutorial with plenty of help and testing.
II	10–12	Preparation for CEEB in American history.
II	10–12	Preparation for CEEB in American history.
II, MS	7–12	Gamelike drill on historical characters.
II	4–10	Factual and higher-level questions on American history.
II, 64	7–12	Several games review facts of American history.
II	7–12	Guess vocabulary words related to U.S. history from clues.
II, 64	4–8	Facts about Native Americans from all parts of U.S.
II, 64	5–10	Facts about and impact of six major inventions.
II, 64	5–12	Quiz/game on facts about U.S. history.

TITLE	VENDOR	TOPIC
AMERICAN PRESIDENCY	MicroEd	History, Government
AMERICA'S PRESIDENTS	Intellectual Software	History
ANASAZI CIVILIZATION	Harcourt Brace Jovanovich	History
ANCIENT CIVILIZATIONS	MicroEd	History
ANCIENT CIVILIZATIONS	Right On	History
ANCIENT CIVILIZATIONS AND THE MIDDLE AGES	Focus Media	History
ANCIENT CIVILIZATIONS KEYWORD	Focus Media	History
ANCIENT ROME	Teach Yourself by Computer	History
AND IF REELECTED	Focus Media	Government
ANNAM: A DEVELOPING COUNTRY	Educational Activities	History
APPLEWORKS	Claris	General
AROUND AND ABOUT THE CIVIL WAR	Orange Cherry	History
AROUND AND ABOUT THE REVOLUTIONARY WAR	Orange Cherry	History
ASK: A SURVEY KIT	William K. Bradford	General
ATLAS EXPLORER	Springboard	Geography
ATLAS*MAPMAKER	Strategic Mapping	Geography
AWARD MAKER PLUS	Baudville	General

COMPUTER	GRADES	COMMENT
64	4–10	Facts about duties and history of American presidency.
II	9–12	Facts about the presidents.
II, MS	7–12	Simulation dealing with the disappearance of the Anasazi Indian tribe.
64	4–8	Geographical locations of ancient civilizations.
II, 64	6–10	Facts about early Greece and Rome.
II	6–12	Tutorial and review questions on stated topic.
II	7–12	Guess vocabulary related to ancient history from clues.
II	6–12	Facts about daily life in ancient Rome.
II, MS	9–12	Excellent simulation requires student to run for president.
II	6–12	Simulation requires student to serve as dictator in Southeast Asia.
II	4–Adult	Word processor integrated with database and spreadsheet programs.
II, 64	4–10	Gamelike quiz on facts about Civil War.
II, 64	4–10	Gamelike quiz on facts about Revolutionary War.
II	9–12	Tool to enable students to conduct surveys and analyze data.
Mac	4–12	Detailed map of the world that zooms in for information and details.
Mac	9–12	Tool for creating professional-quality maps.
II	4–Adult	Generates certificates that can be used as awards for achievement.

TITLE	VENDOR	TOPIC
AZIMUTH	Graphsoft	Geography
BALANCE OF POWER	Mindscape	Government
BALANCE OF POWER 1990	Mindscape	Government
BALANCE OF THE PLANET	Chris Crawford Games	Ecology
BANK STREET FILER	Broderbund	General
BANK STREET SCHOOL FILER	Scholastic	General
BANK STREET WRITER	Scholastic	General
BARON	Britannica Software	Economics
BEGINNING GEOGRAPHY	Right On	Geography
BEYOND THE RISING SUN: DISCOVERING JAPAN	Educational Activities	Geography
BIFS: BASICS IN FORECASTING	Conduit	General
BIG BOOK MAKER: TALL TALES AND AMERICAN FOLK TALES	Pelican	History
BOOKWORM	MECC	General
BUSINESS CLASS	MEDIAGENIC	Geography
BUSINESS ORGANIZATION	Queue	Economics
BUSINESS SIMULATIONS PACKAGE	Queue	Economics
CALENDAR	MicroEd	Elementary
CALENDAR CRAFTER	MECC	General

COMPUTER	GRADES	COMMENT
Mac	9–12	Tool to create maps from various perspectives.
II, 64	7–12	Simulation using maps and database to direct global politics.
Mac	7–12	Uses post–1987 events to update BALANCE OF POWER.
Mac, MS	8–12	Students simulate a balance of economic and ecological factors.
II	4–12	Simple database program—many social studies files available.
II, 64	5–12	Simple database management program with many applications.
II, 64	5–12	Simple word processing program with many applications.
Mac	6–12	Simulation of activity on the real estate market.
II, 64	1–4	Geography facts for very young learners.
II	7–12	Simulation of being member of Japanese family to learn about culture.
MS	10–Adult	Students simulate population and economics projections.
II, MS	4–10	Story-starter graphics for stories on folk tales.
II	3–8	Students compile databases of information about books they read.
Mac	7–12	Uses hyperstacks to present information of interest to travelers.
II	9–12	Factual information on different types of businesses.
II	9–12	Simulations teach economics principles.
64	K–2	Learn days of week, etc.
IIGS	5–Adult	Generates calendars that can focus on specific activities.

TITLE	VENDOR	TOPIC
CAMPAIGN	Queue	History
CAMPAIGN MATH	Mindplay	Government
CANADA	Intellectual Software	Geography
CANADIAN FACTS STACKS	Palm Island	Geography
CARAVAN: THE ADVENTURES OF MARCO POLO	Queue	History
CASTELLON	Harcourt Brace Jovanovich	Government
CERTIFICATE MAKER	Springboard	General
CHILDREN'S WRITING AND PUBLISHING CENTER	Learning Company	General
CHOICE OR CHANCE?	Rand McNally	History
CHOICES, CHOICES: ON THE PLAYGROUND	Tom Snyder	Elementary
CHOICES, CHOICES: TAKING RESPONSIBILITY	Tom Snyder	Elementary
CHRISTOPHER COLUMBUS	MicroEd	History
CIVIL WAR	Hartley	History
CLIMATES OF THE WORLD	William K. Bradford	Geography
COAST-TO-COAST AMERICA	Beard Sales	Geography
COLONIAL MERCHANT	Educational Activities	History

COMPUTER	GRADES	COMMENT
II	9–12	Simulation of military campaign in Hundred Years' War.
II, MS	3–10	Simple simulation of election campaign.
II, MS	9–12	Facts about Canada.
Mac	4–12	Hyperstacks on Canada and provinces.
II	5–12	Simulation of Marco Polo's trip to the Orient.
II, MS	9–12	Simulation of political science activity for secondary students.
II	5–Adult	Generates certificates that can reward achievement.
II	2–10	Desktop publishing easily accessible to young people.
II	7–12	Factual coverage of history focusing on cause and effect.
II, MS	K–6	Simulation of decision-making skills when kid moves into new school.
II, MS	K–6	Simulation of decision-making skills when tattling is possible.
64	4–10	Facts about Christopher Columbus.
II	8–10	Simulation of American Civil War.
IIGS	4–6	Simulation requiring students to understand climates and predict weather.
II, MS	3–9	Review of facts about the states.
II	6–12	Simulation of activity of a colonial merchant before Revolutionary War.

TITLE	VENDOR	TOPIC
COLONIAL TIMES DATABASES	Sunburst	History
COMMUNICATION	Right On	History
COMMUNITY HELPERS	Right On	Elementary
COMMUNITY HELPERS: PUBLIC AND PRIVATE	Orange Cherry	Elementary
COMMUNITY SEARCH	McGraw-Hill	History
COMPTON'S MULTIMEDIA ENCYCLOPEDIA	Encyclopedia Britannica	General
CONGRESS	Scholastic	Government
CONGRESSIONAL BILL SIMULATOR	Focus Media	Government
CONGRESS STACK: 101ST CONGRESS 1989–90	Highlighted Data	Government
CONSTITUTIONAL AMENDMENTS	Queue	History, Government
CONSTITUTIONAL LAW	Intellectual Software	Government
CONSTITUTION AND GOVERNMENT OF THE U.S.	Educational Activities	Government
CONSTITUTION OF THE UNITED STATES	Learning Arts	History, Government
CONSUMERS AND THE LAW	Educational Activities	Economics
CONTINENTS AND COUNTRIES	Mindscape	Geography
CONTRACTS LAW	Queue	Government
CONVERSATIONS WITH GREAT AMERICANS	Focus Media	History

COMPUTER	GRADES	COMMENT
II	3–8	Database files for BANK STREET SCHOOL FILER.
II, 64	6–10	Facts about the history of communication.
II, 64	2–4	Facts about community helpers.
II, 64	3–6	Facts about community helpers.
II	5–10	Simulation of search for a new homeland after a drought.
MS, Mac	4–Adult	Comprehensive electronic encyclopedia.
II	7–12	APPLEWORKS databases regarding Congressional activities.
II	8–12	Simulation of the progress of a bill through Congress.
Mac	11–12	Comprehensive Hypertext stacks (will be updated).
II, MS	8–12	Facts about amendments to the Constitution.
II	10–12	Basic principles of constitutional law.
II	7–12	Facts about Constitution based on case studies.
II	7–12	Historical background for each article and amendment.
II	7–12	Basic facts about consumer law.
II	5–12	Database on worldwide facts.
II	9–Adult	Facts about contractual law.
II	6–12	Students use famous people as "primary sources" to learn history.

TITLE	VENDOR	TOPIC
COUNTRIES AND CAPITALS	Micro Learningware	Geography
COUNTRIES OF THE WORLD	Grolier	Geography
CREATE LESSONS	Hartley	General
CREATE LESSONS—ADVANCED	Hartley	General
CREATING THE U.S. CONSTITUTION	Educational Activities	History
CREDIT AND BANKING	Queue	Economics
CREDIT: THE FIRST STEPS	MCE	Economics
CRIMINAL LAW	Intellectual Software	Government
CRIMINAL PROCEDURE	Intellectual Software	Government
CROSSCOUNTRY CALIFORNIA	Didatech Software	Geography
CROSSCOUNTRY CANADA	Didatech Software	Geography
CROSSCOUNTRY TEXAS	Didatech Software	Geography
CROSSCOUNTRY USA	Didatech Software	Geography
CROSSWORD MAGIC	Mindscape	General
CULTURE 1.0	Cultural Resources	History
DAY TO FIND OUT	Orange Cherry	General
DECADES	Queue	History
DECISIONS	EMC	Economics
DECISIONS, DECISIONS: COLONIZATION	Tom Snyder	History

COMPUTER	GRADES	COMMENT
II	6–9	Drill on facts about nations of the world.
II	6–12	Information on nations of the world.
II	4–12	Authoring system to generate tutorials and drills.
II	6–12	Authoring system to generate tutorials and tests.
II	7–12	Student simulates participation in the Constitutional Convention.
II	9–12	Basic facts regarding credit and banking.
II	9–12	Basic facts about using credit.
II	9–12	Basic principles of criminal justice.
II	9–12	Basic principles of criminal justice.
II	5–12	Simulation of transporting commodities throughout California.
II	5–12	Simulation of transporting commodities throughout Canada.
II	5–12	Simulation of transporting commodities throughout Texas.
II	5–12	Simulation of transporting commodities throughout the U.S.
II	3–Adult	Generates well-designed crossword puzzles.
Mac	9–12	Humanities information for units on Western Civilization.
II	7–10	Simulations of four major roles in society.
II	7–12	Guess dates of events in U.S. history.
II	9–12	Tutorials and simulations on economics (10 disks).
II, MS	5–12	Students simulate colonization in outer space using historical info.

TITLE	VENDOR	TOPIC
DECISIONS, DECISIONS: FOREIGN POLICY	Tom Snyder	History
DECISIONS, DECISIONS: IMMIGRATION	Tom Snyder	Economics, Government
DECISIONS, DECISIONS: ON THE CAMPAIGN TRAIL	Tom Snyder	Government
DECISIONS, DECISIONS: REVOLUTIONARY WARS	Tom Snyder	History
DECISIONS, DECISIONS: TELEVISION	Tom Snyder	General
DECISIONS, DECISIONS: THE BUDGET PROCESS	Tom Snyder	Economics, Government
DECISIONS, DECISIONS: URBANIZATION	Tom Snyder	History, Government
DEMOCOMP	Focus Media	History
DEMOCRACY	Right On	Government
DEMO-GRAPHICS: POPULATIONS AND PROJECTIONS	Conduit	General
DESERT	William K. Bradford	Geography
DIFFUSION GAME	Conduit	General
DINOSAUR DAYS	Teach Yourself by Computer	History
DINOSAUR DIG	Mindscape	History
DIRECTION AND DISTANCE	MicroEd	Geography
DISCOVER THE WORLD	Hartley	History

COMPUTER	GRADES	COMMENT
II, MS	8–12	Simulation of superpower decision making.
II, MS	8–12	Students simulate decision regarding admission of immigrants.
II, MS	7–12	Students simulate campaign for president.
II, MS	5–12	Students govern a province during a revolutionary movement.
II, MS	8–12	Simulation studies role of media and media ethics.
II, MS	8–12	Students simulate vote on a controversial spending bill in Congress.
II, MS	5–12	Simulation of conflicts that arise during urbanization processes.
II, 64	6–12	Maps of various eras of U.S. history.
II, 64	5–10	Basic facts about government, especially democracy.
II	9–12	Database and tools to make population projections.
IIGS	3–6	Graphics and animation support writing about the desert.
II	9–12	Students simulate the role of a change agent in the diffusion process.
II	2–6	Facts about dinosaurs.
II, MS	3–6	Facts about dinosaurs.
64	K–4	Basic facts about directions and distance.
II, MS	5–12	Students simulate a voyage to the Orient.

TITLE	VENDOR	TOPIC
DISRAELI AND THE EASTERN QUESTION	Queue	History
DOUBLE 'N' TROUBLE	Hartley	General
DR. KNOW'S GEOGRAPHY	MicroEd	Geography
EARLY HUMANS	Right On	History
EARTHQUEST	Earthquest, Inc.	Geography
EASTERN EUROPE	MicroEd	Geography
EASY SEARCH	Focus Media	Geography
EASY SEARCH: AMERICAN STUDIES	Focus Media	Geography
ECONOMIC INDICATORS	Heizer Software	Economics
ECONOMICS	Merrill Publishing Company	Economics
ECONOMICS KEYWORD	Focus Media	Economics
ECONOMICS: WHAT, HOW & FOR WHOM?	Focus Media	Economics
EDITORIAL FORUM SERIES	MicroEd	History
ELECTION OF 1912	Eastgate Systems	History
ELECTRONIC ENCYCLOPEDIA	Grolier	General
ELECTRONIC MAP CABINET	Highlighted Data	Geography
ELEMENTS OF ECONOMICS	Queue	Economics
EUROGRAPHICS	Sunshine Computer Software	Geography

COMPUTER	GRADES	COMMENT
II	9–12	Students take role of Disraeli in British foreign policy.
II	3–6	Gamelike review of many topics, including social studies.
64	5–10	Facts about countries and capitals.
II, 64	6–10	Facts about prehistoric people.
Mac	5–Adult	Hypertext presentation of facts about our planet.
64	5–12	Facts about Eastern Europe.
II	5–12	Database and simulation on countries around the world.
II	6–12	Database and simulation on information about the U.S.
Mac	9–12	Hypertext stack of 50 economic indicators 1960–1987.
II	9–12	Tutorial and simulation of economic concepts.
II	9–12	Development of vocabulary for economics.
II	10–12	Basic facts about economics (five disks).
II, 64	9–Adult	Problem-solving scenarios for current events discussions.
Mac	12	Hypertext simulation of presidential election of 1912.
Mac, MS	4–Adult	Electronic encyclopedia.
Mac	4–12	CD-ROM tool with MACDRAW software for designing maps.
II	9–12	Basics of elements (two disks).
MS	7–12	Basic facts about Europe—with maps.

TITLE	VENDOR	TOPIC
EUROPEAN NATIONS AND LOCATIONS	Edu-Tron	Geography
EUROPEAN STATES AND TRAITS	Britannica Software	Geography
EUROPEAN THEATRE	Hartley	History
EVALUATING PRESIDENTIAL LEADERSHIP	Focus Media	Government
EVENTS DAY-BY-DAY	Slippery Disks	History
EVIDENCE	Queue	Government
EXPEDITION TO SAGGARA	Intellectual Software	History
EXPLORATION TO THE JEFFERSONIAN ERA	Queue	History
EXPLORE AUSTRALIA	William K. Bradford	Geography
FACTORY	Sunburst	Economics
FACTS & FACES OF U.S. PRESIDENTS	Visatex	History
FACTS AND OPINIONS	Hartley	Geography, History
FACTS AND OPINIONS	MicroEd	Elementary
FACTS ON FILE NEWS DIGEST CD-ROM	Facts on File	History, Geography
FAMOUS BLACKS IN U.S. HISTORY	Frontier Software	History
FAMOUS WOMEN IN U.S. HISTORY	Frontier Software	History
FARM LIFE	Right On	Elementary
FINANCIAL COOKBOOK AND CONSUMER'S GUIDE	South-Western	Economics

COMPUTER	GRADES	COMMENT
II, 64	4–10	Basic facts about European countries.
II, MS	9–12	Sophisticated guessing game about European facts.
II	9–12	Simulation of activity in Europe during World War II.
II	9–12	Students conduct research; computer analyzes and presents data.
Mac	3–12	Hypertext stacks with events on various dates from 1905 to present.
II	9–Adult	The concept of evidence in courts of law (two disks).
II	6–12	Simulation of discovery of archaeological site in Egypt.
II, MS	7–12	Facts about pre-Jeffersonian explorers.
IIGS	4–6	Interactive exploration of geography and history of Australia.
II, MS	4–12	Thinking skills program that uses a factory environment.
Mac	6–12	Hypertext quiz format for U.S. presidents.
II	7–9	Review of facts on geography and history with focus on misconceptions.
64	3–6	Learn to distinguish fact from opinion.
Mac	7–12	Vast amount of information—access to 500,000 articles.
II	4–10	Facts about famous black Americans.
II	4–10	Facts on famous American women.
II, 64	K–3	Basic facts about farm life.
II, MS	9–12	Students solve financial problems.

TITLE	VENDOR	TOPIC
FOREIGN GOVERNMENTS AND THE UNITED NATIONS	SEI	Government
FREDWRITER	CUE	General
FRENCH REVOLUTION	Frontier Software	History
GAME OF PRESIDENTS	Intellectual Software	History
GAME SHOW	Advanced Ideas	General
GEOGRAPHIC JIGSAW	Eclat Microproducts	Geography
GEOGRAPHICS	Sunshine Computer Software	Geography
GEOGRAPHY GAMES	Intellectual Software	Geography
GEOGRAPHY KEYWORD	Focus Media	Geography
GEOGRAPHY QUIZ SERIES	Learning Arts	Geography
GEOGRAPHY SEARCH	McGraw-Hill	Geography
GEOWHIZ	Silver, Burdett & Ginn	Geography
GEOWORLD	Tom Snyder	Geography
GLOBAL EXPRESS ATLAS: THE WORLD	Orange Cherry	Geography
GLOBAL RECALL	World Games Institute	History, Geography
GLOBE MASTER II	Learning Arts	Geography
GOLDEN SPIKE	National Geographic	History
GOLD RUSH	Sierra Online	History

COMPUTER	GRADES	COMMENT
II	9–12	Basic introduction to foreign relations.
II	4–Adult	Public domain word processing program.
II	7–12	Facts about the French Revolution.
II	7–12	Creative format to teach facts about presidents.
II, MS	3–10	TV gameshow format—uses existing questions or allows additional.
II	6–12	Game that drills on geography facts.
MS	7–12	Select a state from a map and name capitals and cities.
II	5–10	Competitive game on facts about the states.
II	7–12	Development of vocabulary for geography.
II	7–12	Quizzes on basic facts, including major regions of world.
II	5–10	Students make decisions as they navigate around the world.
II	4–8	Drill on geography facts.
II	5–12	Develops ability to interpret maps, charts, etc. and use databases.
IIGS	5–Adult	Drill on facts about the world.
Mac	6–12	Hypertext stacks emphasizing maps and statistics.
II	5–12	Computer gives maps of continents, students answer questions.
II	5–10	Multimedia simulation teaches problem solving and decision making.
II	6–12	Adventure game that simulates California gold rush.

TITLE	VENDOR	TOPIC
GOVERNMENT AND THE MARKET	Queue	Economics, Government
GOVERNMENT KEYWORD SERIES	Focus Media	Government
GRAB-A-CAB	Silver, Burdett & Ginn	Geography
GRADE MANAGER	MECC	General
GRAND TOUR OF WESTERN EUROPE	Orange Cherry	Geography
GREAT AMERICAN HISTORY KNOWLEDGE RACE	Focus Media	History
GREAT DEPRESSION	Frontier Software	History
GREAT KNOWLEDGE RACE: U.S. HISTORY SERIES	Focus Media	History
GREAT QUAKE OF '89 HYPERCARD STACK	Voyager Company	History
GREAT STATES RACE	Milliken	Geography
GREAT WORLD HISTORY KNOWLEDGE RACE	Focus Media	History
GREEK MYTHOLOGY	Teach Yourself by Computer	History
GROWTH OF THE UNITED STATES	Right On	History
GTV: A GEOGRAPHIC PERSPECTIVE ON AMERICAN HISTORY	Optical Data	Geography, History
HAIL TO THE CHIEF	K–12 Micromedia	Government

COMPUTER	GRADES	COMMENT
II	9–12	Tutorial on how government policies influence economics.
II	7–12	Development of vocabulary for government classes.
II	4–6	Simulation of cab driving to practice map skills.
II	K–Adult	Gradebook program to manage and report student grades.
II, 64	7–12	Facts about geography, culture, and history of Western Europe countries.
II, MS	9–12	Game provides quiz on American history.
II	6–10	Facts about events and causes of the Great Depression.
II	7–12	Game provides quiz on U.S. history.
Mac	4–12	Accompanied by ABC News videodisc.
II	4–6	Race across the U.S. in balloon while answering geography questions.
II, MS	7–12	Game provides quiz on world history.
II	7–12	Tutorial on popular Greek legends.
II, 64	4–6	Explains how U.S. developed into an industrial nation.
GS, Mac	5–12	Students easily prepare history presentations with geography focus.
II	7–12	Two-player simulation of a presidential election.

TITLE	VENDOR	TOPIC
HALLS OF MONTEZUMA	Strategic Studies Group	History
HAT IN THE RING	MicroEd	Government
HEART OF AFRICA	Edu-Tron	Geography
HIDDEN AGENDA	Scholastic	Government, History
HILL RAILWAY	Queue	Geography
HISTORY AND GEOGRAPHY	Learning Arts	History, Government
HISTORY OF ASIA AND AFRICAN DEMOCOMP	Focus Media	History
HISTORY OF EUROPE DEMOCOMP	Focus Media	History
HISTORY OF JAPAN	Intellectual Software	History
HISTORY OF U.S. DEMOCOMP	Focus Media	History
HISTORY OF WESTERN CIVILIZATION	COMPress	History
HISTORY STUDY CENTER	Teach Yourself by Computer	History
HOLIDAYS AND FESTIVALS	Right On	Elementary
HOMETOWN: A LOCAL AREA STUDY	Active Learning Systems	General
HOMETOWN, U.S.A.	Publishing International	Government
HOW A BILL BECOMES A LAW	Intellectual Software	Government
HOW CAN I FIND IT IF I DON'T KNOW WHAT I'M LOOKING FOR?	Sunburst	General

COMPUTER	GRADES	COMMENT
II	6–12	Simulation of American activity in Mexico.
64	5–10	Tutorial on factors influencing presidential elections.
64	6–12	Learn African facts during simulated search for pharaoh's tomb.
II, Mac	8–12	Problem-solving simulation of governing fictional country.
II	8–12	Read a contour map in order to build a simulated railway.
II	4–10	Drill on facts about history and geography.
II, 64	7–12	Maps of various eras of Asian and African history.
II, 64	7–12	Maps of Europe during various eras of history.
II	9–12	Tutorial on entire history of Japan.
II, 64	6–12	Maps of U.S. during various eras of history.
MS	9–12	Drills of entire western history (12 disks).
II	6–12	Quiz on major areas of history—authoring system included.
II, 64	2–4	Tutorial on major holidays and festivals.
II, MS	6–12	Database tool with demographic information—encourages interviewing.
Mac	K–12	Students easily draw cities, buildings, etc.
II, MS	7–10	Demonstration of how a bill becomes a law.
II	4–9	Tutorial on reference book usage.

TITLE	VENDOR	TOPIC
HYPERCARD	Claris	General
HYPERSTUDIO	Roger Wagner	General
IFS: INTERNATIONAL FUTURES SIMULATION	Conduit	Economics
I LOVE AMERICA SERIES	K–12 Micromedia	History, Government
IMMIGRANT	Sunburst	History
INCREDIBLE BUT TRUE	Orange Cherry	History
INDIANS, INDIANS COMPUTER KIT	Orange Cherry	Elementary
INDIANS OF NORTH AMERICA	Frontier Software	History
INDIAN WARS	Hartley	History
INDUSTRIALISM IN AMERICA	Focus Media	History
INSTANT SURVEY	MECC	General
INTELLECTUAL PURSUITS	Hartley	History
INTERVIEWS WITH HISTORY	Educational Pub. Concepts	History
IN THE HOLY LAND	Optical Data	History, Geography
INTO THE UNKNOWN: A VOYAGE SIMULATION	Focus Media	History
INTRODUCTION TO ECONOMICS	Queue	Economics

COMPUTER	GRADES	COMMENT
Mac	K–Adult	Macintosh hypertext allows development of interactive presentations.
II	K–Adult	Apple II hypertext allows development of interactive presentations.
MS	11–Adult	Simulation of key issues of global development, etc.
II	4–10	Maps skills and facts about American geography and history.
II	9–12	Database compatible with APPLEWORKS on the Irish experience in Boston.
II, 64	7–12	Interesting, amazing facts about U.S. and world history.
II, 64	2–6	Information about Native American culture.
II	3–6	Facts about Native American tribes and their cultures.
II	8–12	Simulation for two students of U.S. troops fighting American Indians.
II	9–12	Covers the industrial revolution to the present in America.
II	7–12	Tool enabling students to create, administer, and analyze surveys.
II	10–12	Drill questions on English and American literature.
II	4–10	Student interviews famous persons and then takes quiz.
Mac	9–12	Interactive videodisc of Middle East produced by ABC News.
II, 64	4–10	Simulation of a sea voyage in the 15th century.
II	9–12	Tutorial on basic concepts of economics.

TITLE	VENDOR	TOPIC
INTRODUCTION TO GEOGRAPHY	Orange Cherry	Geography
INVENTIONS THAT AFFECT OUR LIVES	Orange Cherry	History
IRISH IMMIGRANT EXPERIENCE	Donald M. Morrison	History
JAMESTOWN, AN EARLY SETTLEMENT	Aquarius	History
JENNY'S JOURNEYS	MECC	Elementary
JOURNEY INTO THE UNKNOWN	Focus Media	History
JUNE–DECEMBER 1894	Harcourt Brace Jovanovich	History
JURY TRIAL II	NAVIC	Government
KIDWRITER	Spinnaker	General
KNOW YOUR STATE	Right On	Geography
LABOR	Queue	Economics
LANGUAGE OF MAPS	Focus Media	Geography
LAW IN AMERICAN HISTORY I AND II	Queue	History
LEARNING ABOUT GEOGRAPHY, MAPS, AND GLOBES	Educational Activities	Geography
LESSONS IN AMERICAN HISTORY	COMPress	History
LET'S LEARN ABOUT THE LIBRARY	Troll	General
LEWIS AND CLARK EXPEDITION	MicroEd	History
LINCOLN'S DECISIONS	Educational Activities	History

COMPUTER	GRADES	COMMENT
II	5–10	Drill on maps, 50 states, and other geographical information.
II, 64	3–10	Tutorial on inventions throughout history.
II	6–12	Simulation of experience of Irish immigrants in America.
II, MS	7–12	Mostly tutorial with some simulation on Jamestown settlement.
II, MS	4–6	Children practice skills in map reading and related activities.
II	6–12	Simulation of age of discovery and ocean voyages.
II, MS	7–12	Simulation dealing with the Pullman strike.
II, 64	7–12	Students simulate roles of prosecutor and defense attorney.
II	K–3	Very simple word processor with graphics.
II, 64	3–8	Different factual programs are available for each state.
II	9–12	Examines history of labor movement and current union status.
II	4–10	Basic map-reading skills.
MS, 64	7–12	Simulations of legal cases in American history.
II	4–6	Three programs with good graphs and focusing on map-related skills.
MS	9–12	Comprehensive drills on facts from American history.
II	4–8	Tutorial on library usage.
64	5–12	Students simulate Lewis and Clark expedition.
II, MS	8–12	Tutorial on Lincoln's decisions.

TITLE	VENDOR	TOPIC
LINKWAY	IBM	General
LOCATION AND DISTANCE	Focus Media	Geography
LOLLIPOP DRAGON'S WORLD MAPS AND GLOBES	SVE	Geography
MACATLAS Series	MicroMaps Software	Geography
MACCHORO II	Image Mapping Systems	Geography
MACKIDS: LEMONADE STAND	Nordic Software	Economics
MACROECONOMICS	Queue	Economics
MACTIMELINER	Tom Snyder Productions	History
MAGIC SLATE	Sunburst	General
MAKE–A–FLASH	Teacher Support Software	General
MAP READING	SVE	Geography
MAPS AND GLOBES	SVE	Geography
MAPS AND LEGENDS— THE CARTOGRAPHER	Antic Publishing	Geography
MAP SKILLS	Learning Arts	Geography
MARKET ECONOMY	Queue	Economics
MARKET PLACE	MECC	Economics

COMPUTER	GRADES	COMMENT
MS	K–Adult	MS-DOS hypertext allows development of interactive presentations.
II	3–10	Basic direction, distance, and map-usage skills.
II	K–3	Very basic map and globe skills.
Mac	K–12	Three separate packages for generating high quality maps.
Mac	9–12	Tool to permit easy mapping of statistical information.
Mac	3–8	Inexpensive simulation of the operation of a lemonade stand.
II, MS, Mac	9–12	Tutorial on basics of macroeconomics.
Mac	K–12	TIMELINER with features adapted to the Macintosh computer.
II	K–Adult	Word processor with formats for young and old.
II	7–12	Students make flashcards for study.
II	5–12	Three programs on the basics of map reading.
II, 64	5–12	Nineteen drill programs on important facts related to maps and globes.
II, MS	9–12	Map creation program.
II	1–3	Very basic map-usage skills.
II	9–12	Tutorial on market economy.
II, MS	3–10	Students simulate small business operation, such as a lemonade stand.

TITLE	VENDOR	TOPIC
MARKET PLACE	Learning Arts	Economics
MARTIN LUTHER KING, JR.	Optical Data	History
MAXI TAXI	MicroEd	Economics
MEASURING ECONOMIC ACTIVITY	Focus Media	Economics
MECC DATAQUEST: ASIA AND OCEANIA	MECC	Geography
MECC DATAQUEST: EUROPE AND THE SOVIET UNION	MECC	Geography
MECC DATAQUEST: LATIN AMERICA	MECC	Geography
MECC DATAQUEST: THE FIFTY STATES	MECC	Geography
MECC DATAQUEST: THE MIDDLE EAST AND NORTH AFRICA	MECC	Geography
MECC DATAQUEST: THE PRESIDENTS	MECC	History
MECC DATAQUEST: THE WORLD COMMUNITY	MECC	Geography, Economics
MECC GRAPH	MECC	General
MEDALISTS SERIES	Hartley	History, Government
MEDIA MAGIC	Pelican	History, Geography
MICROECONOMICS	Queue	Economics
MICROSOFT WORD	Microsoft	General

COMPUTER	GRADES	COMMENT
II	7–12	Tutorial and drill on supply and demand and other economic principles.
Mac	4–12	Interactive videodisc by ABC News.
64	4–12	Exercises relating time to money.
II	9–12	Tutorial on economic indicators.
II	6–12	Database exercises with factual and statistical information.
II	6–12	Database exercises with factual and statistical information.
II	6–12	Database exercises with factual and statistical information.
II	5–12	Database exercises with factual and statistical information on states.
II	6–12	Database exercises with factual and statistical information.
II	9–12	Database exercises with factual information about the presidents.
II	7–12	Database exercises with worldwide facts and statistics.
II	7–12	Creates graphs based on data entered.
II, MS	4–10	Drills (with authoring system) on history and geography.
II, MS	3–10	Students or teachers can develop show-and-tell presentations.
II, MS, Mac	9–12	Tutorials on basics of microeconomics.
MS	7–12	Sophisticated word processor for MS-DOS computers.

TITLE	VENDOR	TOPIC
MICROSOFT WORKS	Microsoft	General
MIDDLE AGES	Right On	History
MILLIONAIRE	Britannica Software	Economics
MODERN EURASIA	Focus Media	History
MONARCH	Dynacomp	Government, History
MONEY AND FINANCIAL INSTITUTIONS	Queue	Economics
NATIONAL ECONOMIC POLICY	Queue	Economics
NATIONAL ECONOMY	Queue	Economics
NATIONAL GALLERY OF ART	Voyager Company	History
NATIONAL INSPIRER	Tom Snyder	Geography
NATIONALISM: PAST AND PRESENT	Focus Media	History
NEW CONTINENT IS DISCOVERED	Aquarius	History
NEW WORLD	K–12 Micromedia	History
NON-WESTERN CULTURES	Focus Media	History
NORTH AMERICAN DATABASES	Sunburst	Geography
OCEANS AND CONTINENTS	MicroEd	Geography
OLD IRONSIDES	Edu-Tron	History
ONE WORLD: A COUNTRIES DATABASE	Active Learning Systems	Geography, History

COMPUTER	GRADES	COMMENT
MS, Mac	7–12	Sophisticated word processor, spreadsheet, and database for MS-DOS and Macintosh computers.
II, 64	5–10	Basic information on Middle Ages.
Mac	6–12	Simulation of stock market activity.
II	4–10	Information on Middle East, Europe, Russia, and Asia.
MS	7–12	Students simulate being ruler of a country.
II	9–12	Tutorial on money and related processes.
II	9–12	Tutorial on the interaction of economics with governmental policy.
II	9–12	Tutorial on employment, unemployment, recessions, etc.
Mac	9–12	Interactive videodisc of extensive art collection.
II, MS	5–10	Game for students in small groups to learn facts about states.
II	9–12	Five programs for tutoring, simulations, and problem solving.
II, MS	7–12	Facts about early U.S. history.
II	4–10	Simulation of discovery and colonization of America.
II, 64	7–12	Drills on non-Western cultures.
II, 64	5–12	Databases of facts and statistics about North America.
64	2–5	Students learn to identify and locate oceans and continents.
II	1–4	Students simulate a naval battle.
II, MS	5–12	Database with 30 categories on 178 countries.

TITLE	VENDOR	TOPIC
OREGON TRAIL	MECC	History
OTHER SIDE	Tom Snyder	History
OUR TOWN DATABASES	Sunburst	Government
OUR TOWN MEETING	Tom Snyder	Government, Economics
OUTWIT THE OWL	Hartley	Geography
PACIFIC THEATRE	Hartley	History
PAGEMAKER	Aldus	General
PARKING LOT	MicroEd	Economics
PC GLOBE+	PC Globe	Geography
PC USA	PC Globe	Geography
POINT OF VIEW	Scholastic	History
POLITICAL GENIE: HOUSE VERSION	Boring Software Company	Government
POLITICAL GENIE: SENATE VERSION	Boring Software Company	Government
POLLS AND POLITICS	MECC	Government
POWER GRID	HRM	Economics, Government
POWER OF NATION STATES	Data Disc International	Government

COMPUTER	GRADES	COMMENT
II	4–12	Simulation of a trip along the Oregon Trail.
II, MS	7–12	Teams of students simulate interaction between two nations.
II	4–12	Students gather and analyze database information about their own towns.
II, MS	5–12	Simulation to enhance town's image without bankruptcy.
II	4–7	Students use databases to answer questions about social studies.
II	9–12	Simulation of activity in the Pacific during World War II.
MS, Mac	9–Adult	Sophisticated desktop publishing program.
64	4–10	Simulation of laws of supply and demand.
MS	6–12	Maps with zoom capability and database information.
MS	6–12	Maps with zoom capability and database information.
Mac	8–12	Extensive information on history packed into a single program.
II, MS	7–12	Database of House members and their votes on 100 issues.
II, MS	7–12	Database of Senate members and their votes on 100 issues.
II, MS	7–12	Tutorial and simulation about political polling.
II	6–12	Simulation of principles involved in electrical power distribution.
Mac	4–12	Uses databases and spreadsheets to show interdependence of nations.

TITLE	VENDOR	TOPIC
PRESIDENCY SERIES	Focus Media	Government
PRESIDENT ELECT	Strategic Simulations	Government
PRESIDENTIAL CANDIDATES	Heizer Software	History
PRESIDENTIAL DATABASE 2.0	Heizer Software	History
PRESIDENTS	Data Disc International	History
PRESIDENT'S CHOICE	Edu-Tron	Government, Economics
PRINT SHOP	Broderbund	General
PRINT SHOP COMPANION	Broderbund	General
PRINT SHOP GRAPHICS LIBRARIES	Broderbund	General
PROFESSIONAL SIGN MAKER	Sunburst	General
PROPERTY	Queue	Government
PUBLISH IT!	Timeworks Platinum	General
PUZZLES AND POSTERS	MECC	General
QUEST FOR FILES: SOCIAL STUDIES	Mindscape	History
QUICK FLASH	MECC	General
QUICK MAP	MicroMaps Software	Geography

COMPUTER	GRADES	COMMENT
II	7–12	Tutorial and simulation on the office of the president.
II	9–12	Simulation of presidential election.
Mac	4–12	Database of 400 presidential candidates.
Mac	11–12	Database on presidents.
Mac	4–12	Hypertext stacks with information on presidents of U.S.
MS	8–12	Simulation of the president making economic decisions.
II, MS, Mac	3–Adult	Most popular graphics program for young people.
II, MS, Mac	3–Adult	Enhancements for PRINT SHOP, including good calendar program.
II, MS, Mac	3–Adult	Graphics to expand the possibilities of PRINT SHOP.
II	5–Adult	Generates posters.
II	9–Adult	Three-disk tutorial on legal aspects of property.
IIGS, MS, Mac	9–Adult	Sophisticated desktop publishing program.
II	3–Adult	Generates wordsearch and crossword puzzles.
II, MS	9–12	Three databases—immigration, Congress, and presidents.
II	3–12	Students, teachers, or peers generate flashcards for study.
Mac	9–12	Utility program for creating maps.

TITLE	VENDOR	TOPIC
RACE FOR THE WEST	Hartley	History
RAILS WEST	Strategic Simulations	History, Economics
READING A MAP	Aquarius	Geography
REGIONS OF THE UNITED STATES	Educational Activities	Geography
RENAISSANCE	Right On	History
REPORT CARD	Sensible Software	General
REVIEW QUESTIONS IN AMERICAN HISTORY	Queue	History
REVIEW QUESTIONS IN WORLD HISTORY	Queue	History
REVOLUTION	Britannica Software	History
REVOLUTION AND CONSTITUTION	Mindscape	History
REVOLUTIONS: PAST, PRESENT, AND FUTURE	Focus Media	History
RIPLEY'S BELIEVE IT OR NOT!	SVE	General
RIPPLE THAT CHANGED AMERICAN HISTORY	Tom Snyder	History
RISE AND FALL	Heizer Software	History
RIVERS AND ANCIENT CULTURES	Teach Yourself by Computer	History
ROAD RALLY U.S.A.	Edu-Tron	Geography

COMPUTER	GRADES	COMMENT
II	5–10	Students simulate exploration of the American Northwest.
II	9–12	Simulation of economic decisions set in 1870.
II	2–4	Drill on basic map-reading skills.
II, 64	5–12	Review of factual information about the states.
II, 64	6–10	Tutorial on facts about the Renaissance.
II, MS	K–Adult	Grade-management program with many options.
II	9–12	Two disks with over 400 questions on American history.
II	9–12	Two disks with over 400 questions on world history.
GS	6–12	Simulation of American Revolution (program runs very slowly).
II	7–12	Facts about American Revolution and Constitutional Era.
II	9–12	Tutorial using historical analysis to compare various revolutions.
II	5–10	Practice library research skills by looking up incredible facts.
II, MS	5–12	Time machine approach to American history.
Mac	7–12	Hypertext stacks related to World War II.
II	4–8	Review of Egyptian and Sumerian civilizations.
II, MS	5–10	Simulation of road rally develops geography and problem solving skills.

TITLE	VENDOR	TOPIC
RUN FOR PRESIDENT	Edu-Tron	Geography
RUSSIAN REVOLUTION	Frontier Software	History
SAILING SHIPS GAME	Queue	History
SALAMANDRE	Voyager Company	History
SAMP: SURVEY SAMPLING	Conduit	General
SANTA FE TRAIL	Educational Activities	History
SATELLITE DOWN	Focus Media	Geography
SAVE THE !KUNG	Edu-Tron	History
SCARE CITY MOTEL	MicroEd	Economics
SCHOLASTIC PFS: WORLD GEOGRAPHY DATABASE	Scholastic	Geography
SCHOLASTIC PFS: WORLD HISTORY DATABASE	Scholastic	History
SEARCH AND RESCUE: GEOGRAPHY SKILLS	Learning Arts	Geography
SEA VOYAGES	Mindscape	History
SECOND VOYAGE OF THE MIMI	Wings for Learning	General
SEE THE U.S.A.	Compu-Tech	Geography
SETTLING AMERICA	Edu-Tron	History
SEVEN CITIES OF GOLD	Edu-Tron	History

COMPUTER	GRADES	COMMENT
II	6–12	Presidential election game provides review of U.S. geography.
II	6–12	Tutorial on Russian Revolution.
II	7–12	Simulations of navigation of ship on oceans of the world.
Mac	7–12	Videodisc with comprehensive collection of French art.
II, MS	9–Adult	Simulation of various sampling methodologies.
II	7–12	Simulation of trip along the Santa Fe Trail.
II	7–12	Satellite game reviews geography—world and U.S. editions.
II	9–Adult	Simulation of survival of a tribe.
64	4–10	Tutorial on supply and demand.
II	5–12	Databases related to world geography.
II	5–12	Databases related to world history.
II	4–10	Game in which students apply geography knowledge to find stolen object.
II, MS	3–10	Game format teaches facts about explorers.
II	6–12	Integrated, interdisciplinary package of CAI and video materials.
II	6–12	Students simulate a trip across U.S.A. on a high-resolution map.
II	6–12	Simulation of settlement of Ohio River valley.
II, MS	4–12	Simulation of exploration of America.

TITLE	VENDOR	TOPIC
SHORE FEATURES	Teach Yourself by Computer	Geography
SIM CITY: THE CITY SIMULATOR	Broderbund	Government, Ecology
SIM EARTH	Broderbund	Government
SIMPOLICON	Cross Cultural Software	Economics
SIMULATION CONSTRUCTION KIT	Hartley	General
SIMULATIONS IN AMERICAN HISTORY	Harcourt Brace Jovanovich	History
SOCIAL STUDIES (Series)	MECC	General
SOCIAL STUDIES EXPLORER: AMERICAN HISTORY	Mindscape	History
SOCIAL STUDIES EXPLORER: WORLD GEOGRAPHY	Mindscape	History
SOCIAL STUDIES REGIONS	MicroEd	Geography
SOCIAL STUDIES SKILL BUILDER	Queue	General
SOCTERMS: SOCIOLOGICAL DEFINITIONS	Conduit	General
SOUTH AMERICAN GEOGRAPHY	Sunshine Computer Software	Geography
SOUTH DAKOTA	Educational Activities	Economics
SPACE COMMANDER: STATES AND CAPITALS GAME	Gamco	Geography

COMPUTER	GRADES	COMMENT
II	7–12	Tutorial on features of shores and beaches.
Mac	6–Adult	Student simulates very realistic construction and government of a city.
Mac	7–12	Student simulates very realistic construction and government of Earth.
II	9–12	Simulation of political and economic factors in government.
II	7–12	Teachers and students can design their own simulations.
II	7–12	Various simulations of American history.
II	4–12	Original versions of several early social studies programs.
II, MS	5–10	Game requires insight to answer questions on American history.
II, MS	5–10	Game requires insight to answer questions on world history.
64	4–6	Tutorial on vocabulary related to geographic regions.
II	6–10	Reading and writing skills related to social studies.
MS	10–Adult	Drill on sociology terms.
MS	7–12	Drill on South America map and facts.
II	9–12	Simulation of operation of a grain cereal farm.
II, 64	3–6	Drill game on states and capitals.

TITLE	VENDOR	TOPIC
SPELL M-O-N-E-Y	MicroEd	Economics
SPY'S ADVENTURES IN NORTH AMERICA	Polarware	Geography
STANDING ROOM ONLY	Sunburst	General
STATES	Ventura Educational Systems	Geography
STATES	Queue	Geography
STATES AND CAPITALS	Gamco	Geography
STATES AND CAPITALS	MicroEd	Geography
STATES AND TRAITS	Britannica Software	Geography
STATE-SMART 3.0	HyPerFormance	Geography
STATES OF THE UNION DATABASE 2.0	Heizer Software	Geography
STICKYBEAR TOWN BUILDER	Weekly Reader	Elementary
STOCK MARKET SIMULATION	Queue	Economics
STORYBOOK STARTERS	Mindscape	Elementary
STORY STARTERS: SOCIAL STUDIES	Pelican	Elementary, History
STRANGE ENCOUNTERS	Orange Cherry	General
STREET MAP	Micro Power and Light	Geography
STRUGGLE FOR INDEPENDENCE	Aquarius	History

COMPUTER	GRADES	COMMENT
64	5–10	Tutorial on definitions of basic economic terms.
II	5–12	Use geography clues to find spy. (Also SOUTH AMERICA and other continents.)
II	8–12	Tool for making and studying population projections.
Mac	4–8	Quizzes on geographical information about states.
II, 64	3–6	Drill on state shapes, locations, and facts.
II, 64	3–6	Game provides drill on states, capitals, and cities.
64	3–6	Drill on states and capitals.
II, MS	9–12	Students move states to proper locations and identify facts.
Mac	4–9	Hypertext stacks on U.S. geography.
Mac	4–12	Database with extensive information on states.
II, 64	1–3	Students build town and then drive around in it.
II	7–12	Students simulate buying and selling on the stock market.
II	3–8	Story starters to integrate social studies and language arts.
II, MS	3–8	Story-starter graphics for topics related to social studies.
II	4–10	Students discuss "strange encounters" such as Bermuda Triangle and Bigfoot.
II	4–10	Students follow map to drive car in various cities.
II, MS	7–12	Figures from American Revolution speak to students.

TITLE	VENDOR	TOPIC
STUDY GUIDE	MECC	General
STUDY SKILLS	Houghton Mifflin	General
SUPER QUIZ COMPUTER GAME	Queue	History
SUPREME COURT DECISION	Intellectual Software	Government
SURFACE OF THE EARTH	Focus Media	Geography
SURVEY KIT	William K. Bradford	General
SURVEY TAKER	Scholastic	General
TAXES AND GOVERNMENT	Queue	Economics, Government
TEDDYTRONIC	Queue	Economics
TESTWORKS	Milliken	General
TEXAS HISTORY	Frontier Software	History, Geography
THIRTEEN COLONIES	Aquarius	History
TICKET TO PARIS	William K. Bradford	Geography
TICKET TO WASHINGTON DC	William K. Bradford	Geography
TIME AND SEASON	Rand McNally	Geography
TIME-LINE	Intellectual Software	History
TIMELINER	Tom Snyder	History
TIME-LINES IN HISTORY	Queue	History

COMPUTER	GRADES	COMMENT
II	4–12	Generates multiple-choice, true/false, matching, and completion questions.
II	3–8	Lessons on reference skills and organizing information.
II	4–8	Game asks questions about American history.
II, MS	9–12	Students simulate a case from local trial through Supreme Court.
II	3–10	Tutorial on terms used with maps.
II	6–12	Enables students to conduct and interpret surveys.
II	4–10	Tool for conducting and analyzing survey data.
II	9–12	Tutorial on how government collects and spends taxes.
II	9–12	Students try to make money while running a teddy bear factory.
II	3–Adult	Computerized test construction, including interactive testing.
II	4–10	Drill on events and cities of Texas.
II, MS	7–12	Figures from pre–Revolutionary War speak to students.
II	7–12	Simulations of activities in foreign countries.
II	7–12	Simulation of trip to Washington, D.C.
II	4–8	Basic facts about time and season.
II	9–12	Students use or add to a database to create timelines.
II	5–12	Tool for creating timelines—easy to add personal data.
II	7–12	Databases with hundreds of events to create timelines.

TITLE	*VENDOR*	*TOPIC*
TIME MACHINE TRAVELER	Queue	History
TIME NAVIGATOR	MECC	History
TIME NAVIGATOR LEAPS BACK	MECC	History
TIMEOUT Series	Beagle Brothers	General
TIME TABLE OF HISTORY: SCIENCE AND INNOVATION	Xiphias	History
TIME TUNNEL: AMERICAN HISTORY SERIES 1	Focus Media	History
TIME TUNNEL: AMERICAN HISTORY SERIES 2	Focus Media	History
TIME TUNNEL: AMERICA SERIES	Focus Media	History
TIME TUNNEL: EUROPEAN HISTORY	Focus Media	History
TIME TUNNEL: THE PRESIDENTS	Focus Media	History
TORTS	Queue	Government
TRAGEDY OF WAR: A SIMULATION	Focus Media	History
TRAIL WEST	MicroEd	History
TRANSCONTINENTAL RAILROAD	MicroEd	History
TRANSPORTATION	Right On	Elementary
TRAVELS WITH ZA-ZOOM	Focus Media	Geography

COMPUTER	GRADES	COMMENT
II	3–6	Students determine how they would have handled historical dilemmas.
II	6–12	Time travel game on U.S. history since 1900.
II	6–12	Time travel game on U.S. history from beginning to 1900.
II	5–Adult	Supplementary tools for APPLEWORKS such as spelling checker.
Mac	3–12	CD-ROM database with HYPERCARD access to information on science.
II	7–12	Students travel in time to guess mystery persons from U.S. history.
II	7–12	Students travel in time to guess mystery persons from U.S. history.
II	4–12	Students travel in time to guess mystery persons from U.S. history.
II	7–12	Students travel in time to guess mystery persons from European history.
II	4–12	Students travel in time to guess mystery president.
II	9–Adult	Two disks on torts for advanced students.
II	7–12	Simulation of activity on Western Front in World War I.
64	3–8	Tutorial on traveling west as a pioneer.
64	5–12	Tutorial on how the first transcontinental railroad was built.
II, 64	2–4	Basic facts on transportation and its history.
II, MS	4–10	Students are taken to strange places and figure out where they are.

TITLE	VENDOR	TOPIC
TREATY OF VERSAILLES	Intellimation	History
TUT, A BOY KING	MicroEd	History
TYCOON	Britannica Software	Economics
UNDERSTANDING CONTRACTS	MCE	Economics
UNDERSTANDING THE UNITED STATES CONSTITUTION	Mindscape	Government
UNITED STATES GEOGRAPHY Series	Intellectual Software	Geography
UNITED STATES REGIONAL STUDIES	Orange Cherry	Geography
UNLOCKING THE MAP CODE	Rand McNally	Geography
U.S.A. GEOGRAPH	MECC	Geography
USA IN PROFILE	Active Learning Systems	Geography
U.S. ATLAS ACTION	Edu-Tron	Geography
U.S. CONSTITUTION	Classroom Consortia Media	Government
U.S. CONSTITUTION	Queue	Government
U.S. CONSTITUTION: NATIONALISM AND FEDERALISM	Focus Media	History
U.S. CONSTITUTION THEN AND NOW	Scholastic	History
U.S. DATABASES	Sunburst	General
U.S. GEOGRAPHY ADVENTURE	Intellectual Software	Geography

COMPUTER	GRADES	COMMENT
Mac	10–12	Exercises related to the conclusion of World War I.
64	5–10	Tutorial on King Tut.
Mac	6–12	Simulation of the commodities market.
II	7–12	Tutorial on rights and responsibilities regarding contracts.
II	7–12	Tutorial leads to factual understanding of Constitution.
II, MS	7–12	Tutorials and drills on wide range of geography concepts.
II, MS	3–10	Tutorial on how geography influenced development of U.S.
II	5–10	Tutorial and game on map skills.
IIGS	5–12	Easily accessed maps and databases on U.S. states.
II, MS	6–12	Database with 29 categories for states.
II	3–10	Students locate states and give facts.
II, MS	8–12	Tutorial on the U.S. Constitution.
II, MS	8–12	Tutorial on the U.S. Constitution.
II	7–12	Three programs on background and development of Constitution.
II	7–12	Database enables students to role-play Constitutional Convention.
II, 64	5–12	Databases for U.S. history, geography, and government.
II, MS	5–12	Students travel through states and possessions to identify facts.

TITLE	VENDOR	TOPIC
U.S. GEOGRAPHY Series	Intellectual Software	Geography
U.S. HISTORY	Bureau of Electronic Publishing	History
U.S. HISTORY	Hartley	History
U.S. HISTORY: GROWTH OF A NATION	Focus Media	History
U.S. HISTORY Series	Queue	History
U.S. HISTORY: THE YOUNG REPUBLIC	Focus Media	History
U.S. TIME ZONES	MicroEd	Elementary
VALDEZ	K–12 Micromedia	History
VAN GOGH	Voyager Company	History
VCR COMPANION	Broderbund	General
VIETNAM REMEMBERED	Wayzata Technology	History
VIETNAM WAR 2.0	Regeneration Software	History
VIKING RAIDERS	Orange Cherry Media	History
VOYAGE OF THE MIMI	Wings for Learning	General
VOYAGES OF DISCOVERY	Learning Arts	History
WAGONS WEST	Focus Media	History
WAGON TRAIN 1848	MECC	History
WARBIRDS OF WORLD WAR II	P-Productions	History

COMPUTER	GRADES	COMMENT
II, MS	5–10	Separate disks drill on facts of states by region.
Mac	7–12	CD-ROM with extensive information on U.S. history.
II	10–12	Factual drill on U.S. history.
II, 64	5–12	Two disks drill students in game format on U.S. history.
II	6–12	Five programs cover U.S. history comprehensively.
II, 64	7–12	Two disks cover U.S. history through Revolution.
64	3–6	Basic facts on time zones.
II	9–12	Navigation of a supertanker develops map-reading skills.
Mac	9–12	Hypertext access to a videodisc on Van Gogh.
II, IIGS, MS	5–Adult	Adds titles, transitions, credits, and closings to videotapes.
Mac	7–12	CD-ROM with extensive information on Vietnam War.
Mac	6–12	Hypertext stacks with extensive information on Vietnam War.
II	6–12	Simulation of activity of Vikings.
II	6–12	Integrated, interdisciplinary package of CAI and video materials.
II	4–10	Simulation of explorations by Columbus or Lewis and Clark.
II	5–10	Simulation of pioneer journey westward.
Mac	5–12	Version of OREGON TRAIL designed for local area networks.
Mac	10–12	Hypertext stacks with information about war planes of World War II.

TITLE	VENDOR	TOPIC
WAR SIMULATIONS	Hartley	History
WASHINGTON'S DECISIONS	Educational Activities	History
WATER POLLUTION	EME Corporation	Economics
WEALTH BUILDER	Reality	Economics
WEALTH STARTER	Reality	Economics
WEATHER FRONTS	Diversified Educational Enterprises	Geography
WEATHER FRONTS	Teach Yourself by Computer	Geography
WESTERN CIVILIZATION	Focus Media	History
WESTERN EUROPE	MicroEd	Geography
WESTERN EXPANSION	Aquarius	History
WHAT DO THEY DO IN OUAGADOUGOU?	Educational Activities	Geography
WHATSIT CORPORATION	Sunburst	Economics
WHERE IN EUROPE IS CARMEN SANDIEGO?	Broderbund	Geography
WHERE IN THE USA IS CARMEN SANDIEGO?	Broderbund	Geography
WHERE IN THE WORLD IS CARMEN SANDIEGO?	Broderbund	Geography
WHERE IN TIME IS CARMEN SANDIEGO?	Broderbund	History
WHO BUILT AMERICA?	Right On	History
WHO CAN BE PRESIDENT?	Focus Media	History

COMPUTER	GRADES	COMMENT
II, MS	8–12	Simulation of activities in major American wars.
II	7–12	Tutorial on decisions made by George Washington.
II, MS	9–12	Simulation of the impact of pollution on water environment.
MS, Mac	9–12	Tool for tracking finances and assets.
MS, Mac	9–12	Tool for tracking finances and assets.
II	7–12	Students simulate the prediction of weather.
II	7–12	Tutorial on weather fronts and their activity.
II, 64	8–12	Three disks deal with ancient, medieval, and modern history.
64	5–12	Students identify Western European countries on a map.
II, MS	7–12	Review of westward expansion in U.S.
II	6–12	Students score points by recognizing countries from cultural clues.
II, MS	5–10	Students simulate production and sale of goods.
II, MS	8–12	Students travel Europe in search of thief.
II, MS	6–12	Students travel U.S. in search of thief.
II, MS	6–12	Students travel world in search of thief.
II, MS	8–12	Students travel through time in search of thief.
II, 64	4–6	Tutorial on basic facts about immigrants.
II	7–12	Students compare themselves to actual presidents.

TITLE	VENDOR	TOPIC
WHOLE NEIGHBORHOOD	Pelican	Elementary
WHO WILL SAVE ABACAXI?	Focus Media	History
WOMEN IN HISTORY SERIES	MicroEd	History
WORLD ATLAS ACTION	Edu-Tron	Geography
WORLD COUNTRY DATABASE	Heizer Software	Geography
WORLD DATA	Data Disc International	Geography
WORLD DESERT REGIONS	Right On	Geography
WORLD GEOGRAPH	MECC	Geography
WORLD GEOGRAPHY ADVENTURE I–IV	Intellectual Software	Geography
WORLD GEOGRAPHY Series	Intellectual Software	Geography
WORLD HISTORY ADVENTURE	Queue	History
WORLD MOUNTAIN REGIONS	Right On	Geography
WORLD OF ECONOMICS	South-Western	Economics
WORLD POLAR REGIONS	Right On	Geography
WORLD TIME ZONES	MicroEd	Elementary
YESTERDAY'S EXPLORERS	Orange Cherry	History
YOU AND THE LAW	Queue	Government
ZANDER	SVE	Economics

COMPUTER	GRADES	COMMENT
II, MS	3–8	Story-starter graphics for units on neighborhoods.
II	7–12	Students simulate being president of a country called Abacaxi.
II, 64	9–12	Several disks on women in various cultures.
II	4–10	Game teaches locations and facts about countries around the world.
Mac	7–12	Database information on 160 countries.
Mac	7–12	Hypertext stacks on countries of the world.
II, 64	3–6	Tutorial on animals and plant life in deserts.
IIGS	5–12	Easily accessed maps and databases on countries around world.
II, MS, Mac	7–12	Four programs drill on Americas, Europe, Asia, and Africa.
II, MS	9–12	Several disks drill on countries around the world.
II, MS	9–12	Students connect events with persons from history.
II, 64	3–6	Tutorial on animals and plant life or mountain regions.
II, MS	9–12	Three disks introduce economics to high school students.
II, 64	3–6	Animals and plant life of polar regions.
64	4–10	Students identify day and hour in various time zones of the world.
II, 64	4–10	Tutorial on French, Spanish, and British explorers.
II, MS	7–12	Eight programs focus on legal rights and responsibilities.
II	9–12	Students simulate governing a developing nation.

APPENDIX C

Annotated Bibliography

- Ainsa, Trisha. "The Writing Center." *Teaching and Computers*, 1988, *6* (September), 67–69.

    The computer as a tool in the writing center is the main topic of this article, which includes management tips, software resources, and sample lesson plans for primary teachers. The author incorporates ideas for introducing word processing to young students through message board activities and journal writing. Writing centers merge easily with social studies instruction.

- Alvermann, D. "Strategic Teaching in Social Studies." In Beau Fly Jones, Annemarie Sullivan Palinscar, Donna Sederburg Ogle, and Eileen Glynn Carr (Eds.), *Strategic Teaching and Learning: Cognitive Instruction in the Content Areas.* Alexandria, VA: ASCD, 1987.

    This book discusses "strategic teaching" in several curriculum areas. This chapter focuses on helping students develop process skills through strategic teaching in the social studies.

- Bitter, Gary. "CD-ROM Technology and the Classroom of the Future." *Computers in the Schools*, 1988, *5*(1/2), 23–34.

    This article presents some good definitions, descriptions, and applications of CD-ROM.

- D'Ignazio, Fred. "The Multimedia Sandbox: Creating a Publishing Center for Students." *Classroom Computer Learning*, 1989, *10* (October), 22–29.

    According to this article, multimedia doesn't have to be highly expensive to be highly productive. The author takes a very positive approach to creating a multimedia publishing center from available resources. His suggestions are upbeat and practical.

- D'Ignazio, Fred. "The Multimedia Classroom: Making It Work." *Classroom Computer Learning*, 1989, *10* (November/December), 36–39.

    The author describes the endless possibilities for connecting technology in a multimedia center. He focuses on hardware, software, and connections—both technology based and people-based. This is the second article in a two-part series on multimedia in the classroom.

- Dockterman, David. *Teaching in the One Computer Classroom.* Cambridge, MA: Tom Snyder Productions, 1989.

    The author views the computer in the classroom from several perspectives: as a tool for professional teacher tasks, such as grade and information management, home-school communication, and generating instructional materials; as a smart chalkboard consisting of computer and projection system; as a discussion generator; and as a group activator. This book offers practical suggestions for making the best use of one computer, especially in a social studies setting.

- Hohmann, Charles. *Young Children and Computers.* Yspilanti, MI: High/Scope Press, 1990.

  After several years of working with young children and computers within the framework of the High/Scope curriculum, the author has compiled a valuable resource. This book answers questions that concern teachers of young children who would like to incorporate computer activities into their program. It offers practical suggestions that cover every imaginable topic from room arrangement to hardware/software decisions. The book describes developmentally appropriate computer activities for young children. It describes the role of the teacher in providing the young child with a balance of direction and freedom to explore.

- Kenworthy, Leonard S. *Guide to Social Studies Teaching.* Belmont, CA: Wadsworth, 1987.

  This work describes the characteristics of student-centered activities and the responsibility of the teacher to create the proper learning environment. These principles are useful in applying the computer to the social studies curriculum.

- King, Rebecca, and Edward L. Vockell. *The Computer in the Language Arts Curriculum.* Watsonville, CA: Mitchell McGraw-Hill, 1991.

  A companion to the present volume, this book goes into specific detail on strategies for using the computer to help students develop language arts skills. Language arts skills and social studies activities often overlap at the computer.

- National Council for the Social Studies. *Curriculum Guidelines.* Washington, DC: NCSS, 1983.

  This publication provides an excellent synopsis of the theory and goals of social studies education, including abstracts from major educational theorists, such as Piaget, Bloom, Bruner, Skinner, and others.

- Naylor, David T., and Richard Diem. *Elementary and Middle School Social Studies.* New York: Land Akers, Inc., 1987.

  On pages 9–13 the authors address the problems in dealing with citizenship education by dividing learning into smaller components—

knowledge, skills, and valuing. Programs like TOWN BUILDER and TOWN MEETING can be integrated with these ideas to meet these objectives.

- Pogge, Alfred F., and Vincent N. Lunetta. "Spreadsheets Answer 'What If ...?' " *The Science Teacher*, 1987 (November), *54*(8), 46–49.

    This article gives several examples of spreadsheets for population and ecology studies. The computer does the calculations, freeing students to question and analyze the problems.

- Sherwood, Robert D. "Optical Technologies: Current Status and Possible Directions for Science Instruction." In J. D. Ellis (Ed.), *Information Technology and Science Education*. 1988 AETS Yearbook. Columbus, Ohio: ERIC, 1989.

    This chapter discusses such questions as what are the major hardware and software technologies currently in use in videodiscs and CD-ROM? Why might their use provide a learning environment especially useful for such areas as science and social studies instruction?

- Solomon, Gwen. "Going On-Line to Expand the Classroom." *Electronic Learning* Special Supplement 1989, 44–47.

    This article describes a telecommunications project in Ramapo Central School District in New York. The project was designed to expand students' audience for writing and to extend the scope of their research skills. The author shares the success of the project by relating its "humble beginnings" through the successful application of a $100,000 grant to expand the initial project. The telecommunication, research, and collaborative publishing activities that connected students within the school district and eventually around the world are shared.

- Vockell, Edward L., and Robert van Deusen. *The Computer and Higher-Order Thinking Skills*. Watsonville, CA: Mitchell McGraw-Hill, 1989.

    This book, a companion volume to the present book, focuses in detail on using the computer to teach higher order thinking skills in all curriculum areas. It advocates a use of guided discovery with a focus on generalizing skills to new areas.

- Vockell, Edward L., and Eileen Schwartz. *The Computer in the Classroom*. (2nd Ed.) Watsonville, CA: Mitchell McGraw-Hill, 1992.

    This book provides a good introduction to the whole range of instructional applications of the microcomputer to education. It is a useful tool for training teachers to use computers more effectively.

APPENDIX D

List of Vendors

Ability Systems
P.O. Box 5888
Lynnwood, WA 98046

Active Learning Systems
2515 Ashman
Midland, MI 48640

Advanced Ideas
2902 San Pablo Ave.
Berkeley, CA 94702

Aeius Corporation
P.O. Box 700457
San Jose, CA 95170

Aldus Corporation
411 First Ave., Suite 200
Seattle, WA 98104

Alphatel Systems Limited
11428 - 168th St.
Edmonton, Alberta T5M 3T9

Antic Publishing
544 Second St.
San Francisco, CA 94107

Aquarius People Materials
P.O. Box 128
Indian Rocks Beach, FL 33535

Baudville
1001 Medical Park Dr. S.E.
Grand Rapids, MI 49506

Beagle Brothers
6215 Ferris Square, Suite 102
San Diego, CA 92121

Boring Software Co.
P.O. Box 568
Boring, OR 97009

William K. Bradford Publishing
Company
310 School St.
Acton, MA 01720

Britannica Software
345 Fourth St.
San Francisco, CA 94107

Broderbund Software
17 Paul Dr.
San Rafael, CA 94903

Bureau of Electronic Publishing
P.O. Box 779
Upper Montclair, NJ 07043

Classroom Consortia Media
One Edgewater Plaza, Suite 209
Staten Island, NY 10305

Compact Publishing Company
P.O. Box 40310
Washington, DC 20077-4962

COMPress
P.O. Box 102
Wentworth, NH 03282

Compu-Teach
78 Olive St.
New Haven, CT 06511

Conduit
University of Iowa
Oakdale Campus
Iowa City, IA 52242

Chris Crawford Games
P.O. Box 360872
Portland, OR 95036

Cross Cultural Software
5385 Elrose Ave.
San Jose, CA 95124

Cross Educational Software
P.O. Box 1536
Ruston, LA 71270

CUE SoftSwap
P.O. Box 271704
Concord, CA 94527-1704

Cultural Resources
30 Iroquois Rd.
Cranford, NJ 07016

Data Disc International
1430 Willamette, Suite 577
Eugene, OR 97401

Didatech
3812 William St.
Burnaby, BC V5C 3H9

Digital Vision
270 Bridge St.
Dedham, MA 02026

Diversified Educational
Enterprises
725 Main St.
Lafayette, IN 47901

Dynacomp
1064 Gravel Rd.
Webster, NY 14580

Earthquest
125 University Ave.
Palo Alto, CA 94301

Eastgate Systems
P.O. Box 1307
Cambridge, MA 02238

Eclat Microproducts
P.O. Box 570756
Miami, FL 33257-0756

Educational Activities
P.O. Box 392
Freeport, NY 11520

EduSoft
P.O. Box 2560
Berkeley, CA 94702

EMC Publishing
300 York Ave.
St. Paul, MN 55101

E.M.E. Corp.
P.O. Box 2805
Danbury, CT 06813-2805

Excelsior Software
P.O. Box 3416
Greeley, CO 80633

Facts on File
460 Park Avenue South
New York, NY 10016

Focus Media
P.O. Box 835
Garden City, NY 11530

Gamco Industries
P.O. Box 1911
Big Spring, TX 79720

Graphsoft
8370 Court Ave., Suite 202
Elliott City, MD 21043

Great Wave Software
5353 Scotts Valley Dr.
Scotts Valley, CA 95066

Grolier Electronic Publishing
Old Sherman Turnpike
Danbury, CT 06816

Harcourt Brace Jovanovich
1250 Sixth Ave.
San Diego, CA 92101

Hartley Courseware
123 Bridge
Dimondale, MI 48821

Heizer Software
P.O. Box 232019
Pleasant Hill, CA 94523

Houghton Mifflin Educational
Software Division
One Beacon St.
Boston, MA 02107

HRM Software
175 Tompkins Ave.
Pleasantville, NY 10570

HyPerFormance
P.O. Box 1591
Corvallis, OR 97339

Image Mapping Systems
516 South 51st St.
Omaha, NE 68106

Intellectual Software
562 Boston Ave.
Bridgeport, CT 06610

Intellimation
P.O. Box 1922
Santa Barbara, CA 93116

K–12 Micromedia
6 Arrow Rd.
Ramsey, NJ 07446

The Learning Company
6493 Kaiser Dr.
Fremont, CA 94555

MCE Inc.
157 S. Kalamazoo Mall,
Suite 250
Kalamazoo, MI 49007

McGraw-Hill Publishing
1221 Avenue of the Americas
New York, NY 10020

MECC - Minnesota Educational
Computing Corporation
3490 Lexington Ave.
St. Paul, MN 55126-8097

MEDIAGENIC
3885 Bohannon Dr.
Menlo Park, CA 94025

Microcomputer Workshops
Courseware
225 Westchester Ave.
Portchester, NY 10573

Micro-Ed
P.O. Box 444005
Eden Prairie, MN 55344

Micro Learningware
P.O. Box 307
Mankota, MN 56002

MicroMaps Software
P.O. Box 757
Lambertville, NJ 08530

Micro Power & Light Company
12820 Hillcrest Rd., #219
Dallas, TX 75230

Microsoft Corporation
16011 N.E. 36th Way
Redmond, WA 98073

Midwest Software
P.O. Box 214
Farmington, MI 48024

Milliken Publishing Company
P.O. Box 21579
St. Louis, MO 63132

MindPlay
3130 N. Dodge Blvd.
Tucson, AZ 85716-1726

Mindscape
3444 Dundee Rd.
Northbrook, IL 60062

Misty City Software
10921 129th Place N.E.
Kirkland, WA 98033

National Geographic
Educational Services
17th & M Streets, NW
Washington, DC 20036

Nordic Software
3939 N. 48th St.
Lincoln, NE 68504-1401

Optical Data Corporation
30 Technology Dr.
Warren, NJ 07060

Orange Cherry Media
7 Delano Dr.
Bedford Hills, NY 10507

Palm Island
Bag 800
Vegreville, Alberta T0B 4L0

PC Globe
4700 South McClintock
Tempe, AZ 85282

Pelican Software
768 Farmingham Rd.
Farmingham, CT 06032

Polarware
P.O. Box 311
Geneva, IL 60134

P-Productions
2514 Illinois St.
Racine, WI 53405

Prodigy Service Company
445 Hamilton Ave.
White Plains, NY 10601

Publishing International
333 W El Camino Real, Suite 300
Sunnyvale, CA 94087

Queue
338 Commerce Dr.
Fairfield, CT 06430

Rand McNally
8255 No. Central Park
Skokie, IL 60076

Reality Technologies, Inc.
3624 Market St.
Philadelphia, PA 19104

Regeneration Software
377 Collado Dr.
Scotts Valley, CA 95066

Right On Programs
1737 Veteran's Memorial Dr.
Central Islip, NY 11722

Scholastic
730 Broadway
New York, NY 10003

SEI
2360-5 George Washington Hwy.
Yorktown, VA 23692

Sensible Software, Inc.
335 East Big Beaver, Suite 207
Troy, MI 48083

Sierra On-Line
36575 Mudge Ranch Rd.
Coarsegold, CA 93614

Silver, Burdett & Ginn
250 James St.
Morristown, NJ 07960-1918

Slippery Disks
P.O. Box 1126
Los Angeles, CA 90069

Tom Snyder Productions
90 Sherman St.
Cambridge, MA 02140

South-Western Publishing
Company
5101 Madison Rd.
Cincinnati, OH 45227

Spinnaker Software
One Kendall Square
Cambridge, MA 02139

Springboard Software
7807 Crekridge Circle
Minneapolis, MN 55435

Strategic Mapping
4030 Moorpark Ave., Suite 250
San Jose, CA 95117

Strategic Simulations
N. Rengstorff Ave.
Mountain View, CA 94043-1983

Strategic Studies Group
1747 Orleans Ct.
Walnut Creek, CA 94548

Sunburst Communications
39 Washington Ave.
Pleasantville, NY 10570

Sunshine Computer Software
1101 Post Oak Blvd.
Houston, TX 77056

SVE - Society for Visual
Education
1345 Diversey Pkwy.
Chicago, IL 60614

Teacher Support Software
502 NW 75th St., Suite 380
Gainesville, FL 32601

Teach Yourself by Computer
Software
2128 W. Jefferson Rd.
Pittsford, NY 14534

Unicorn Software
2950 E. Flamingo
Las Vegas, NV 89121

Ventura Educational Systems
3440 Brokenhill St.
Newbury Park, CA 91320

Visatex
1745 Dell Ave.
Campbell, CA 95008

Voyager Company
1351 Pacific Coast Hwy.
Santa Monica, CA 90401

Roger Wagner Publishing Co.
1050 Pioneer Way
El Cajon, CA 92020

Wayzata Technology
P.O. Box 87
Prior Lake, MN 55372

Weekly Reader Family Software
245 Long Hill
Middletown, CT 06457

Wings for Learning
1600 Green Hills Rd.
Scotts Valley, CA 95067-0002

World Games Institute
3508 Market St.
Philadelphia, PA 19104

Xiphias
8758 Venice Blvd.
Los Angeles, CA 90034

INDEX

DATE DUE

DE 19 95			